TRAILS
OF
EASTERN
IDAHO

Pinyon pines at City of Rocks.

TRAILS
OF
EASTERN
IDAHO

Second edition, revised and updated

Margaret Fuller and Jerry Painter

TRAIL GUIDE BOOKS

Published by
Trail Guide Books
P.O. Box 148
Weiser, Idaho 83672

Revised and updated Second edtion
© 2001 Margaret Fuller and Jerry Painter

Manufactured in the United States

Edited by Beth Butler and Jon Jensen
Maps by Jerry Painter
Cover and book design by Jerry Painter of Trail Guide Books
Section icons from Fonthous Art Parts collection
All photographs by the authors, unless otherwise noted

Cover photograph: Scrambling up Mount Idaho in the Lost River Range

Library of Congress Catalog Card Number: 98-85447
Painter, Jerry, 1955–
Fuller, Margaret, 1935–

ISBN 0-9664233-1-3

Foreword

When I heard that Idaho trail disciples Margaret Fuller and Jerry Painter had teamed up for a new hiking guidebook on Eastern Idaho, I knew the result would be well worth waiting for. Margaret's and Jerry's experience in researching and writing about Idaho trails goes way back. In fact, if there are any two Idaho authors that could form a sort of dream team of hiking guide writers, it is these two.

This dream team has produced no fluff. They have meticulously done their research and present the plain and accurate facts of Eastern Idaho trail hiking. Here and there, trail descriptions are supplemented with tidbits of natural and social history. You can see Margaret Fuller's influence here. Her longtime and passionate love affair with the Idaho outdoors has given her a sensitivity for natural history – a topic to which she has devoted two previous books. And you can also see Jerry Painter's touch in the carefully drawn maps and the crisp, no-nonsense approach to trail descriptions that comes naturally from his years working as a journalist and editor of a trails newsletter.

What a place to do their research! I envy their forays into the hidden-away nooks and crannies of Eastern Idaho. From the forbidding desolation of the Great Rift to the graceful curving summits of the Beaverheads on the Continental Divide, this part of Idaho is a varied, wide open and blessed land. Just the names of the ranges are poetry and ring with a kind of allure that draws our thoughts away from cluttered offices and glowing computer screens: the Salmon River Mountains, the Lemhis, the Pioneers, the Lost Rivers, the Boulders, the Bannocks, the Big Holes.

"A hell of a lot of state, this Idaho," Ernest Hemingway once remarked to a friend. But busy with his novels and running off on far-flung adventures, Hemingway saw relatively little of Idaho. This book will help you see much of what Hemingway missed – a part of Idaho that superficially deceives and leads many to believe that much of it is dry and unappealing. Unappealing? Not in the eyes of Fuller and Painter. Not in the eyes of anyone who takes the time to explore it.

There are no tourist attractions described here, but rather out-of-the-way places and uncrowded sanctuaries with a special charm and character, places with some elbow room where you can leave the trail and amble along a ridge or an open hillside, and where your view, and the thoughts of your mind, are clear and unobstructed.

So don't stay home. Let the poetry of the Eastern Idaho outdoors pull you away from the office. Use this book to see the real Idaho. Wander and explore its hills and vales: lose yourself, surprise yourself, discover the hidden-away treasures waiting at the trail's end, hold onto them, savor them, take them home, and live, truly rich and fulfilled.

Ron Watters

Idaho State University Outdoor Education faculty
Author of "Never Turn Back," "Ski Camping" and "Guide to Idaho Paddling"
with Katherine Daly.

Acknowledgements

The authors would like to express our appreciation to the Forest Service, Bureau of Land Management, Idaho State Parks, City of Rocks National Reserve, and Craters of the Moon National Monument personnel who suggested trails to include, shared their knowledge of trails, and reviewed the hike descriptions and appendix trail notes for accuracy. Thanks to Rick Baugher for his wealth of knowledge on the high peaks of Idaho and suggestions for this book. Thanks to Paul McCarthy for his contributions on the Hells Half Acre trail and the 12,000-foot peak descriptions. Thanks to Beth Butler and Jon Jensen for their copy editing, and to friends who were caught in front of our cameras and allowed their pictures to be included in this book. We would also like to thank the relatives and friends who hiked with us or provided lodging, transportation or information. Most of all we, the authors, would like to thank our families for hiking with us and encouraging us with this book: Julie, Sam, Naomi, Sarah, Leah, and Levi Painter and Wayne, Doug, Neal, and Stuart Fuller, Leslie Fuller Magryta, and Hilary Fuller Renner.

A word about safety

It is important to take the proper precautions in all outdoor activities. It is impossible to alert you to every hazard or anticipate all the limitations of every reader or group in a guidebook. Because of this, the descriptions of trails, routes and natural features in this book do not necessarily mean that a particular place or trip will be safe for your group. It also helps to remember that to fully enjoy many of the trails described in this book a certain level of physical conditioning is required – especially trails rated as strenuous. When you follow any of the trips described in this book, you assume any responsibility for the safety of yourself or your party. Under most normal conditions, excursions require that you pay the proper attention to driving conditions, traffic, roads, trails, weather, terrain, the capabilities of your group members and other factors.

It is also important to remember that the lands described in this book are subject to development and ownership changes. Access and other conditions may have changed since this book was published that may make it unwise to use the exact routes described. Always check for current conditions ahead of time, respect posted private property signs, and avoid confrontations with property owners or managers. We have provided information sources with each trail description. Staying informed on current conditions and using common sense are the best ways to enjoy fun and safe outings.

LEGEND

-⑮-	Interstate highway	✳--1.0--✳	Distance points
-⑳-	U.S. highway	⚠	Primitive campground
•③①•	State highway	⚠	Improved campground
⊣272⊢	County or Forest Service Road	·---	Boundary
▬▬	Paved road	⇇N⇇	North
══	Dirt or gravel road	■	Building or site
▪ ▪ ·	Main trail	⩓	Mountain peak
- - -	Other trails	⤬	Mine
•••••••	Cross-country route	◠◡◠	River or creek
= = =	Primitive road	⬬	Lake or pond

How to use this book

At the beginning of each trail description are the **elevation gain and loss**, the highest point reached, and the topographic and/or other maps needed. If you are using a Forest Service map be sure it is the current "travel plan" map rather than the general forest map because the travel plan maps are more up to date. For the easier trails, a Forest Service map and the maps and descriptions in this book will get you on your way. Topographic maps are especially recommended if you plan to do any off-trail hiking or follow trails in poor condition. Notes on whom to contact for **more information** and current conditions are also found at the beginning of each trail description. You will find a list of phone numbers and addresses in the appendix.

In the trail descriptions there are estimates of the difficulty, and the **round trip time** on foot. If you are in good physical condition, your time will probably be much less. The beginning also tells **how to reach the trailhead**. For most trails the mileage has been measured from the farthest point a two-wheel-drive vehicle can reach. Reaching some of the trailheads requires a high-clearance vehicle, but only a few require four-wheel drive. A few of the trails are described in sections. For these hikes the information at the top reads "This section x miles, y feet elevation gain."

The difficulty of each trail has been estimated according to the following scale: **Easy** is less than seven miles, less than 1,000 feet elevation gain, and a good, well-marked trail. **Moderate** is 7 to 10 miles and 1,000 to 2,000 feet elevation gain. Anything more than 10 miles or 2,000 feet elevation gain is **strenuous**. Trails that are hard to find or have poor footing or there is no trail for part of the route are listed as **expert**. This is not to say that these trails are for experts only, but that trekkers should be experienced in rough mountain conditions and path finding or go with experienced friends.

If obtaining **water** is a problem, water sources are mentioned. It is advisable to filter or boil all water to prevent intestinal illnesses such as giardia.

For quick reference information on specific trails refer to the **trails chart** in the appendix. This chart is a good starting point for finding trails with certain features such as campgrounds, fishing opportunities, or mountain biking.

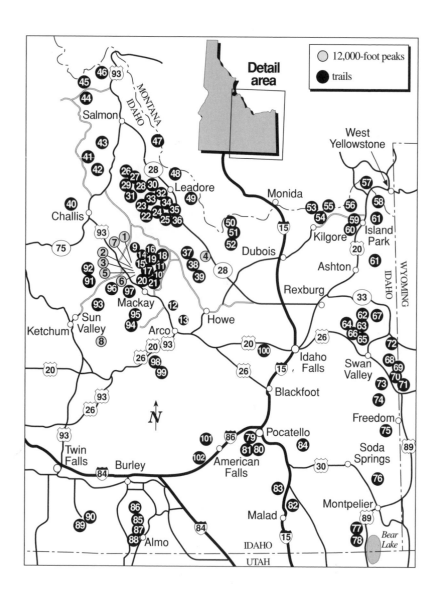

TABLE OF CONTENTS

INTRODUCTION 12
SCRAMBLING UP IDAHO'S 12,000 FOOT PEAKS 15
  1. Mount Borah 19
  2. Leatherman Peak 22
  3. Mount Church and Donaldson Peak 26
  4. Diamond Peak 29
  5. Mount Breitenbach 31
  6. Peak 12,078 (Lost River Peak) 33
  7. Mount Idaho 36
  8. Hyndman Peak 38

LOST RIVER RANGE - WEST
  9. Carlson Lake 42
 10. Bear Creek Lake 43
 11. Wet Creek – Long Lost Trail to Big Creek 45
 12. Ramshorn Canyon 47
 13. Natural Arch 48

LOST RIVER RANGE – EAST
 14. Merriam Lake 50
 15. Pass Lake 52
 16. East Fork of the Pahsimeroi 54
 17. Unnamed Lake, 9,682' 56
 18. Dry Creek Trail 57
 19. Swauger and Copper Lakes 59
 20. Upper Long Lost Creek 61
 21. Shadow Lakes 62

LEMHI RANGE – WEST
 22. North Fork of Big Creek 63
 23. Devils Basin and the Park Fork Loop From Yellow Lake 65
 24. Timber Creek Pass 67
 25. Mill Creek Lake 69

LEMHI RANGE – EAST
 26. Bear Valley Lakes and Buck Lakes 70
 27. Mill Lake 72
 28. Stroud Lake 74
 29. Everson Lake 76
 30. Dairy Lake 77
 31. Big Eightmile Creek 77
 32. North Fork of Little Timber Creek Lake 79
 33. Middle Fork of Little Timber Creek and Yellow Lake 81
 34. Big Timber Creek 83
 35. Nez Perce Lake 86
 36. Meadow Lake Trail 89
 37. Bell Mountain Canyon 90
 38. Rocky Canyon 91
 39. Pass Creek Lake 93

SALMON RIVER MOUNTAINS – NORTH OF CHALLIS
 40. Challis Creek Lakes 95
 41. Opal Lake 97

SALMON RIVER MOUNTAINS – WEST AND NORTH OF SALMON
42. Hat Creek Lakes 98
43. Old Thunder Mountain Trail 100
44. Pine Creek Ridge Trail and the Clipper Bullion Mill 102
45. Divide Trail from the Spring Creek Road 104
46. Allan Lake 105

BEAVERHEAD MOUNTAINS
47. Lewis and Clark Trail at Lemhi Pass 108
48. Gilmore and Pittsburg Railroad Grade 110
49. Hawley Creek, the Continental Divide, and Morrison Lake 111
50. Divide Creek Lake 113
51. Divide Creek Lake to Webber Creek 114
52. Webber Lakes 115

CENTENNIAL RANGE
53. Salamander Lakes 117
54. Aldous and Hancock Lakes 119
55. Blair and Lillian Lakes 121
56. Mount Jefferson and Rock Creek Basin 123

HENRY'S LAKE MOUNTAINS
57. Targhee Creek and Lakes 126
58. Tygee Creek Basin 128
59. Coffee Pot Rapids 130
60. Golden Lake 131
61. Warm River Rail Trail 133

BIG HOLE MOUNTAINS
62. Big Hole Crest Trail 138
63. Moody Swamp Trail To Thousand Springs Valley and Castle Lake 141
64. Hell Hole Trail 143
65. South Fork Snake River 144
66. Black Canyon, Little Burns Creek and Burns Creek 146
67. Packsaddle Lake 147

SNAKE RIVER MOUNTAINS
68. Palisades Lakes 149
69. Waterfall Canyon 150
70. Little Elk Creek and Mount Baird 153
71. Big Elk Creek 154
72. Oliver Peak (the Mike Harris Trail) 155

CARIBOU MOUNTAINS
73. Bear Creek 157
74. Caribou Mountain 158

WEBSTER RANGE
75. Historic Lander Cut-off of the Oregon Trail 161

PREUSS RANGE
76. Snowdrift Mountain 164

10

BEAR RIVER RANGE
77. Bloomington Lake and the High Line Trail 167
78. St. Charles Canyon, the High Line Trail, and Snowslide Canyon 169

BANNOCK RANGE
79. City Creek 171
80. Scout Mountain Nature Trail and East Mink Trail 173
81. West Fork of Mink Creek Trail 175
82. Oxford Peak 177
83. Wright Creek National Recreation Trail 179

PORTNEUF RANGE
84. Boundary Trail 181

ALBION MOUNTAINS
85. Independence Lakes 184
86. Skyline Trail on Mount Harrison 186
87. City of Rocks: Boxtop Trail, Stripe Rock, the Lost Arrow, Flaming Rock . 187
88. City of Rocks: Creekside Towers and the South Fork of Circle Creek ... 189

GOOSE CREEK MOUNTAINS
89. Third Fork of Rock Creek 191
90. Harrington Fork 192

BOULDER MOUNTAINS
91. Hunter Creek Summit 194
92. North Fork Lake 196

PIONEER MOUNTAINS
93. Wildhorse Lakes 197
94. Iron Bog and Fishpole Lakes from Antelope Valley 199
95. Brockie Lake 200

WHITE KNOB MOUNTAINS
96. Wildcat Trail to the Wildhorse Lookout 202
97. Corral Creek 203

SNAKE RIVER PLAIN
98. Craters of the Moon: North Crater Trail 205
99. Craters of the Moon: Big Cinder and Echo Crater 208
100. Hells Half Acre 210
101. Wapi Lava Flow 212
102. Massacre Rocks 214

APPENDIX:
Notes on Other Selected Trails 217
Useful addresses and phone numbers 224
Tips for Leave-No-Trace Camping 225
Suggested Equipment List 226
About the Authors 227
Guide to Trail Features 228

11

Introduction

This latest edition of "Trails of Eastern Idaho" offers the most up-to-date information on more than 100 routes in book form. The most exciting new part of this book is a scrambler's guide to Idaho's 12,000-foot peaks. Like all the other trail guides, these descriptions include what to expect, how to get there and photos.

Eastern Idaho is a landscape of variety. It includes black lava, grotesque granite towers, multicolored cliffs, and unearthly turquoise water. The trees range from pinon pine, juniper and sagebrush to whitebark pine, subalpine fir, and Engelmann spruce. Sagebrush is the dominant shrub at lower altitudes, but higher up the shrubs are varied. Some of them are mountain mahogany, mountain snowberry, and huckleberry. Wildlife species of both desert and mountains live here: badger, pronghorn antelope, and desert cottontail, as well as pika and mountain goat. Most of the mountain ranges in eastern Idaho run north and south, with the great arc of the Snake River plain flattening them out in the middle.

Most eastern Idaho communities are small and friendly, and the people have a sense of their history. In Mormon farming communities like Paris and resort communities like Driggs and Island Park, history seems to have happened only yesterday. Many buildings have been preserved and displays tell the stories of explorers, fur traders, and travelers on the Oregon Trail, which bisects the area. Today people still make their living largely from agriculture, with help from tourism, the Idaho National Engineering and Environmental Laboratory, and four colleges: Idaho State University, BYU-Idaho, the College of Southern Idaho and Eastern Idaho Technical College. Mining and logging are still important to the economy but less so than they were 50 years ago.

Eastern Idaho has about 22 mountain ranges, the exact number depending on what you consider a separate range. Trails in 19 of these ranges are covered here. They are suitable for a variety of user groups, from hikers to mountain bikers.

The book begins with Mount Borah, Idaho's highest peak, at 12,662 feet. Then it moves clockwise around eastern Idaho, ending with trips on the Snake River Plain. For this book, eastern Idaho is the land east of a line drawn along U.S. Highway 93 from the Nevada border to Shoshone, and then along Idaho Highway 75 to Ketchum. Then it goes up the east side of the Sawtooth National Recreation Area and along the east side of the Frank Church-River of No Return Wilderness to the Montana border.

The base of the Lost River Range east of Sun Valley is marked by the 11-foot scarp left by the 1983 Mount Borah earthquake, which was 7.3 in magnitude. The scarp is about 23 miles long. Besides Borah Peak, several other peaks, such as Leatherman and Breitenbach also are over 12,000 feet. Many of the peaks have twisted layers of multicolored rock. Boulders and ruts in the access roads assure solitude. The Lost River is "lost" because it disappears in the lava of the Snake River Plain and appears again a hundred miles away at Thousand Springs on the

Snake River near Hagerman.

East of the Lost River Range, the Lemhi Range runs north and south for a hundred miles with no road crossing it other than a four-wheel-drive track. The Lemhis are much more wooded than the ranges east and west of them and have more lakes. Peaks vary from rounded talus summits to jagged peaks with cliffs as their east faces. The ghost town of Gilmore and the four charcoal kilns that once provided charcoal for a smelter at nearby Nicholia give evidence of the Lemhis' history.

North and west of the Lemhis roll the gentle granite peaks of the Salmon River Mountains, split by the chasms of the Salmon River and its Middle and South forks. Much of this range is in the Frank Church-River of No Return Wilderness, which is not included in this book, but east of the wilderness the range is still rugged and beautiful, and this section is included.

The dry peaks called the Beaverheads, a subrange of the Bitterroots, run along the Montana border from Lost Trail Pass on the north to Monida Pass on Interstate 15 on the east. The Beaverheads look bald and bare on their west side, the side that faces Idaho, except for a small section near Salmon, where they are spectacular on both sides. However, private land curtails access to the Idaho side in that section. The Continental Divide Trail, which goes along the crest of the range, will, when completed, make it possible to backpack easily from Lost Trail Pass to Yellowstone National Park with only a few detours into Montana. It is possible for those with good route-finding skills to do so now.

Grizzly habitat, amazing wildflowers, and the world-famous trout-fishing river the Henry's Fork, make the Centennial and Henry's Lake mountains great places to go. The Centennials begin at Monida Pass on Interstate 15 and go east and then north along the Montana border to Red Rock Pass southwest of Henry's Lake. From Red Rock Pass to Yellowstone the range along Idaho-Montana is called the Henry's Lake Mountains. The terrain of these ranges varies from steep wooded hills littered with granite blocks to high cliffs with rock layers that curve into waves and circles.

Although you get a wonderful view of the Teton Mountains from Teton Basin in eastern Idaho, all but the lowest part of the west side access roads are in Wyoming. Therefore, hikes in the Tetons are not included in this book. For information on a half-dozen hikes on the west side of the Tetons as well as many others inside Grand Teton National Park, see Jerry Painter's book, "Great Trails for Family Hiking: The Tetons."

East of Idaho Falls, the Big Hole Mountains sit to the northeast of the Snake River. The river here is also known as the South Fork of the Snake River to distinguish it from the Henry's Fork to the north. Red and gray outcrops, and lush wildflowers make the Big Hole Mountains colorful country. In late summer, the huckleberries are usually plentiful. On the southeast side of Idaho Highway 31 this range continues along the east side of Palisades Reservoir, but here it is called the Snake River Range. This section is noted for thick forests, many avalanche chutes, beautiful waterfalls, and mountain goats.

The Caribou, Webster, and Preuss ranges west and south of Palisades Reservoir are characterized by their views of distant ranges like the Tetons and of a quilt of farms in the valleys below them. They are also interesting historically, with places like the vanished mining town of Caribou City and the historic Lander Cutoff of the Oregon Trail.

The high grassy hills west of Bear Lake are called the Bear River Range. They are covered with wildflowers, patches of forest, and cream and pearl gray limestone outcrops. They also give a view of the milky turquoise water of huge Bear Lake. All of these features are so pretty they make it seem as though the Bear River Range is a set of mountains in a watercolor painting.

The high wooded hills of the Portneuf and Bannock ranges south of Pocatello are distinguished by crumbled cliffs and fine displays of wildflowers and flowering shrubs. They also have good views of the farms and the Portneuf River in the deep valleys around them.

The Goose Creek Mountains south of Twin Falls begin with semidesert canyons lined with brown and black lava cliffs progressing to slopes wooded with juniper, fir and aspen. The black cliffs of Rock Creek Canyon are especially scenic.

The Albion Mountains south of Burley are surprisingly beautiful, with aspen groves, a chain of alpine lakes, and the world-famous City of Rocks, now a mecca for rock climbers. The City of Rocks was a landmark on the California Trail, and visitors can still see names of pioneers written in axle grease. Some of the flowers are species usually found farther south, and all the wildflowers here grow prolifically. That is because this range receives more snow than most other Idaho mountains, often 20 feet or more in a winter.

The cream, gray, black, and rose-colored crags of the Pioneer Mountains are just east of Sun Valley. Their canyons rise to sheer headwalls. Some of the headwalls are of layered rock, reminiscent of that seen in Glacier National Park.

Most of the Boulder Mountains north of the Pioneers are of gray and black rock, but a few of them are red and orange. There are fewer lakes but you may see mountain goats.

The White Knob Mountains east of the Pioneers are mostly orange and have much sagebrush, few trees, and many white and orange outcrops. This range separates the Pioneers from the Lost River Valley to the east.

Idaho's only national monument, Craters of the Moon, is south of the Pioneers between Carey and Arco. Here, cones and craters of black and reddish lava, and black and occasionally iridescent blue lava flows cover thousands of acres. Some of the lava is smooth, but much of it is broken into sharp blocks. Here grows a variety of plant life from limber pine to a buckwheat that is white and hairy to help it keep cool. Trails, campgrounds, interpretive displays, and a visitor center serve the public. Other nearby lava fields and cones are also fun to explore.

Because the elevation of the trails in this book varies from 2,700 feet to more than 12,000 feet, there is somewhere to go almost all year. They vary in difficulty from gentle maintained trails suitable for horses and mountain bikes to steep paths best for hikers and scramblers.

Because it can rain or even snow in the Idaho mountains any day of the summer, and storms can come up suddenly, always bring long pants, a warm jacket, wool hat and rain gear even on a day hike. Most storms in Idaho come from the west, so on the east side of these ranges you often won't see a storm coming.

A list of suggested equipment, and tips for leave-no-trace camping are given in the appendix, which also contains notes of selected other trails.

We hope this book will help make your trips on eastern Idaho trails wonderful ones.

14

Scrambling up
Idaho's 12,000-foot peaks

Introduction to Idaho's giants

"The nine 12ers," some people call them. There are only nine peaks in Idaho that top the 12,000-foot mark. They are Idaho's rooftop — the crown jewels of Idaho's many beautiful mountain ranges. Reaching the top of these peaks is a goal that many outdoor enthusiasts have. The good news is that getting to the top of these peaks can be accomplished by most advanced hikers *IF* they are in good shape, are equipped and prepared for all kinds of weather, get good directions on the routes — and use common sense. Unlike high peaks in other states, the accessibility of these giants means that any of them can be knocked off in a summer's day.

Even people who consider a walk across the mall parking lot a long hike will often pull the car over and snap a photo of these big mountains. Getting in shape for and trekking to the top of any of them can be the highlight of any summer or fall. A comment found stuffed into a jar on top of Diamond Peak is typical of the comments found on summit registers on many of the "nine 12ers." "Hola fellow hikers. What a beautiful, breath-taking mountain. Well worth the grunt! (8-25-95) Cynthia Tyler"

A couple of the mountaintops are magnets for peak baggers. Borah Peak and Leatherman Peak get a great deal of traffic. The other named peaks on the list: Diamond Peak, Mount Breitenbach, Donaldson Peak and Hyndman Peak also get a good deal of traffic. The third-, seventh- and eighth-highest — unofficially known as Mount Church, Mount Idaho and Lost River Peak — see fewer scramblers in a season.

The nine peaks are found in three different mountain ranges: Pioneer, Lost River and Lemhi. Seven of the peaks, including the three highest, are found in the Lost River Range northeast of Mackay. The Pioneers have one peak, Hyndman; and the Lemhi Range has one, Diamond Peak, the fourth highest. On a clear day, this pyramid-shaped mountain can be seen on the northwest skyline from Idaho Falls or Rexburg.

By 1991, about 12 people had climbed all nine 12ers. An additional two dozen scramblers join the 12ers club each year. Mike Howard of Idaho Falls has climbed all nine 12ers in winter. Buck Horton, also of Idaho Falls, has climbed all nine 12ers in one week (twice).

Before you write off the nine 12ers as a goal that's over your head, consider

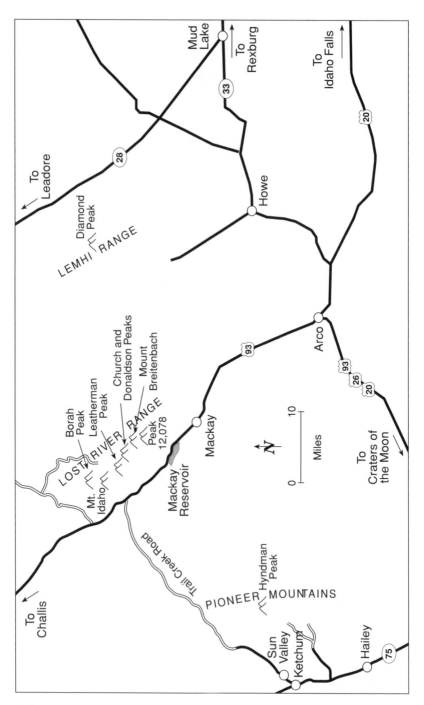

16

that many people have bagged these peaks after their retirement. Others start young as evidenced by this comment on Lost River Peak's summit register: "(7-24-96) Dan, Justin and Merinda Bodily climbed to the top. Took 4 hours. Merinda, who is 9, was just a little slow." Borah Peak's summit sees a broad range of ages and abilities — one typical August Saturday a 10-year-old, a man in his late 60s and a spotted hound were seen on top.

Still, people have contrasting views of these peaks as is shown by two comments in the Leatherman summit register: "This mountain sucks. Never ever again. Jeremy Schwarts." and "Great view. Enjoyed the climb. Hope to have my kids up here in a few years. Jeff Geist."

Most people start up Borah and the other peaks well before the crack of dawn and plod at a steady pace for several hours until they gain the summit. Others, obviously in excellent shape, practically run to the top in back in just a few hours.

While 12,000 feet may not sound like a big deal when compared to other state's 13,000- or 14,000-foot peaks, keep in mind that it's not necessarily how high a peak is, but the distance and elevation gain from start to finish and the roughness of the terrain that determine a peak's difficulty. How long it takes you depends on many variables such as conditioning, age, and reaction to altitude. Borah Peak takes some people as long as 15 hours, so it is wise to start climbing at or before dawn on the longer climbs. "Highpointers" — climbers who bag the highest peak in every state — rank Borah Peak in the top six among the 50 states for difficulty, partly because the elevation gain is 5,400 feet. Idaho's 12,000-foot peaks have climbs from 4,600 to 5,700 feet, and several are at least as difficult as Borah. Each of the nine 12ers has several different routes of ascent, but all have at least one "easy" scrambler's route to the top.

Here are a few guidelines to help make your bid to the top of Idaho's 12ers a success:

❏ **Get in shape.** Out-of-shape hikers often climb these peaks, but their bodies will pay for it later. It is also dangerous to get most of the way up a peak and lack the energy to retreat or help others retreat in the face of an oncoming storm or medical emergency. A good measuring stick is to be able to jog two to three miles without stopping. If jogging is not your thing, then build up to 30 or 40 minutes without stopping either climbing hills in your neighborhood or at medium resistance on a stairstepper machine. If you're in shape, you'll enjoy the trip a lot more.

❏ **Get some experience.** Hike some intermediate-size mountains first to get experience with route finding, bushwhacking, exposure to high places and the stamina required. Hike up some easier mountains like Mount Baird in the Snake River Range near Palisades Reservoir, Oxford Peak south of Pocatello, or McDonald Peak in the Sawtooths. They are good warmups for the tougher 12ers.

❏ **Be aware of the dangers and how to avoid them.** Know how to read the oncoming weather and what to do if it decides to rain, snow or shoot lightning bolts. Know basic first aid to help yourself or others who have problems. Know how to cope with steep snowfields, falling rock and exposure to cliffs or heights.

❏ **Get good directions.** After getting in shape, the hardest part about climbing a mountain is finding your way up. All of these mountains can be climbed by advanced hikers if they take the right route to the top. But we would like to warn you that if you get off the proven route you could find yourself in some serious scrambling or even technical rock climbing. Finding the right way to the top of the right peak can be tricky on some of these mountains. Just having a topographic map is no guarantee, but a topographic map is an essential piece of equipment for

Climbing down the "Nose" on the way up the Mount Borah trail in the Lost River Range.

these climbs. Many of the canyons and peaks are so similar to nearby formations that it is easy even for experienced hikers to mix them up. If you have doubts, have someone who has already gone point the way on the ground or, better yet, go with you. For extra route-finding tips, contact Rick Baugher of Idaho Falls or Jerry Painter for directions. (Please bring your topographic and national forest maps with you.)

❑ **Hike prepared.** Take plenty of drinking water; most climbs don't have any water sources at higher elevations. Two quarts is a minimum; three is recommended. Take lots of high-energy snacks or candy in addition to a lunch. Bring along a warm sweater and/or light jacket, gloves, a wool or fleece hat and rain gear. It can be a mild 70 degrees on the valley floor and snowing on the summit. Wear good boots or trail-running shoes. Sure, you can hike these peaks in sneakers, but boots offer better support, traction and protection from the miles of loose scree and rocks. A walking stick gives stability especially when hiking down steep scree and we strongly recommend that you use one.

❑ **Use an altimeter**. While many people hike or climb without one, an altimeter helps you find yourself on a topographic map precisely and quickly.

18

Table of Idaho peaks higher than 12,000 feet

Name	Elevation	Elev. gain	Round trip	Scrambling?
Borah Peak	12,662+*	5,412 feet	9.2 miles	yes
Leatherman Pk	12,228	4,068	8	minimal**
Mount Church	12,200+***	5,100	8.6	yes
Diamond Peak	12,197	4,600	5.5	yes
Mt Breitenbach	12,140	5,140	7.6	minimal
"Lost River" Pk	12,078	4,478	5	minimal
Mount Idaho	12,065	5,065	7	yes
Donaldson Pk	12,023	4,600	7	yes
Hyndman Pk	12,009	5,009	13.6	easy

Because of the 1983 central Idaho earthquake, Borah Peak gained at least one foot of elevation while the surrounding valley dropped several feet. This change is not noted on USGS maps.

**Scrambling is minimal for the east side approach, but serious for the northwest ridge approach.*

***Mount Church doesn't have an official elevation and is listed in most sources as 12,200 "plus." The summit is slightly higher than the 12,200 foot contour shown on the USGS map.*

---

1. BORAH PEAK

Round trip: 9.2 miles
Elevation gain: 5,412 feet
Elevation loss (return climb): 120 feet
Highest point: 12,662 feet
Time: 6 to 12 hours, depending on conditioning, age, and response to high altitude
Difficulty: very strenuous, no water, scrambling required
Maps: USGS topographic: Borah Peak; U.S. Forest Service: Challis National Forest
Information: Lost River Ranger District
Getting there: Turn east from U.S., 93, 26 miles south of Challis or 14 miles north of Mackay on the signed Mount Borah access road (279). Just before the road crosses the fault scarp from the 1983 earthquake a new road runs right and goes .5 mile to a small developed campground and trailhead about 4 miles from the highway. The jeep trail shown on the topographic map that used to allow hikers to drive .6 mile farther is no longer open to motor vehicles.

From the top of Mount Borah, the Lost River Range extends north and south in immense pleated summits, ribboned with a narrow band of forest. At 12,662-plus feet it is the highest mountain in Idaho. From the summit only one small lake is visible, and Mount Borah's glacierette is hidden below cliffs. Below to the east

19

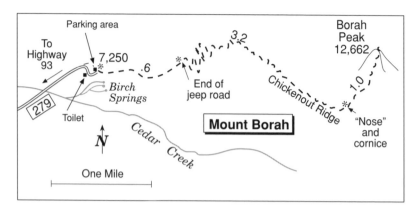

are the irrigated valleys of the Pahsimeroi River, which flows north, and the Little Lost River, which flows south. East of those valleys rises the massive wall of the Lemhi Range. West of Mount Borah is the valley of the Big Lost River, and to the west of it are the pale blue scallops of the Boulders and the White Clouds. To the north float the dim shapes of the Salmon River Mountains.

Mount Borah is a memorable climb because of the large vertical ascent, difficult footing, rock scrambling, and a knife-edge ridge with drop-offs of several hundred feet. With an arsenal of mostly poor trail, steep inclines, a narrow heart-stopping ridge, nearly perpendicular snow fields and its ultimate weapon the weather, this tallest of Idaho's peaks is a formidable foe. An early start is a good idea most days because of the threat of afternoon thunderstorms. It can be a dawn-to-after-dark effort, depending on your conditioning and how you react to the effects of high altitude. Backpacking partway up requires extra effort because you must carry all the water needed for the climb.

The first ascent of Borah was by T.M. Bannon, a United States topographer, in 1914. The peak is named for William Borah, U.S. senator from Idaho after it was determined in 1929 that it was the state's highest point. Prior to that time the mountain was known as "Beauty."

The speed record for Borah Peak is an incredible 90 minutes from parking lot to summit. Borah has been climbed every month of the year by one person: David Ferguson. Chuck Ferguson claims the most ascents of Borah: 25. The first woman, Miriam Underhill of Boston, Mass., climbed Borah Peak in 1934. You can climb Borah with a licensed guide service, but the price is not cheap; expect to pay around $400. A few hardy souls have climbed the peak at night, lingering on the summit for the sunrise or perhaps a glimpse of the aurora borealis.

The trail leads out of the trailhead above the parking area. At .6 mile, when the old roadbed ends, follow an unsigned trail northeast across the dry creek bed. The trail climbs in switchbacks that have recently been built through groves of limber pine, curving north to a saddle at 1.1 miles, just east of the hill marked 8,714 on the topo map.

From the saddle the route turns east up the end of a ridge and at 2 miles after climbing 2,300 feet emerges from the timber. Here there is a campsite with two flat, rocky places for sleeping. The trail follows the ridge, which climbs ever upward and hooks around to the north in the general shape of a question mark. At the edge of the 10,000-foot elevation plateau you might be lucky enough to find

20

*Crossing the
snowfield after
Chickenout Ridge
on Borah Peak.
Some years the
snowfield melts
below the ridge
and permits a dry
crossing in late
summer.*

trickles of running water from snowmelt before July 4.

From the campsites as the trail continues up the ridge, it is less steep and circles north of two gray and brown striped hills at 2.3 miles. From this flatter section, to the right (southwest) you look down on a flat spur that meets the main ridge at 90-degree angle. Beyond the second striped hill at 10,600 feet is another rocky campsite, with a rock windbreak.

The path climbs steeply again, then disappears on yellow ledges. Here where the ridge top narrows to the width of a school bus, with drop-offs of 600 to 800 feet on either side, the mountain asks a big question of the climber. Because so many people turn back here, this section has become known as Chickenout Ridge.

The scramble over Chickenout Ridge is not hard but is a bit scary. Best advice is don't look down. If this ridge is snow covered or icy, turn around and come back another day unless you brought along an ice ax and know how to self-arrest. To negotiate the ridge, when climbing along it becomes too difficult, drop down off the crest to the right (southeast) through a narrow notch. Using hands and feet climb down a 40-foot inclined chimney into a gully. Next, climb up the gully to a side gully and take it northeast back to the crest of the ridge.

From here on the route depends on the season and conditions. The ridge soon drops in a 30-foot cliff to a saddle (11,750 feet). A snow cornice clings to this saddle until mid- to late summer, above steep, treacherous snow slopes. If snow still covers the saddle and the slopes below it, it is best to reach the saddle by climbing down the cliff. Then you will need to walk carefully across the saddle, keeping between the cornice and the drop-off to the east. This is another don't look down section. You may need to stomp or hack steps in the snow. Do not try to cross the snow slope below (west of) the saddle as the snow is too steep to be safe.

If the snow in the saddle and on the slope below it has melted, you can climb down before the cliff ends onto the talus to the left of the saddle and follow a faint path across the steep slope to a path along the left side of the next hill on the ridge, which is labeled 11,898 feet. Take this path to another saddle at 4 miles (11,800 feet).

The last 850 feet from this saddle to the summit at 4.6 miles is slow going because of the steepness, loose rock, and high altitude. There are two routes from here. One is following a sketchy path that climbs loose rock left (west) of the ridge crest. The other is climbing the ledges and cliffs along the ridge crest. This route avoids the loose rock and provides a nice view most of the way up, but requires the use of hands as well as feet. On a clear day the view from the top includes dozens of mountain ranges.

On your descent use great care because gravel on the steep dirt of the trail acts like ball bearings. Be sure to stick to the route on the descent. People have been killed taking shortcuts. Lightning is also a hazard, so if a thunderstorm comes up, it is best to beat a fast retreat.

2. LEATHERMAN PEAK

Round trip: 8 miles (10 without four-wheel drive)
Elevation gain: 4,068 feet from W. Fork Pahsimeroi (5,128 from Sawmill Gulch)
Highest point: 12,228 feet
Time: 6 to 8 hours
Difficulty: Strenuous to very strenuous depending on your route
Maps: USGS: Leatherman Peak. Forest Service: Challis National Forest
Information: Lost River Ranger District
Getting there: There are two popular routes to the top of Leatherman Peak: one from the west side up Sawmill Gulch and one from the east side from the West Fork of the Pahsimeroi Road. First, we'll describe how to drive to the end of the West Fork of the Pahsimeroi Road. To reach the West Fork of the Pahsimeroi Road drive 23 miles south of Challis or 16 miles north of Mackay on U.S. 93 to the Doublesprings Road (116). Turn east on this road for 10.5 miles. Then turn right (south) on the primitive Horseheaven Pass Road (117). At a short, steep hill just past the turn, keep right for a gentler grade that rejoins the road at the top of the hill. Keep right at the Y where the road accessing Carlson Lake turns left. The main road crosses unmarked Horseheaven Pass at 14.3 miles, and at 16.7 miles a road from Burnt Creek joins from the left. This is a better road than the Horseheaven Road but much harder to find. At 17.8 miles, a sign warns the road is not suitable for passenger cars. The track descends into the canyon of Mahogany Creek and fords it at 18.2 miles. Just past the creek a side road turns off to the right through a gate. Keep straight ahead. Immediately the road branches again, with the

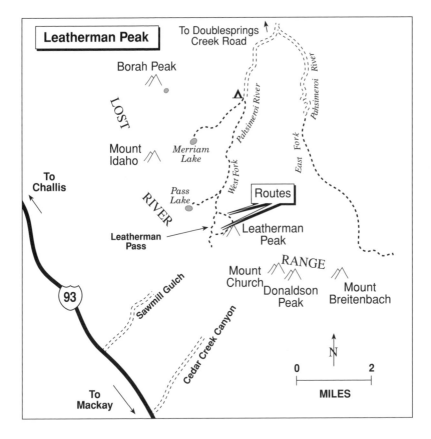

Leatherman Peak

left branch climbing a steep hill. To avoid the steep hill keep right and then left on a detour that rejoins the main road above the hill. Soon the road drops into the canyon of the Pahsimeroi River. Pahsimeroi is Shoshone for "water one grove" or "a grove by a stream" and honors the one grove of trees that used to be the only trees on the lower part of the river. At 21.8 miles is a cattleman's cabin and corral with a fine view of folded and tilted rock layers on the canyon walls. Just beyond that you must open and shut a gate to continue. At 22.1 miles the road splits. Take the right (north) branch (Road 267) up the West Fork of the Pahsimeroi. From here high clearance is essential. At 24.1 miles the road worsens. Most drivers without four-wheel drive will want to park here. After a rocky, rutted mile, park beside an informal campsite 25.1 miles from U.S. 93. The road ends within 200 yards.

WEST SIDE: The drive to the west-side route up Leatherman Peak is much easier. Go north on Highway 93 about 8 miles north of Mackay and turn right (northeast) on the Sawmill Gulch Road. About 1.5 miles up, the road has a rough, washed-out section and becomes rough even for high-clearance vehicles. You can park here and hike or ride a mountain bike or try and sneak your vehicle through the rough section. The road continues toward Leatherman Pass for another two miles. At this point, leave the road and take a trail that heads straight for the pass.

Standing on top of Leatherman Peak and looking south toward Mount Church and Donaldson Peak.

Leatherman Peak was probably first climbed in 1914 by T.M. Bannon, a U.S. Geological Surveyor. The peak is named for Henry Leatherman, a regional freighter of the late 1800s. Leatherman is buried at Battleground Cemetery along the Mackay Reservoir, in sight of the mountain named for him. The peak was officially named in 1917.

The two most popular routes to the top of Idaho's second-highest peak offer a few trade-offs. You can climb the peak from the west side by going up Sawmill Gulch to Leatherman Pass, then up the steep west ridge or you can attack the mountain from the northeast side by hiking up the West Fork of the Pahsimeroi River canyon and climbing the north ridge. It's easy enough to drive to Coyote Spring in Sawmill Gulch, but it is a steeper and harder climb that way with 1,000 feet more elevation gain and danger of dislodging rocks once you get above Leatherman Pass. On the other hand, it's a grueling drive up the Pahsimeroi Valley to the West Fork of Pahsimeroi River but 1,000 feet less climbing and a gentler trek up the northeast gully to the top from there. We'll describe both routes.

This first description is of the easier east-side route.

At the end of the road on the West Fork of the Pahsimeroi River, there is a well-marked trail, which forks after about 50 yards. The trail to the right goes to Merriam Lake about 2 miles away. Continue on the trail to Pass Lake, which fords the west fork immediately. That crossing and one at 1.5 miles could be difficult in late spring or early summer. This trail follows the West Fork of the Pahsimeroi for the next two miles. For the most part, walking this trail is a breeze. You gain 850 feet in two miles. It's a refreshing change when you're used to bushwhacking most mountain approaches. After two miles the trail enters an open meadow section. This is where you leave the trail. Leatherman Pass is directly in front of you about 1.5 miles away, with the huge Leatherman Peak to the left (south) of the pass.

The easiest route is found by not continuing to the pass, but by leaving the trail and taking a gully to the left (east) of the prominent north ridge. Cross the stream to the southeast of the meadow and climb a steep scree slope. After .3 mile, you'll be in the gully. This is where the work really begins. For the next 1.2 miles it's almost all up. The going is mostly slippery, loose scree. After about 2,000 feet of elevation gain, you reach the summit ridge at 3.4 miles, northeast of the summit.

From here it's another 400- to 500-foot climb southwest to the summit at 4 miles. To reach it keep on or next to the ridge all the way to the top. A faint trail occasionally appears along this ridge, made by the passing of previous climbers. Leatherman's summit register sits inside of an old-style, bolt-down military box with holes that have allowed mice to chew up some of the names and notes in the register box.

From the top of Leatherman, you can spot climbers on Borah Peak with your binoculars. On a clear day you should be able to see all eight of the other 12,000-footers in Idaho. Church, Donaldson, Breitenbach and Lost River are only a couple miles to the southeast along the main crest of the Lost River Range. Two others are to the north: Borah Peak and Mount Idaho. Diamond Peak is at the southern end of the Lemhis to the east, and Hyndman Peak is to the southeast in the Pioneer Range near Sun Valley.

It is evident from the summit register that Leatherman Peak gets a lot of visitors. It appears that as many as two dozen or more visited some years, many from up from the west side.

Now for the description of climbing Leatherman from the west side:
After you leave the Sawmill Gulch Road, continue on a trail that aims directly for Leatherman Pass. Sawmill Gulch tops out and the trail takes you to a point high above the Lone Cedar Creek Canyon. Some climbers have mistakenly tried accessing Leatherman Pass via Lone Cedar Creek Canyon and found themselves bushwhacking for hours before making the pass.

The mostly easy trail from Sawmill Gulch takes you through occasionally thick timber and a few small meadows. The trail disappears through a large talus field above the canyon. Don't worry; the trail is easily found again above the rocks. Sawmill Gulch and Lone Cedar Creek canyons nearly meet at the base of Leatherman Pass. The trail leaves all the trees behind and climbs steeply for about a mile up to the pass. At the pass — at 10,600 feet — you are treated with a wonderful view of two of Idaho's great mountain valleys: The Pahsimeroi on the east and the Lost River on the west.

From the pass, follow a faint trail up Leatherman Peak's west ridge. This is where the scrambling begins. You will climb about 1,600 feet in the next half-mile. The first few hundred are hiking on steep loose scree. Stay close to the ridgeline as much as possible.

After climbing the ridge about 500 feet up, you come to more solid rock. Several spires, chutes and ramps begin to present themselves. In some places, the incline exceeds 45 degrees and hikers are compelled to become scramblers. Resist the temptation to move right off the ridge. The easiest approach up is to stay on the ridge or, when faced with a decision of going right or left, go to the left of the ridge. At the very least, this route is class 3 scrambling, but there are a few borderline class 4 scrambling spots. This is not a beginner's route up the mountain. This route is also fairly sustained scrambling. It doesn't let up until you reach the summit. On the descent, we recommend down climbing the easier east-side route and circling around to Leatherman Pass to return to Sawmill Gulch. If you do choose to return, via the northwest ridge, take great care on the scree-filled chutes which can quickly eject an unsuspecting scrambler off the mountain.

3. MOUNT CHURCH AND DONALDSON PEAK

Round trip for both peaks: 8.6 miles (7 for Donaldson by itself)
Elevation gain: 4,600 feet for Donaldson, 500 additional feet for Mt. Church
Highest points: 12,023 for Donaldson Peak, 12,200 for Mt. Church,
Time: 9 to 12 hours
Difficulty: Very strenuous, scrambling required
Maps: USGS: Leatherman Peak. Forest Service: Challis National Forest
Information: Lost River Ranger District.
Getting there: Follow maps carefully; the right canyon can be difficult to find. From Mackay, drive northwest on Highway 93 to Mackay Reservoir. About halfway along the reservoir there are three prominent canyons along the Lost River Range to the northeast. The first canyon is Upper Cedar Creek. The second is Pete Creek and the third is Jones Creek. Jones Creek is your destination. Between Pete and Jones creeks about three miles past the reservoir at milepost 117 turn right (northeast) on Forest Service Road 415, which is shown on the Challis Forest Service Map. This dirt road heads straight for the mountains. After 1.5 miles the road passes power lines. After two miles it comes to an intersection. Turn right and in a quarter mile the road will swing left and head north to the mouth of Jones Creek canyon where it ends at about 7,500 feet. There are often confusing jeep roads that intersect with the road you want. Use your Leatherman Peak map to find the correct road.

While everyone has a little different experience when climbing a mountain, most who have climbed Idaho's highest peaks rate Mount Church and Donaldson next to climbing Borah Peak as a wonderful but difficult experience. The two peaks, Idaho's third- and eighth-highest, are usually climbed together. They are connected by a half-mile ridgeline that is part of the main crest of the Lost River Range.

Mount Church is unofficially named after Sen. Frank Church, an Idaho senator from 1956 to 1980, who, during the 1970s, fought for wilderness protection for the Sawtooths, the Gospel Hump, and the wilderness that now bears his name. The peak has also been called Ken Williams Peak by the Chuck Williams family of Pocatello who climbed the peak in 1975. They wanted the peak named after their deceased son. The family may have made the first ascent of the peak. They built a cairn at the summit and left an ax handle at the top. In 1998, the summit register still contained the message from the Williams family visit, but neither name is official with the U.S. Bureau of Geographic names.

Climbing these two peaks is a workout. The first part of the climb involves a lot of bushwhacking up Jones Creek. The jeep road ends at the mouth of the canyon at 7,600 feet. The perennial Jones Creek can be an obstacle in itself, especially during the early summer at the height of runoff. Bear in mind that early in the summer the morning creek levels can rise by as much as a foot by late afternoon from snow melt. It can be difficult to avoid wet feet.

At about 1.5 miles up the canyon, look for a large talus slope on the northwest (left) side of the canyon. There is also a small spring that trickles out of the canyon wall here. Climb this steep talus slope about a mile to a prominent saddle

26

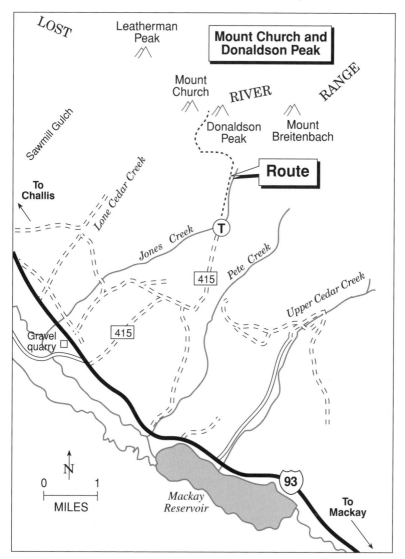

sitting at 10,000 feet. There are a few game trails that may help some, but much of the going is loose scree. Once on the saddle at 2.4 miles, try to contour around north to an obvious notch. As you climb up this notch, the mountain eventually opens up into an enchanting cirque. Three miles up at the base of the cirque are two ponds. One is shown at 10,800 feet on the USGS map. In late summer this pond is only a foot or two deep, but in early to mid-summer, the water takes on the appearance of a small lake.

This is a good place to pause and pick out your route up to the crest of the range. There is a class three (scrambling, but no need for ropes) route directly east

27

A hiker scrambles along the narrow ridge between Donaldson Peak (upper right) and Mount Church. Mount Breitenbach is top center a couple of miles away.

of the tarn. The going is steep and full of loose scree ramps, but if you take your time and scout around as you move upward you can avoid some of the nastier-looking rock. If you go too far to the left side (north direction) of the cirque you will quickly find yourself climbing rock that requires ropes and technical skills.

After about 1,100 feet of elevation gain you will be on the ridge top near the summit of Donaldson Peak. Once on the crest it's a few minutes walk to the top of Donaldson. Donaldson, at 12,023 feet, is officially named after the late chief of the Idaho Supreme Court Charles Russell Donaldson. The name has yet to appear on the USGS or BLM maps. Most of the climbers logging in the summit register on Donaldson mentioned that they were on their way to climb the nearby Mount Church as well.

From the top of Donaldson the crest of the range heads runs northeast in one direction and west in the other. The next big peak to the northeast, about three-fourths of a mile away, is Peak 11,972, commonly called No Regret Peak. About another three-fourths of a mile along the crest and almost directly east of Donaldson is Mount Breitenbach, 12,140 feet.

The summit of Mount Church is a little more than half a mile along the crest to the west. The ridge drops about 300 feet before climbing 500 feet to the summit at 4.3 miles. The ridge looks tougher than it is, but expect some serious class 3 scrambling. There is one 30-yard stretch of ridge that narrows to about two feet wide with exposure on both sides. The climbing is not hard but can be unnerving.

The summit of Church had a rock cairn with a weathered ax handle in it as late as 1999 and a register tucked inside the cairn. From the top of Mount Church you can see all the highest peaks in Idaho, weather permitting — an amazing view. Because the other sides of Mount Church drop off steeply, it is best to descend via

28

the ridge and the route you came up.

4. DIAMOND PEAK

Round trip: 5.5 miles
Elevation gain: 4,600 feet
Highest point: 12,197 feet
Time: 7 to 8 hours
Difficulty: Strenuous, requires scrambling
Maps: USGS topographic: Diamond Peak. Forest Service: Island Park and Dubois Ranger Districts, Targhee National Forest
Information: Dubois Ranger District

GETTING THERE: From Idaho Falls, take I-15 north to the Salmon-Rexburg exit. Turn west and drive to Mud Lake. Just after Terreton turn north on Highway 28 heading to Leadore. About 13 miles past the INEEL boundary look for the area marked Blue Dome on the maps. There is not much there today except for a road up Skull Canyon to the east. About 1 mile past it is a sign on the left for Pass Creek. Take the Pass Creek Road (181); then in less than .3 mile take the first jeep road to the right, then the next jeep road to the left a quarter-mile later. This road heads northwest and hooks into a jeep road going due west toward the mountain. The road winds around and passes two barbed-wire gates and at about 5.5 miles a water tank for cattle. Be sure to close any gates you pass through. The jeep trail you want leads another .7 mile into the North Fork Pass Creek Canyon at the base of Diamond Peak.

Butte County's Diamond Peak, at 12,197 feet, is the highest peak in the Lemhi

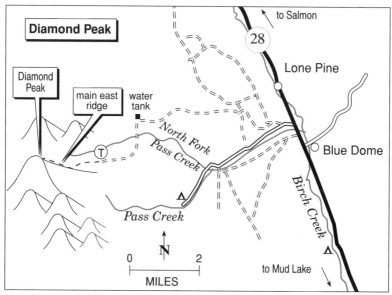

Scrambling up the main east ridge of Diamond Peak with the dry Birch Creek Valley in the background.

Range and the state's fourth highest peak behind Borah, Leatherman Peak and Mount Church, which are in the Lost River Range. The peak was first climbed in 1912 by T.M. Bannon of the U.S. Geological Survey. The peak was also skied from the summit by the late Duane Monte, a Forest Service ranger.

It is less physically demanding than Borah but more psychologically taxing. It lulls you up the slope — then wham! You find yourself scrambling on all fours up the last steep ridgeline. This ridge becomes for many a "Chickenout Ridge," like Borah's famous narrow section. But Diamond's tight spot is not hard, just spooky.

The peak shoots 6,000 feet out of the flat Birch Creek Valley. If you have a high-clearance vehicle you can drive right to the base of the mountain. From that point, it's less than 3 miles to the top, but it is much steeper than Borah because you climb 4,600 feet in those three miles.

To begin the climb go up a steep two track to the top of the peak's prominent east ridge, then follow that ridge all the way to the summit. The first mile of the ridge is still covered with soil. The route — mostly a faint trail — takes you through grass and sagebrush for the first half-mile, then into a stand of fir trees at .7 mile. At about 9,500 feet at 1.2 miles the soil disappears along with the trees and most other vegetation. Shell fossils from an ancient seabed are often seen in this section.

Now halfway up, you begin to climb over loose, broken rock. In some places, it's like walking up a steep soft pile of gravel. Eventually the ridge becomes more pronounced and the rock more solid, but here at about 2 miles the route becomes a scramble. If you're not used to scrambling, the next third of a mile can be grueling. It's not technically difficult, just a bit scary. Plan on it taking more time than you anticipate for the scrambling section. The route is almost all on the right side of the ridge, but stay as close to the ridge top as you can. If you don't, you may get stuck on hairy cliffs and never reach the summit. About 100 yards from the summit, the ridge gives way to an easy walk to the top at 2.75 miles.

The views of the nearby ranges are superb, except that in late summer and fall, range and forest fires may obscure the vista. From the summit you can see Borah

Peak to the west and Bell Mountain to the north. The Beaverhead Range to the east is most impressive. The summit is marked by a small pile of rocks forming a wind break and containing a summit register.

On the trek down, which is not as scary as you might expect, follow the ridge-line as much as possible. Beyond the scrambling section is a constant steep down-hill that can make your knees sore.

5. MOUNT BREITENBACH

Round trip: 7.6 miles
Elevation gain: 5,140 feet
Highest point: 12,140 feet
Time: 8 to 10 hours
Difficulty: Very strenuous, minimal scrambling
Maps: USGS: Leatherman Peak. Forest Service: Challis National Forest
Information: Lost River Ranger District
Getting there: Follow the maps carefully. The right canyon can be difficult to find. From Mackay, drive northwest on Highway 93 to Mackay Reservoir. Beginning about halfway up the reservoir there are three prominent canyons along the Lost River Range to the northeast. From south to north the first canyon is Upper Cedar Creek. The second is Pete Creek and the third is Jones Creek. About two miles north of the reservoir dam turn right (northeast) on Forest Service Road 127. This road is shown on the Challis Forest map as Upper Cedar Creek Road. Follow this dirt road straight for the mountains. After about three miles a left fork crosses a canal (a high-clearance vehicle is advised) and heads northwest along the base of the mountains. Take this road for about 1.8 miles to its end just below the mouth of Pete Creek Canyon.

Hiking up above Pete Creek Canyon below the summit ridge of Mount Breiten-bach over a dusting of late summer snow. In the back-ground is Mackay Reservoir.

This peak is a hybrid of Hyndman Peak and Peak 12,078 (Lost River Peak). There's a long approach similar to Hyndman and a narrow ridge to the summit akin to Lost River Peak. As is the case with most

31

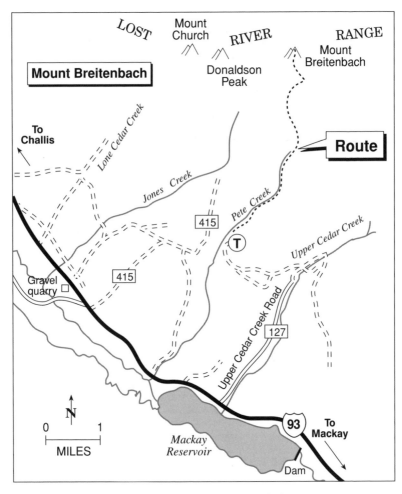

"named" peaks, Breitenbach receives a good share of visitors.

Mount Breitenbach is named after Jake Breitenbach, a well-known Teton mountaineer and guide in the 1950s. He died on Mount Everest in an ice fall during a trip that put the first American, Jim Whittaker, at the top of the world in 1963. In the 1930s, this peak was unofficially known as Hawley Peak after one of Idaho's governors.

The easiest way to the top of Mount Breitenbach is up Pete Creek Canyon. From the mouth of the canyon prepare for serious bushwhacking. If you don't want to wear long pants, you might consider wearing gaiters to protect your legs from the stinging nettle that infests the creek banks. After spring and early summer, the creek shrinks down and often disappears for several hundred yards, then reappears aboveground for a hundred feet or so, before disappearing again. It usually disappears for good 1.5 miles up the canyon. You'll have a much easier time keeping your boots dry if you climb this peak in late summer.

Hiking along the narrow ridge leading to the summit of Peak 12,078 (Lost River Peak).

The first two miles up the canyon gain 1,000 feet of elevation. After this the going steepens. At the top of the canyon at 2 miles you take a left turn (north) up a wide, steep gully with fairly stable footing. This steep gully eventually arrives at the headwall of the mountain. It is possible to go from the gully straight up to the southern end of the summit ridge, but it is easier to turn right and hike northeast up a relatively easy grade to a saddle between Peak 12,078 (Lost River Peak) and Mount Breitenbach. This saddle is on the crest of the Lost River Range at 11,400 feet at 3 miles.

When you arrive at the saddle, go left (north) and follow the ridge up to the summit ridge of Breitenbach at 3.3 miles at about 12,000 feet. As with most of the other 12,000-footers Breitenbach's east side is nearly vertical. Unlike Hyndman, its last big climb to the summit ridge is not ankle-popping talus, but fairly stable scree. Once at the top of the ridge, it's another half-mile north of up and down over a couple of smaller points to the summit at 3.8 miles. There are a few knife-edge stretches along this ridge. A faint route is apparent along some of the ridge and on the last uphill to the summit the ridge widens.

A plastic water bottle has served as a summit register in recent years. While most people climbed the peak up Pete Creek, a few traverse the crest from Lost River Peak, and a few come up the steeper Jones Creek Canyon. The mountain is too steep on the Pahsimeroi River side of the range to recommend approaching from the east or northeast for casual scrambling.

6. PEAK 12,078 (LOST RIVER PEAK)

Round trip: 5 miles
Elevation gain: 4,478 feet

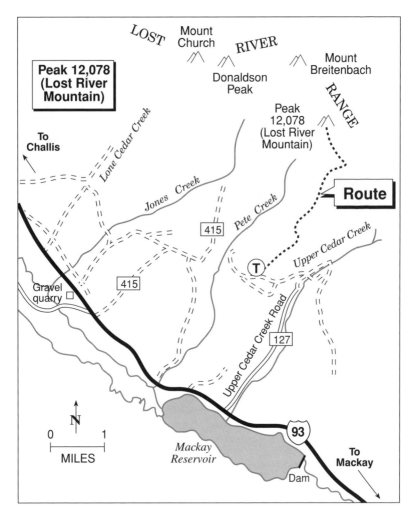

Highest point: 12,078 feet
Time: 5 to 8 hours
Difficulty: Strenuous, minimal scrambling
Maps: USGS: Leatherman Peak. Forest Service: Challis National Forest
Information: Lost River Ranger District.
   Getting there: Follow maps carefully; the right canyon can be difficult to find. From Mackay, drive northwest on Highway 93 to Mackay Reservoir. Beginning about halfway along the reservoir there are three prominent canyons along the Lost River Range to the northeast. The first canyon is Upper Cedar Creek. The second is Pete Creek and the third is Jones Creek. About two miles north of the reservoir dam, turn right (northeast) on Forest Service Road 127. This road is shown on the Challis Forest Service Map as Upper Cedar Creek Road. Follow this dirt road straight for the mountains. After about three miles a left fork crosses a canal (a

high-clearance vehicle is advised) and heads northwest along the base of the mountains. Within .3 mile it heads straight north to the mountains, going about a mile before ending at the base of the mountain wall next to an intermittent stream. Park below a prominent dirt bike trail that heads up the mountainside a few hundred yards.

The route up this peak is one of the shortest in distance and time of all the 12,000-footers, but what it lacks in distance, it makes up for in the climb of more than 5,000 feet and a unique personality.

This peak was known in the 1930s as Dorion, after an early fur trapper. In 1991, the name Mount Andrus (Idaho's governor during the 1980s) was proposed. Lost River Peak is probably its most currently popular name.

After an exciting, bumpy trip along the jeep trail to its base, you will find yourself staring up the monster supergully of the mountain. This peak is the last of the 12,000-footers on the southern end of the Lost River Range. Unlike some of the other big boys of the range that are tucked away behind a few lesser peaks, this peak is right up front, in your face. The jeep road takes you right to its base.

As with most mountains, if you're in good shape, this is a fun climb. And in the case of Peak 12,078, nearly every step takes you higher. That boils down to a fast climb. But expect a serious heart-lung-calf muscle workout.

The basic route up the peak is via the south-southwest-facing supergully, which is the intermittent stream about a half-mile to the right (east) of Pete Creek. Once in the supergully you follow it to the summit ridge. But obvious cliffs, pinnacles and escarpments block the lower part of the gully.

Here's how to avoid them. Begin the climb by taking an eroded motorcycle path that heads straight up the steep brush-covered slope. After about a fourth of a mile, the path disappears and you soon enter the trees. The trees are mostly weather-beaten junipers and an occasional mountain mahogany. The steepness of the slope is constant. As you climb through the trees, angle to the left across a small wash and head for a knoll (8,881 feet). This gets you onto the tree-covered ridge that parallels the gully on the right (east) side. Continue up this ridge until you reach its last tree at about 1.3 miles. Here turn left (west) into the supergully and climb up it. Here is where you start the scree section of the hike. The higher you get the narrower and more enclosed the gully becomes. About midway up the gully you are surrounded by deep cliffs and escarpments. In some places it looks like a warped and distorted stadium for giants. The higher up the gully, the steeper and looser the hiking becomes. We found ourselves hugging the left side of the gully for firmer footing.

The gully is often called a bowling alley by many who climb this peak. Indeed, any rocks that start rolling may go for several hundred yards. Stick close together or stay well spread out to avoid kicking rocks loose on others.

At the top of the supergully at about 2 miles, it narrows to a "gate" about 15 yards wide. This point is around 11,000 feet. Above the gate is a huge loose scree field that leads to the summit ridge. From the gate to the summit ridge is less than a half-mile, but the loose rock and added steepness make it seem farther. To reach the ridgeline sooner and avoid a steep slope straight ahead, angle to the right (left will work also) above the gate.

Once on the ridgeline, the views are wonderful and the way to the summit becomes obvious: Just stick to the ridge. A worn path can be seen in places here from previous climbers. Because of the angles, though, you won't be able to spot the summit until you almost clear the first big point on the ridge. During the late

1990s there was a weathered wooden post stuck in the top of the first high point along the ridge at 12,000 feet. From here you will spot the summit about a half-mile away along the ridge. It is marked by a large rock cairn. In several places the ridge narrows to less than 3 feet wide. Although there is some exposure along the knife-edge section of the ridge, the climbing is not difficult and is mostly level. Fortunately, the summit at 2.5 miles is much more accommodating than the ridge that leads to it.

On a clear day, the views of Mount Breitenbach to the north and Diamond Peak and Bell Mountain to the east are super. A military ammo can tucked inside the rock pile has been used as a register box.

The way down Peak 12,078 is a joy. What takes hours to ascend is skidded down in mere minutes on the loose scree. If you aren't adept at scree skiing, take it slow. Some sections that appear to be skiable are often solid and can throw you off balance. It takes about 15 minutes for the intrepid scree skier to fly down from the summit ridge to the lower end of the supergully at the top of the ridge of trees.

Although when snow-filled the avalanche danger can be extreme, this peak's supergully is becoming a classic descent for skiers and snowboarders who like their adventures a bit more wild.

7. MOUNT IDAHO

Round trip: 7 miles
Elevation gain: 5,065 feet
Highest point: 12,065 feet
Time: 8 to 10 hours
Difficulty: Very strenuous, scrambling required
Maps: USGS: Elkhorn Creek. Forest Service: Challis National Forest
Information: Lost River Ranger District
Getting there: Go north from Arco on Highway 93 about 6 miles north of Mackay Reservoir to Elkhorn Creek, which is just south of where Trail Creek Road turns off to the west. Turn right and drive along a bumpy road about a mile to a parking area along Elkhorn Creek at about 7,000 feet.

A friend who led the way to the top of this 12,000-foot peak said, "If you can do Mount Idaho, you won't have any trouble with the rest of the 12,000-foot peaks." It is not that it is particularly difficult and all the rest are easier. It just offers a little taste of what all the rest will throw at you. There's some heavy-duty bushwhacking and route finding, steep ups, steep scree, narrow ridges and crumbly towers on ridges to sneak around. There's also the time element. Unless you're a speed hiker, expect to spend around nine hours to go up and back.

Getting to the top of Mount Idaho is a three-part trek. The first part is the bush-whack up Elkhorn Creek canyon. The second is the climb up to and along the ridge that connects Mount Morrison and Mount Idaho. The third part is the scramble up the face of the peak to the top.

The climb starts out by following what's left of a jeep trail up the canyon. The trail quickly gives out and becomes mostly a cow trail paralleling Elkhorn Creek. It is necessary to cross the dry creek bed a couple of times to negotiate the narrow canyon. Elkhorn Creek is one of those "now you see it, now you don't" mountain streams that goes underground for long stretches at a time before reappearing as a

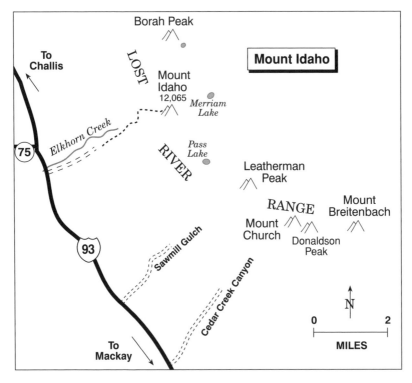

full-fledged creek again. As the route begins to gain in elevation, the cow trail disappears. Once it does, keep to the south side of the canyon which is thick with large firs, pines and junipers. This forest blocks most views of the goal ahead. Map reading and intuition are helpful during this part of the trip. It is easier to stay out of the creek's canyon from about .5 to 1.5 miles and go up a little gully south of the creek.

After climbing about 2.5 miles up the canyon and gaining 2,800 feet in elevation you want to move north (left) to reach a saddle on the ridge that connects the mountain sometimes called Morrison (11,367 feet) to Mount Idaho. This is where the sweating and panting begins. Begin climbing left (north) out of the canyon near a large field of boulders under which you can hear percolating water. The canyon becomes a headwall here anyway. These open areas give fine views of Mount Idaho high above at the top of the canyon. At this point, the peak is less than a mile away as the crow flies, but it looks much farther.

There are different possible approaches to the top of the ridge that connects Morrison to Mount Idaho. Perhaps the best is to keep to the sparsely forested slope above the boulder field on the left side of the canyon below Mount Morrison. This route avoids some of the scree and talus of other barren routes up to the ridge. After about 1,000 feet elevation gain, you come to the saddle and base of the pillars at 3 miles. At this point, the way to the top of Mount Idaho becomes obvious. Angle northeast to the top of the ridge, where you are treated to one of the best views of Mount Borah in the entire Lost River Range. The north side of the ridge

drops away dramatically. This is a good place to stop, catch your breath, and with binoculars watch a few people daintily picking their way across Chickenout Ridge toward the top of Mount Borah.

Once on the ridge, part two of the Mount Idaho climb begins. Physically, this is the easy part. The ridge climbs gently up, but you have to get past some crumbly sandstone pillars along the way. With a bit of care and scouting about, the way is usually obvious. At each pillar you basically only have three choices: left, right or straight over the top. Mostly you should stay left of the pinnacles. There is some exposure, but it's minimal. This ridge continues for less than a halfmile before climbing sharply to the top.

Pausing along the ridge between Mount Morrison and Mount Idaho. Mount Idaho is in the background. The route follows the ridge, then moves right up the face.

When the ridge turns up sharply, move over to the right (east) onto the face of the peak. Here you are presented with some steep loose scree and more solid rock best climbed on all fours.

It is a little easier if you climb along the dividing line between loose and solid rock. About a quarter mile up this steep slope, you come to the northeast ridge and can follow it northwest (left) to the summit. The summit is slightly higher on the northern end of this ridge. In the late 1990s, the top had a military ammunition can for a summit register.

8. HYNDMAN PEAK

Round trip: 13.6 miles
Elevation gain: 5,009 feet
Highest point: 12,009 feet

Time: 8 to 13 hours

Difficulty: Strenuous, easy scrambling required

Maps: USGS Topographic: Hyndman Peak, Grays Peak. Forest Service: Sawtooth National Forest

Information: Ketchum Ranger District

Getting there: Five miles south of Ketchum on Idaho 75 turn east on the East Fork of Wood River Road and drive 8.5 miles. Turn north on the Hyndman Creek Road, crossing to the north side of Hyndman Creek on a bridge 2.5 miles from the East Fork. Drive to the gate at the North Fork of Hyndman Creek 4 miles from the East Fork.

Old Hyndman Peak dominates the view looking south from the saddle between Old Hyndman and Hyndman Peaks.

At 12,009 feet, Hyndman is the shortest of the 12,000-footers. Its other claim to fame is that it is the only 12,000-footer in the Pioneer Range. Before surveyors checked out the Lost River Range, it was thought to be the state's highest peak. Hyndman Peak is Idaho's first 12er to be climbed and named. It was first climbed by the U.S. Geological Survey party of W.T. Griswold and E.T. Perkins in 1889. The peak is named for Maj. William Hyndman, a Civil War veteran and local mine superintendent. From 1889 to 1929 this peak was recognized as Idaho's highest mountain, at a bogus height of 12,078 feet. Because Hyndman is close to Sun Valley, it may be the second-most climbed 12,000-footer, after Borah Peak.

The trailhead to Hyndman Peak requires a Forest Service trailhead parking pass. This means that scramblers will need to purchase a use sticker from a Forest Service office to place on their vehicle when parking at the trailhead. Another concern for this area is the water. Because this area sees intense grazing by domestic sheep, it is important to filter or treat all water you intend to drink from area streams.

Snowfields can be a problem on this climb if you go too early in the season — usually before July. You won't need to worry about hard technical climbing or even much exposure with Hyndman, but you should expect a long, tiring trip. What adds to Hyndman's long day is hiking to its base. Several years ago it was possible to drive a bumpy jeep trail much closer to the base of the peak. Today, the

39

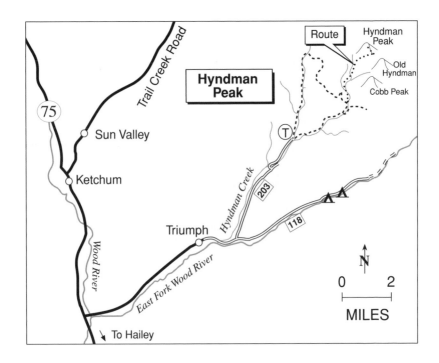

jeep trail is closed to motorized vehicles with a locked gate three miles farther down. The extra three miles are fairly easy hiking through beautiful Pioneer Mountain country along Hyndman Creek. Because of the long hike, if you live far from the peak, the climb will be easier if you camp at or near the trailhead the night before. The nearest developed campgrounds are at Federal Gulch and Sawmill on the East Fork Road a few miles beyond your turnoff.

The signed, easy-to-follow trail (along the old jeep road) begins near the north and south forks of Hyndman Creek. Fortunately it starts out with a footbridge across the creek. The next three miles winds through a variety of canyon habitats that include fir, aspen and willow, climbing only 1,000 feet. Avalanches have scoured chutes and left piles of debris on the steep southern side of the canyon.

At 2.5 miles an old jeep trail leads across the creek to the right. Stay on the left side of the creek. At 3 miles the trail turns left (north) off the jeep track and begins to climb as it goes around the southwestern end of the base of Cobb Peak. It climbs high above the creek and eventually reaches a flat meadow with a small pond at 3.5 miles. On our visit, we found near the pond a well-kept yurt belonging to and used by outfitters for their clients. The area is a beautiful setting with Cobb Peak dominating the background and pointy Hyndman Peak off in the distance.

Just up from the meadow, the trail toward Hyndman crosses to the right side of the creek and begins to switch back northeast up into the large basin formed by the three peaks — Hyndman, Old Hyndman and Cobb. (Another trail continues north from the pond to the top of a 9,500-foot saddle. It will eventually tie in with the Pioneer Cabin Trail.) These three peaks have been getting national recognition as an Idaho classic mountaineer's challenge. The "Triple Traverse" is a grueling technical climb of all three peaks in one day.

Once in the basin, the hard work begins. The higher you go, the more sparse the trees become. After about a mile the route climbs into the upper basin area where the trees all but disappear and vegetation consists mostly of high alpine tundra scrub. The views are impressive of the three peaks — Hyndman, Old Hyndman and Cobb — which are connected by saddles. Several hundred feet of nasty-looking cliffs rise straight to the summits of Old Hyndman and Cobb. Fortunately, Hyndman looks less intimidating. The goal here is the saddle between Old Hyndman on the right (southeast) and Hyndman on the left. On the way up the basin, there are a couple of beautiful tarns; one deep and shaped like a warped heart is at 5 miles.

Beyond this tarn you hike on talus (boulders) the size of apple boxes. You can avoid some of them by staying in the basin as long as you can while climbing to the saddle between Old Hyndman and Hyndman. It is much easier to climb along the ridgeline to the summit from the saddle than straight up to the summit from the basin. When you arrive at the saddle between the two peaks, you've already hiked 5.8 miles. On the edge of the saddle, you'll be treated to some wonderful views to the east over a 500-foot drop-off. To identify the lakes and peaks you'll need the USGS maps: Phi Kappa Mountain and Wildhorse Lakes.

As you follow the ridgeline from the saddle to the top of Hyndman, don't let the northeastern side's sheer cliffs intimidate you. It doesn't take as long as you may anticipate to get to the summit at 6.5 miles. You'll be going up the relatively straightforward route along the northwestern side of the ridgeline, although you have to do some easy scrambling up steep talus. The best route is found by staying 10 to 20 yards to the left of the cliff. Occasionally, a useful path presents itself.

The summit offers commanding views of the Pioneer, Lost River and Sawtooth ranges. In every direction you see mountains. There hasn't been a summit register on top. As is the case for many summits, coming down is the hairiest part of the climb. Because of the huge talus field, you must concentrate on every step. This is ankle-twisting country. Don't get in a hurry.

Lost River Range – West

9. CARLSON LAKE

Round trip: 7 miles
Elevation gain: 1,040 feet
Highest point: 8,593 feet
Time: 5 hours
Difficulty: moderate
Maps: USGS topographic: Doublesprings; Forest Service: Challis National Forest
Information: Challis Ranger District

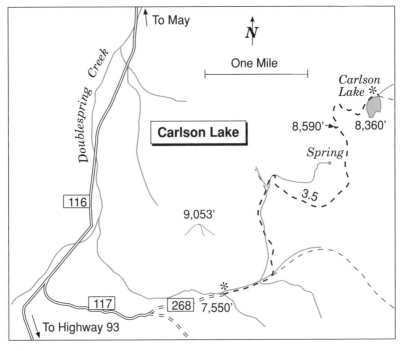

Getting there: On U.S. 93, 30.4 miles south of Challis turn left (north) on the Doublesprings Pass Road (116). Turn right (east) on the primitive Horseheaven Pass Road (117) at 10.9 miles. At 12.2 miles from the beginning of the Doublesprings Road, turn left (east) on the Carlson Lake Road (268). Park at 13.1 miles where the road fords a wash. (Those with four-wheel drive can continue on the rutted, rocky road to the top of the ridge at 16.1 miles.)

The jeep trail to the ridge above this lake gives a spectacular view of the cliffs and snowbanks of Mount Borah and the Lost River Range. The lake perches on a sagebrush bench below rust-colored cliffs with a view of the Lemhis. In early July, the pink flowers of bitterroot bloom among the rocks. The .5-mile descent from the ridge to the lake is so steep that hikers have to zigzag across the track.

To reach the lake from the deep wash at 13.1 miles, walk or drive a four-wheel-drive vehicle along the road in the sagebrush. Keep left at a junction with a side road at .5 mile. The track fords the main stream of the little canyon at 1 mile and continues along its left bank to a junction at 1.5 miles. Keep right here. At 1.6 miles the road swings right (east), fords the stream, and climbs 800 feet in a mile. At 2.3 miles it curves left, then at 3 miles reaches a junction on the saddle above the lake. The jeep trail to the right that goes to the lake is not open to motor vehicles.

Descend this trail 450 feet in a half-mile to the lake.

At 3.5 miles, the track splits and goes around either side of the lake. There are a couple of small campsites in the trees above the upper end.

---

10. BEAR CREEK LAKE

Round trip: 6 miles
Elevation gain: 1,600 feet
Highest point: 8,800 feet
Time: 6 hours
Difficulty: Moderate, with some route-finding
Maps: USGS topographic: Methodist Creek, Mackay; Forest Service: Challis National Forest
Information: Lost River Ranger District

Getting there: Turn east from U.S. Highway 93 onto the Pass Creek Road (122) one-half mile north of Leslie, which is 18 miles north of Arco. Keep right at a junction at 1.3 miles. At 4.7 miles the road enters Pass Creek Gorge, and at 7.1 miles leaves it. At 8.1 miles is a guard station and at 8.6 miles the Bear Creek Road (430) turns left (west). Take this road, keeping left up a steep hill at a Y at 9.7 miles. The trailhead is at 10.4 miles.

Below Bear Creek Lake, a pearl-gray mountain with three summits separated by chimneys guards the canyon. The three summits are composed of vertical rock layers resting on tilted layers. Splinterlike towers accompany this mountain. Above the upper end of the lake horizontal layers end in scallops. On one side are hills of grass and whitebark pine, and on the other talus and a mountain of lumpy cliffs. Campsites are small and rocky, and the lake has no inlet or outlet most of the summer.

*Bear Creek
Lake in the
Lost River
Range*

From the trailhead, the trail climbs the left side of the canyon of Bear Creek through aspens across from tan cliffs. At .3 mile the route fords the creek to the right (north) side on rocks. In late summer it is dry. The trail next goes along through river bottom shrubs. At .8 mile it turns uphill to the right. Here, the canyon forks, with Methodist Gulch to the left and Bear Creek to the right. Across the canyon is a mountain with a dent in the top ringed by semicircular layers of rock like half a bull's-eye.

The trail continues up Bear Creek. At 1.2 miles, it crosses a talus slope with a view of an old road across the canyon. In the woods at 1.6 miles a trail to Wet Creek turns off to the right. The trail to the left that goes on up the right side of Bear Creek is not shown on the topographic map, but that is the one you take to reach the lake.

At 1.8 miles, the trail angles above the creek in the open. Then it descends a rock outcrop to the brushy edge of the creek. Watch your footing here. At an open area of stumps at 2 miles, the trail becomes fainter. It continues through a Douglas fir forest on the right side of the creek.

At a cairn at 2.2 miles the trail crosses to the left (south) side of the creek and runs along through thick forest. At 2.3 miles it crosses a rock slide. Then the route returns to the right (north) side of the now invisible creek. It goes through trees, crosses a meadow, and skirts a talus slope. At 2.7 miles the route turns right (northwest) up a small side canyon where you glimpse splintery towers. The path goes through a long narrow basin and over a sagebrush hill to the lake at 3 miles.

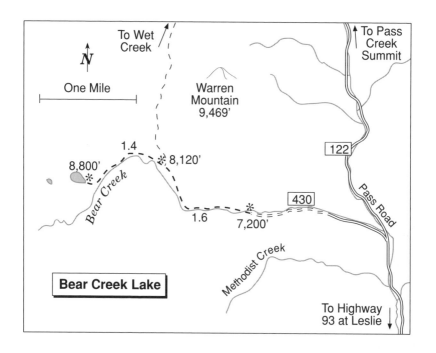

To Wet Creek

To Pass Creek Summit

N

One Mile

Warren Mountain 9,469'

122

1.4

8,800'

8,120'

Bear Creek

430

Pass Road

1.6

7,200'

Bear Creek Lake

Methodist Creek

To Highway 93 at Leslie

11. WET CREEK-LONG LOST TRAIL TO BIG CREEK

Round trip: 8.6 miles
Elevation gain: 1,260 feet
Elevation loss (return climb): 860 feet
Highest point: 8,880 feet
Time: 7 hours
Difficulty: strenuous
Maps: USGS topographic: Warren Mountain, Massacre Mountain; Forest Service: Challis National Forest
Information: Lost River Ranger District
Getting there: From U.S. 93 at Leslie, 18 miles north of Arco, turn right (east) on the gravel Pass Creek Road (122). Drive up to Pass Creek Summit (7,637 feet) at 12.2 miles. Turn left (north) here on an unsigned but improved dirt road (416) and drive to a signed trailhead at 14.2 miles. The access road no longer goes through the Loristica group campsite as shown on the maps. Keep straight ahead at 13.8 miles where a road turns downhill to the right to the campground through a gate. A new road leads .3 mile to the trailhead.

This is an old trail that leads past dramatic rock outcrops to a view of Big Creek Canyon, one of the most beautiful in eastern Idaho. Here above immense limber pines, vertical layers of limestone rib the west canyon wall. Farther up are three yellow-orange striped peaks, one with a split knob on top. Nestled below the layered headwall is a small trailless lake. Near the trailhead, a row of brown tow-

45

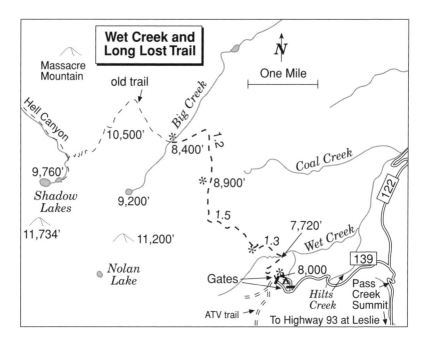

Wet Creek and Long Lost Trail

Massacre Mountain

old trail

One Mile

Hell Canyon

Big Creek

10,500'

8,400'

1.2

Coal Creek

9,760'

8,900'

Shadow Lakes

9,200'

1.5

7,720'

Wet Creek

11,734'

11,200'

1.3

139

Nolan Lake

Gates

8,000

Pass Creek Summit

Hilts Creek

ATV trail

To Highway 93 at Leslie

122

ers and a triangular gray peak with mustard yellow streaks overlook the canyon of Wet Creek. This trail leads from the Lorostica group campsite near Pass Creek Summit to Long Lost Creek, Dry Creek, and the forks of the Pahsimeroi. By walking along the East and West Fork of the Pahsimeroi roads hikers can continue to Leatherman Pass and descend to the Sawmill Creek Road near Mackay Reservoir. Thus the trail provides the opportunity for a trip of several days.

To reach the trailhead, follow the access directions above. The trailhead is west of the fenced campsite and southwest of the pond shown on the map. At the trailhead the road is closed to motor vehicles by posts. Here a "trail" sign points left up an old road that switchbacks uphill. **Do not take this!** It leads south 4 miles to Bear Creek.

Instead go straight ahead downhill on another old road that is the beginning of the Wet Creek-Long Lost Trail. It switchbacks to the right at .4 mile and is blocked off at .8 mile. Here, ford Wet Creek to the north side. Don't ford before that because there is a bog on that side of the creek.

Once across the creek, take a path up a sagebrush hill to a four-wheel-drive road at 1 mile. This road has come up the canyon of Wet Creek from the Pass Creek Road, but the roads don't connect as the map shows. Walk up the road, which switchbacks twice and ends at 1.3 miles. From the switchbacks there is a fine view up Wet Creek of triangular peaks with swirled rock layers.

From the end of the road, two trails take off. Keep straight ahead on the left trail, marked "trail." This trail is not shown on the topographic map, and at first has no blazes, but it is plain in most places and is slated for reconstruction. It goes along the right side of a stream into a meadow. From the meadow the trail goes up into the timber and along a small ridge, passing left of another small meadow.

The trail continues steeply up this ridge, then crosses to the left side of the stream. At 2.3 miles is a big flat meadow and pond. Here the route crosses back to the right side of the stream on a pole bridge. From the meadow the trail, now blazed, climbs a forested draw to a 8,880-foot, grass-covered divide at 2.8 miles. To the right here looms a 200-foot-high fang.

Beyond the divide the trail disappears in the grass for 200 yards. Avoid paths going left and right. At the end of the open area at 3.2 miles the trail splits, and both branches are blazed. Take the left branch into a sagebrush flat. At the end of this flat at 3.7 miles the trail switchbacks left (southwest) into the canyon of Big Creek, heading upstream. A "trail" sign marks this switchback.

Now the path descends the side of the canyon in Douglas firs to a quarter-mile-long boulder field at 4 miles. Here the view across and up the canyon is so remarkable the spot makes a good destination for a day hike. Below the boulders, the trail drops to ford Big Creek at 4.3 miles. In early summer, the creek is large and rushing, but by late summer it often dries up. To reach the small lake at the head of the canyon, it is probably easier not to cross the creek here but to stay on the left (east) bank of the creek. It is a mile and a 700-foot climb cross-country to the lake.

The trail over the divide to Shadow Lakes from the ford ascends the left side of the intermittent stream shown on the map as joining Big Creek at 8,360 feet. In .3 mile, where the stream splits, the trail climbs the right branch. At the head of the branch the tread disappears, but cairns lead south up a ridge to the top of a 10,535-foot plateau. For directions for the rocky, slid-away trail down to Shadow Lakes from the plateau see Hike 14, Shadow Lakes.

---

12. RAMSHORN CANYON

Round trip: 2.6 miles
Elevation gain: 800 feet
Highest point: 7,400 feet
Time: 3 hours
Difficulty: easy to moderate
Maps: USGS topographic: Ramshorn Canyon; Forest Service: Challis National Forest
Information: Lost River Ranger District
Getting there: From Darlington on U.S. Highway 93, turn east straight toward the mountains on a gravel road. There is no sign. At 2.9 miles the road comes to an intersection with the King Mountain Road (Hill Road on the topographic map). Here you may go straight ahead on a two-wheel track for 2.5 miles or go south 1.7 miles on King Mountain Road to another two-wheel track (Road 276) and take it northeast for 2.5 miles instead. Neither of these tracks is signed. Beyond where the tracks join 2.5 miles from King Mountain Road, the road is rocky and borderline for passenger cars. After another 1.6 miles, park by a big rock outcrop 4.1 miles from the King Mountain Road and 7 miles from Darlington. In another .2 mile the track becomes a steep jeep trail and the trail turns left from it.

More than three miles of the west side of Ramshorn Canyon are covered by fins and sails of pale gray rock. The trail leads to a grassy hillside with a fine view of this wall. The viewpoint is across from three cliffs, each several hundred feet high. One has a shallow cave in it like an oval window. On the other side of the canyon perch two burnt-orange mesas. Beyond them down the canyon rolls the

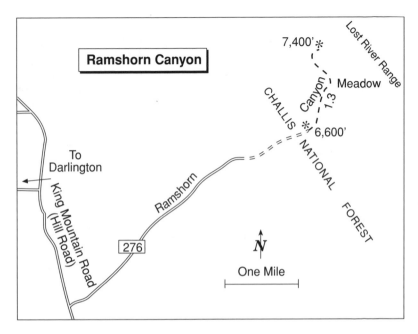

Ramshorn Canyon

7,400' *

Lost River Range

Meadow

CHALLIS

Canyon 1.3

* 6,600'

NATIONAL

To Darlington

Ramshorn

King Mountain Road (Hill Road)

276

N

One Mile

FOREST

black top of King Mountain, 10,612 feet.

To reach the unsigned trailhead follow the access directions above. Where the two-wheel track becomes a jeep trail in mountain mahogany, walk up the jeep trail a few yards until a trail turns off to the left along the hillside. Take this trail to a little swale of junipers and Douglas fir. Beyond the swale, it drops a few feet and goes along the side of a ridge in more firs. At .5 mile, the trail crosses the talus of a rock slide, then cuts over to the left side of the canyon to avoid the rocks. At .7 mile it drops into a meadow 100 yards wide and 150 yards long. The lower end of the rock slide extends into the meadow.

From the head of the meadow the trail climbs a notch between cliffs and a hillside of mountain mahogany. From the hillside a scarp can be seen high on the rock slide. The trail curves right and ends on a grassy hill at 1.3 miles, about .3 mile beyond and 400 feet above the end shown on the topographic map.

---

13. NATURAL ARCH

Round trip: 1 mile
Elevation gain: 540 feet
Highest point: 7,600 feet
Time: 3 hours
Ability: easy to viewpoint, strenuous to arch
Maps: USGS topographic: Arco North, Arco Hills; Forest Service: Challis National Forest
Information: Lost River Ranger District
Getting there: On U.S. 93, .3 mile southeast of its intersection with U.S. 20-

Natural arch northeast of Arco in the Lost River Range.

26 at Arco turn east across the tracks on a road signed "Cemetery." Along this road .3 mile, just across the highway from the Travel Plaza, turn right (east) on a gravel road that goes along transmission lines. At 1.3 miles turn left (north) on a two-wheel track signed Arco Pass. When you reach a steel barn and T intersection at 5.1 miles, turn right (east) on a dirt road. At 6.2 miles turn left (north) through a gate that must be opened and shut. The rutted road beyond the gate is fenced and posted on both sides. It winds and crosses small washes. At 8.7 miles at a corral, take the left fork. On it at 10.3 miles turn uphill to the right on a two-wheel dirt and gravel track that runs through high grass. Four-wheel drive may be needed to reach the end of this track, and a high clearance is advised. Park at the trailhead .2 mile before the track ends at 11.6 miles.

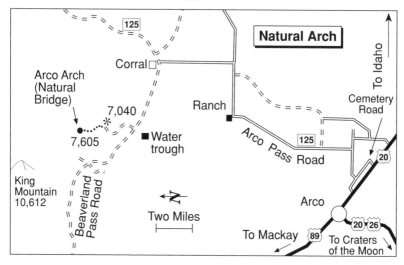

There are other Idaho arches at Craters of the Moon, in Jackknife Canyon near Howe, and at the City of Rocks, but this arch is large and stands on a mountain covered with cliffs. It is gray and beige and about 80 feet across and 60 feet high. A steep, pebbly trail that includes a series of stairs, climbs to an overlook of the arch. Boots and a walking stick are recommended. Climbing into the dell behind the arch is not recommended.

The town of Arco, where the access road begins, got its name from a count who was visiting in Washington, D.C., at the time the residents applied for a post office with the name "Junction." The town had become known as Junction because it was at the junction of the stage route from Blackfoot to the Wood River with the one to Salmon. The U.S. Post Office said there were already too many Junctions.

From the end of the road the trail goes through Great Basin rye and mountain mahogany in a slot between outcrops. Here you look up at 300 feet of jumbled cliffs. At .3 mile the trail enters a flat wooded glade in downed timber, where you can glimpse the arch for the first time.

To climb clear to the arch, look for two cairns marking a path to the left into the mountain mahogany, and take this path, which is less plain than others. It climbs 200 feet in the last 150 yards, at first straight up. Where it splits, take the left branch through mountain mahogany to the base of a cliff. Go left along the cliff to the arch, holding onto the rock as needed. The path goes under the arch and ends in the wooded dell behind it. Be very careful on the way back; the pebbles are like ball bearings.

Lost River Range – East

14. MERRIAM LAKE

Round trip: 6 miles (4 miles with four-wheel-drive)
Elevation gain: 1,440 feet
Highest point: 9,600 feet
Time: 5 hours
Difficulty: moderate, but treacherous footing
Maps: USGS topographic: Burnt Creek, Leatherman Peak, Elkhorn Creek; Forest Service: Challis National Forest

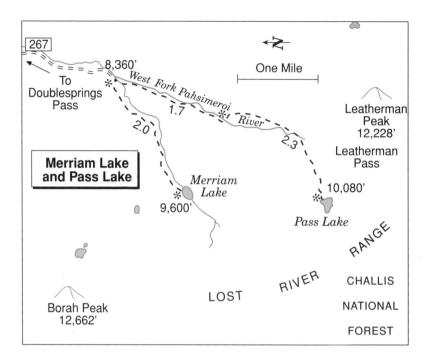

Information: Challis Ranger District

Getting there: Drive to the end of the primitive West Fork of Pahsimeroi Road. To do this, from U.S. Highway 93, go 24 miles south of Challis or 16 miles north of Mackay. Turn east on the dirt Doublesprings Pass Road (116) for 10.5 miles. Then turn right (south) onto the primitive Horseheaven Pass Road (117). At a short steep hill just past the turn, keep straight ahead for a gentler grade that rejoins the road at the top of the hill. Keep right at the Y where the road to Carlson Lake turns left. The main road crosses unmarked Horseheaven Pass at 14.3 miles, and at 16.7 miles a road joins from the left from Burnt Creek. This is a better road than the Horseheaven Road but much harder to find.

At 17.8 miles a sign warns that the road is not suitable for passenger cars. The track descends into the canyon of Mahogany Creek and fords it at 18.2 miles. Just past the creek a side road turns off to the right through a gate. Keep straight ahead. Immediately the road branches again, with the left branch climbing a steep hill. To avoid the steep hill, keep right and then left on a detour that rejoins the main road above the hill. Soon the road drops into the canyon of the Pahsimeroi River. Pahsimeroi is Shoshone for "water one grove" and honors the one grove of trees that used to be the only trees on the lower part of the river. At 21.8 miles is a cattlemen's cabin and corral with a fine view of folded and tilted rock layers on the canyon walls. Just beyond here you must open and shut a gate to continue. At 22.1 miles the road splits. Take the right (north) branch (Road 267) up the West Fork of the Pahsimeroi. From here, high clearance is essential. At 24.1 miles the road worsens. Most drivers without four-wheel drive will want to park here. After a rocky, rutted mile, park beside an informal campsite 25.1 miles from U.S. Highway 93. The road ends within 200 yards.

51

The trail to Merriam Lake is unique because it climbs over high, rounded outcrops of white marble. Talus, scree and a jagged wall of crumbly gray rock barricade the south side of the lake. At its head, frost hummocks and tree islands in a narrow meadow lead toward a jagged headwall and a pointed gray-striped peak. The access road is typical of the poor access roads on the east side of the Lost River Range. The Lost River Mountains are so beautiful that if the roads were better they would be crowded. From a campsite at the end of the West Fork of Pahsimeroi Road, walk along the road that crosses an intermittent stream to a ford of a branch of the West Fork. Just before the ford, the road ends at a trail sign. Here turn right (north) on the Merriam Lake trail. The turn is closer to the West Fork than is shown on the topographic map.

The trail climbs through woods and brush to disappear in a small meadow at 300 yards. Jog to the right across the meadow; do not take the path to the stream. The trail tread resumes, continuing southwest, on a sagebrush slope. After .3 mile it re-enters the woods, then crosses a larger meadow where the tread disappears again. At .5 mile the trail levels for 200 yards around the right side of a shrubby meadow. Here there is a view of folded rock layers on peaks up the West Fork.

The trail climbs steeply at a distance from the creek. At 1.4 miles, the ground flattens at a campsite in a small, hidden meadow. The path resumes climbing, now over benches of white marble. Watch your footing at 1.5 miles because the trail climbs 440 feet in .3 mile. At 1.8 miles the trail curves south around the end of a moraine to the lake at 2 miles. Campsites are along the north shore and among rock knolls at the upper end. Trout fishing is usually good in this lake.

15. PASS LAKE

Round trip: 10 miles (8 miles with four-wheel-drive)
Elevation gain: 1,880 feet
Elevation loss (return climb): 40 feet
Highest point: 10,040 feet
Time: 7 hours
Difficulty: strenuous
Maps: USGS topographic: Burnt Creek, Leatherman Peak, Elkhorn Creek; Forest Service: Challis National Forest
Information: Challis Ranger District
Getting there: Follow the directions under Merriam Lake to reach the end of the West Fork Pahsimeroi Road.

White marble talus and ledges edge Pass Lake with a few whitebark pines and small wildflower meadows for decoration. A bay on the north side of the turquoise lake resembles the handle of a frying pan. This handle points toward a yellowish ridge of notches and towers. To the east, stairsteps of dark rock climb the face of 12,228-foot Leatherman Peak, the second-highest mountain in Idaho.

Park beside the campsite and walk along the road. It fords an intermittent stream on rocks and then in 100 yards ends at a trailhead for the Merriam Lake and Pass Lake trails. These trails begin differently than shown on the topographic map. The West Fork of the Pahsimeroi has split into two branches just below here.

The Pass Lake trail begins by crossing to the left (east) side of the west branch of the West Fork. It then climbs along the right (west) side of the east branch for

Pass Lake in the Lost River Range.

the first part of the hike. Beyond the ford, the trail winds gently through subalpine firs and lodgepoles and outcrops of white marble-like rock. The creek runs in a small gorge. Soon the trail enters a long thin meadow with a view of Leatherman Peak ahead. After passing bits of forest and small meadows, the trail turns left downhill over a grassy slope and disappears. A cairn points to a ford to the left (east) side of the creek at 1.7 miles, with foot logs downstream. Across the creek, the trail cuts uphill in the woods. Avoid other paths by watching for blazes and constructed trail tread. At 2.3 miles is a large, long meadow below cliff-lined peaks.

At the upper end of the meadow is a campsite. An intermittent stream in the meadow splits and the trail goes along the right (west) side of its right branch, then disappears. The trail reappears in a forest of whitebark pines. Past the trees is a much bigger meadow leading to the talus of Leatherman Pass. The trail disappears again here. There are several streams in both meadows, but the main West Fork is over to the right in a ravine. Cross to the west bank of a little stream and head for a tongue of timber at the head of the big meadow. Above it you can see a faint track winding up the talus of Leatherman Pass, but there is no sign of it turning off. This faint trail continues 3 miles down the other side of the pass in a 3,500-foot descent to Road 411 in Sawmill Gulch just off U.S. 93. It allows backpackers to make a through trip from the Lorostica group campsite near the Pass Creek Road to Sawmill Gulch.

The Pass Lake Trail goes up a slot in the center of the tongue of timber, then curves right (northeast) and fords the main creek at 2.8 miles to the right (west) bank.

The trail climbs through partly open forest, then curves farther to the right

53

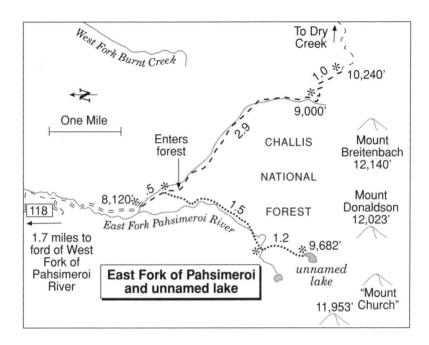

West Fork Burnt Creek

To Dry Creek

1.0 ★ 10,240'
★
9,000'

One Mile

Enters forest

2.9

CHALLIS

Mount Breitenbach 12,140'

NATIONAL

8,120 ★
.5 ★

118

1.5

FOREST

Mount Donaldson 12,023'

East Fork Pahsimeroi River

1.7 miles to ford of West Fork of Pahsimeroi River

1.2
★ 9,682'

East Fork of Pahsimeroi and unnamed lake

unnamed lake

"Mount Church"
11,953'

(north) to a small open area at 3.1 miles with a view of the peaks ahead. At another open area, it turns left toward the talus below the peaks. Here three cairns mark the correct route. Avoid a steep trail to the right to a campsite. The correct trail curves left along a small rocky ridge and climbs over rock ledges to the lake at 4 miles. Campsites near the lake are damp, small, and lumpy or rocky.

16. EAST FORK OF THE PAHSIMEROI

Round trip: 13.8 miles (6.8 miles with four-wheel drive)
Elevation gain: 1,000 to 1,360 feet
Elevation loss (return climb): 120 feet
Highest point: 9,100 feet
Time: 6 to 9 hours
Difficulty: Expert
Maps: USGS topographic: Burnt Creek, Leatherman Peak; Forest Service: Challis National Forest
Information: Challis Ranger District
Getting there: See Hike 14, Merriam Lake. At the junction of the roads up the East and West forks of the Pahsimeroi, 22.1 miles from U.S. Highway 93 via the Doublesprings and Horse Heaven roads, turn left on the East Fork Road (118) in the sagebrush. At 22.8 miles the road fords the West Fork and on the other side pulls up a steep hill. Both the ford and the hill require four-wheel drive, so leave two-wheel-drive cars before the ford. The trail mileage begins here.

From the ford the road climbs gently in the sagebrush. At 1.5 miles, a short,

54

pitted downhill stretch will require four-wheel drive to get back up. Just past this the road splits. Avoid the branch to the left because it has deep ruts, holes and side hills. Take the right-side branch straight ahead. It switches back to the left at the crest of a hill at 2 miles. Beginning at this switchback, there is another steep stretch that requires four-wheel drive to get back up. At the bottom of the hill the roads rejoin. At 2.7 miles the track fords the East Fork to the left (east) bank. At 3 miles is a camp-site at the edge of the woods. At 3.5 miles the road comes close to the creek and peters out within a few yards. A trail, signed Dry Creek Trail, begins where the road comes close to the creek.

Unnamed lake 9,682' in the Lost River Range

The goal of this hike is a grassy basin under the gray columned face of Mount Breitenbach. The mountain was named for Jake Breitenbach, who was killed on the 1963 American Mount Everest expedition. Half a dozen curved chimneys incise the 1,600-foot face of a triangular shoulder of the peak, forming a row of columns. The chimneys are so deep that snow fills them until late summer. Layers of rock corrugate the face horizontally as well. On the way to the basin, the trail passes peaks decorated with zigzag stripes and layers, including one where the stripes create a saddle blanket.

From a sign for Dry Creek Pass, cross the east branch of the East Fork of the Pahsimeroi on logs to the right (west) side. The trail follows this east branch. Once across, the trail goes across the sagebrush hills. At 4.3 miles it enters the forest, accompanied by several cow paths. Keep straight ahead up the canyon. At 4.6 miles the trail is on an open hill across the willow-choked creek from a talus slope. Beginning at 5.5 miles, sagebrush fills the canyon and there are only patches of forest.

Here the trail tread begins to disappear but the trail remains on the right side of the creek. It goes along just below the trees of the canyon wall. It has been rerouted above a slide and then goes through a gate in a pole fence. The trail tread ends in grass and sagebrush opposite a vertical cream-colored streak on the right canyon wall. About 150 yards before the end of this sagebrush-grass area a distinct gully comes down on the left side of the creek. Just beyond it several small whitened logs mark where the trail fords the creek to the left (west) side at 6 miles.

55

Once across, there is a faint path along the valley floor next to the stream. Avoid cow paths leading up into the woods and others on the valley floor. At the end of the big open area at 6.3 miles the canyon narrows, the creek runs in a gorge, and the trail tread ends again. The trail turns off to climb over the pass to Dry Creek, but there is little sign of it.

Game trails lead up either side of the gorge of the East Fork. Take the one that runs up the left side of the creek unless it is late summer and you can easily cross the creek. At 6.9 miles the gorge ends in the grassy basin under Mount Breitenbach.

To reach the pass to Dry Creek from here, climb west up an old avalanche path that is studded with little trees to the talus, where you may find traces of the trail. Follow its disappearing path to the divide. It is 1,200 vertical feet from the basin to the divide in about 1 mile. The top of the divide gives a view of the Dry Creek drainage and provides access to it by an equally faint path.

17. UNNAMED LAKE 9,682'

Round trip: 13.4 miles (6 miles cross-country); 6.4 miles with four-wheel drive
Elevation gain: 1,500 to 2,040 feet
Elevation loss (return climb): 120 feet
Highest point: 9,682 feet
Time: 7 hours from end of four-wheel-drive road, 10 1/2 hours from road ford of West Fork
Difficulty: Cross-country route
Maps: USGS topographic: Burnt Creek, Leatherman Peak; Forest Service: Challis National Forest
Information: Challis Ranger District
Getting there: See Hike 14, Merriam Lake and Hike 16, East Fork Pahsimeroi.

This challenging cross-country hike climbs to a tiny lake under the dramatic black face of a peak unofficially called Mount Church. The 1,500-foot face of this peak is covered with curved rock stairsteps often outlined with snow. The blue lake perches on dark gray talus and ledges, that are softened by grass, larkspur, and elk thistle. On the ridge to the right of the lake, layers of orange rock resemble a stack of smiles. A second, slightly higher lake is only a half-mile from the route to the first.

From the point where the East Fork of the Pahsimeroi Road (118) comes close to the creek 3.5 miles from the place where it fords the West Fork of the Pahsimeroi, take the Dry Creek Pass Trail. The trail first crosses the east branch of the East Fork on logs to its right (west) side.

About .5 mile from this crossing turn off the trail and aim for a string of open rolling areas shaped like a fishhook on the map and go along them until close to the main East Fork at 4.5 miles. Here, stay on the left (east) side and take a game trail going along the top of the ravine the creek runs in. It is a good path that keeps at a distance above the creek, and at 5.1 miles crosses a tongue of talus. At 5.5 miles, just before a side stream, cross the main creek to the right (west) side to avoid a cliff where it curves west and then bends 90 degrees south. Now there is no path. Soon you can see the 200-foot cliff that you crossed the creek to avoid.

At 5.7 miles the canyon widens out into a rocky basin where the creek below turns 90 degrees to the right (west). As you climb along the talus, waterfalls appear on the creek ahead. Continue up until you are above the waterfalls at about 6 miles.

To reach Lake 9,682', turn south from the top of the waterfalls and head toward a grassy basin. Cross the creek to the south side, and aim for the ravine in which the intermittent stream from the lake descends. Walk along the talus on the right (west) of this ravine until a little grassy valley appears on the left side of the stream. Cross into it for a few yards, then return to the right side of the stream and climb to the top of a grassy shelf below a headwall at 6.4 miles. On the left here are cliffs and ledges and on the right boulders. Climb over the boulders because they are more stable than the loose pebbles on the ledges.

At the top of the boulder field is a gully. Walk up it to the lake at 6.7 miles. To reach the other lake at 9,781 feet, back at the top of the waterfalls keep straight ahead and then turn southwest with the creek to the lake about .6 mile from the waterfalls.

In planning your hike, remember that cross-country hiking takes longer than hiking on a trail.

18. DRY CREEK TRAIL

Round trip: 14 miles to valley below divide with the East Fork of Pahsimeroi River (9.6 miles with four-wheel drive); 4 more miles round trip to the divide
Elevation gain: 560 feet
Highest point: 8,240 feet
Time: 6 1/2 to 8 1/2 hours
Difficulty: Strenuous to ford of Dry Creek just below junction with Swauger Lakes trail; expert above that
Maps: USGS topographic: Red Hills, Mulkey Bar, Short Creek, Massacre Mountain, Leatherman Peak; Forest Service: Challis National Forest
Information: Lost River Ranger District
Getting there: Drive to the trailhead beyond the ruins of the old Dry Creek Dam using these directions: On the road from Howe to Patterson and Ellis, 27.7 miles north of Howe, turn left (west) on the Pass Creek Road. The Howe-Ellis Road is paved this far. The gravel Pass Creek Road crosses Wet Creek on a bridge at 33.4 miles. Both topographic and forest maps are needed to find the correct turns from here on. At an unsigned junction at 33.7 miles turn right (north) off the Pass Creek Road. At 34.7 miles this road crosses the Dry Creek Canal. Follow a dirt road along the right (north) side of the old canal and along the left side of the new underground water pipeline. The road heads toward a canyon that curves left into the mountains. Well into this canyon, at 42.5 miles, a road signed "May" joins at an angle in Section 20 on the map. It has come south and then west up the north side of Dry Creek. The road becomes rutted here and at 44.5 miles appears to end below the Dry Creek Dam.

Just before the dam take an unsigned road left that begins by angling northeast back down the valley .3 mile. Then this road turns right (south) up a steep hill to a plateau overlooking the new reservoir. The road continues southwest along the plateau, dropping in and out of a gully. At 45 miles an unsigned road joins from the left. At the end of the plateau at 46 miles the road descends a long switchback

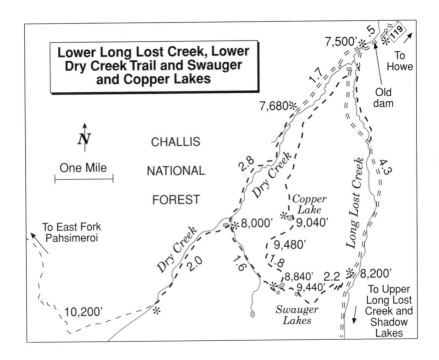

Lower Long Lost Creek, Lower Dry Creek Trail and Swauger and Copper Lakes

CHALLIS

NATIONAL

FOREST

N

One Mile

To East Fork Pahsimeroi

7,500'   To Howe

Old dam

7,680'

Copper Lake

8,000'   9,040'

9,480'

8,840' 2.2 8,200'

9,440'

To Upper Long Lost Creek and Shadow Lakes

Swauger Lakes

10,200'

Dry Creek

Long Lost Creek

1.7

.5

119

2.8

4.3

2.0

1.6

1.8

to the left. From a spur road at the top of the switchback you can look down on the ruins of the old Dry Creek Dam, which was washed out in a cloudburst. At 46.7 miles is the trailhead. Here a sign says "Shadow Lake 9 miles" and another sign "Trail." Leave your car here or back up on the plateau (there is little or no parking at the sign) unless it has four-wheel drive and high clearance. If you choose to drive farther you should be experienced with four-wheel-drive travel and not mind risking damage to your vehicle. The road may be closed to motor vehicles here in the future. The trail mileage for this hike starts here.

From the trailhead walk down the steep four-wheel-drive road, which crosses a talus slope. Just before the junction of the Long Lost and Dry Creek Roads at .8 mile the road fords Long Lost Creek. At the junction take the right branch of the road, which immediately fords Dry Creek to the right (west) side. The roads are a little different here than they are shown on the topographic map. At 1.1 miles a road goes off to the right at a log cabin. At 1.6 miles the road goes through a gate, and at 2 miles it goes up on a side hill that effectively ends it. Don't try to drive farther. From this point you can see the trail to Copper Lake across the creek on the sagebrush ridge. It begins on the road up Long Lost Creek just past its junction with the Dry Creek Road.

From halfway up the canyon of Dry Creek the view is of a caramel-colored peak swirled with white stripes and a dark gray mountain with contorted layers. The trail leads to an immense sagebrush and wildflower flat with a view of the striped headwalls of the three canyons that join here. Beyond the flat there are only traces of trail, but it officially continues over a divide to the East Fork of the Pahsimeroi River.

58

From the point where the road up Dry Creek goes up a side hill, 2 miles from the ruins of the dam, walk along the level road in sagebrush above willows. At 2.8 miles the track is on the right side of a side creek from a spring above. By 3 miles when the trail fords this stream to the left (south) side, the road has become a trail. At 4 miles, high water has carried logs 20 vertical feet above the creek. The trail crosses a sagebrush flat and then edges the steep creek bank. At 4.9 miles the trail fords Dry Creek to the left (east) side. This ford can be difficult in early summer during high water.

At 5 miles, at a beaver pond, the trail to Swauger Lakes turns off to the left. The trail on up Dry Creek is an official trail but is not shown on the topographic map. It goes around the south side of the pond over small sagebrush hills and above marshy ponds. At 6 miles, opposite a dragonlike mountain with a red streak on it, the trail runs right beside the creek. Beyond a patch of forest is an immense sagebrush flat at 6.8 miles. Here two creeks from side canyons on the left come out on the flat. The first is usually dry, but the trail fords the second to a grassy flat where the trail tread ends at 7 miles. There are possible campsites here.

To find the remnants of the trail from here on, look for a path to the right into the woods along the main creek. Take this path across the main creek to the right (west) side. The path climbs a grassy slope, turns left into a patch of forest and at 7.3 miles comes out on a sagebrush hillside with a view of the divide above. On the divide, a faint path can be seen angling across a grassy slope to the summit. Expert route-finding skills are needed to continue to the divide.

19. SWAUGER AND COPPER LAKES

Round trip: 8 miles for both lakes from end of four-wheel-drive road in Long Lost Canyon; 13 miles for loop trip from trailhead beyond ruins of old dam

Elevation gain: 1,120 to 1,820 feet to Swauger Lakes; 520 feet additional for Copper Lake via Swauger Lakes

Elevation loss (return climb): 480 feet for Swauger Lakes; 520 feet additional for Copper Lake

Highest point: 9,320 feet

Time: 6 hours to 2 days

Difficulty: Strenuous

Maps: USGS topographic: Mulkey Bar, Red Hills, Short Creek, Massacre Mountain; Forest Service: Challis National Forest

Information: Lost River Ranger District

Getting there: See Dry Creek for directions for reaching the trailhead below the old Dry Creek Dam. Even though the road beyond the trailhead is open to four-wheel-drive vehicles, it is safer to begin walking at the trailhead. That's because the road plunges over talus with a dropoff on the side toward the creek. This section requires four-wheel-drive low range to come back up. At .7 mile keep right at an unsigned junction. The road fords Long Lost Creek and at .8 mile comes to a signed junction for Long Lost Creek. Turn left (south) here. The road goes up on sagebrush hills and then downhill and fords the creek to the east side. Soon it goes out into a wet meadow at 3.8 miles where in early summer springs may block travel. At 4 miles the track fords the creek back to the right (west) side. At 4.8 miles at a signed junction the Swauger Lakes Trail turns off to the right.

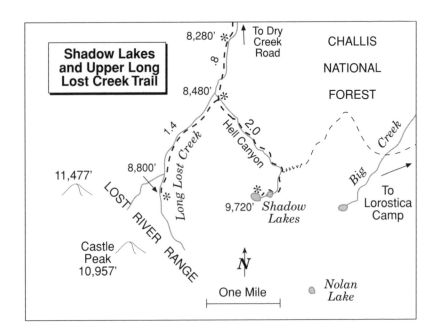

The largest of the two Swauger Lakes is a 100-yard pond set in grass and wildflowers below sagebrush hills. Above it to the east, folded rock layers on a ridge form a row of C's. On the other side of the canyon loom two peaks with crumbly towers and swirled rock layers. Across Dry Creek from the trail to Copper Lake a red streak drips like blood from a red circle on the head of a dinosaur-shaped mountain.

From the Long Lost Road 4.8 miles above the ruins of the old dam the Swauger Lakes trail angles through the sagebrush toward rock layers on the canyon wall. The route differs from that on the topographic map. At first the trail switchbacks up the left (south) side of the intermittent stream shown on the map. A half-mile of it was rerouted in 2000 by adding switchbacks to lessen the grade, so the total distance is now a little more than given here. At 5.7 miles it fords the stream to the right side and goes along in open sagebrush across from a wooded rocky knoll. At 5.9 miles the grade flattens out. The trail follows the creek to its source on a flat divide .3 mile south of the pond shown as being on the trail. Plans are under way to reroute the Swauger Lake Trail to avoid wet places and fix steep places, so by the time you read this the route of the trail may be a little different.

From the flat divide the trail angles down the side of the ridge with a view of the smaller lake ahead. At 7 miles at a signed junction, turn right (north) a few yards to the larger lake, or walk down to the smaller lake below. Because the lakes have grassy shores, be sure to camp well away from them.

A trail leads to Copper Lake from the larger lake. It begins at the lower end of the lake and leads around the left side of the lake to a flat north of the lake at 7.2 miles. (The rerouting will probably put this trail on the right (east) side of the lake and well above it.) From the flat, the trail curves around the left side of a red rock hill (10,297 feet) to a flat saddle at 9,480 feet at 8.1 miles. At the saddle the trail turns east and then north to the lake at 8.8 miles. It is 3 miles from here down to the trailhead on the Long Lost Creek Road near its junction with the Dry Creek Road. When it is rerouted to lessen the grade, it may be as much as a mile longer.

To make a loop trip to Swauger Lakes and back without going to Copper Lake, descend a rocky trail northwest down the fork of Dry Creek that feeds Swauger Lakes. It is 1.6 miles down this trail to the Dry Creek Trail. For .5 mile it descends sagebrush slopes and then crosses back and forth over the creek and goes in it through a narrow canyon. This trail would be difficult in early summer and in a wet year, and the footing is treacherous even when the creek is dry.

20. UPPER LONG LOST CREEK

Round trip: 4.4 miles from end of four-wheel-drive road; 16 miles from trail-head beyond ruins of old dam
Elevation gain: 400 to 1,220 feet
Highest point: 8,720 feet
Time: 5 1/2 hours to 2 days
Difficulty: moderate to strenuous
Maps: USGS topographic: Mulkey Bar, Red Hills, Short Creek, Massacre Mountain; Forest Service: Challis National Forest
Information: Lost River Ranger District
Getting there: Follow directions under Dry Creek Trail for driving to the trail-head below the old Dry Creek dam. Then hike the jeep trail up Long Lost Creek to the end of the road at 5.8 miles.

The road up Long Lost Creek heads towards a triangular mountain whose dozen rock layers resemble a stack of ropes bent back at an acute angle, with the layers ending at the summit. Across the canyon from it, remnants of the same pattern haunt the cliffs. The trail up Long Lost Creek passes this mountain and a meadow of sagebrush and wildflowers. Then it runs below the cliffs of Castle Peak, which rock layers zigzag across.

From the end of the road 5.8 miles from the trailhead below Dry Creek Dam, the trail climbs along the right side of the creek for .6 mile before it fords the creek to a sagebrush bench on the left (east) side. At 6.6 miles a grassy tongue extends up a side canyon called Hell Canyon that leads to Shadow Lakes. Here there is a junction with a trail to the lakes.

Beyond the junction, the Long Lost Creek Trail fords Hell Canyon Creek. Then the trail climbs along in the forest at a distance from the creek. At 7.1 miles it passes beneath two tongues of talus and at 7.2 miles comes out on an open slope above a big flat meadow. At 7.7 miles the trail descends into a big meadow and disappears in talus. Beyond the meadow the path runs through the trees to a sage-brush-covered alluvial fan and stops at 8 miles. Three canyons meet here. Parts of the Long Lost Creek Trail will be rerouted soon, so it may be easier to find by the time you read this.

There is no sign of the old trail going over a divide to Upper Cedar Creek. Beyond the end of the trail, 2 more miles of the main canyon and a side canyon with ponds give opportunities for cross-country exploring.

21. SHADOW LAKES

Round trip: 5.6 miles from end of four-wheel-drive road; 17.2 miles from trailhead beyond ruins of old dam (1 mile cross-country)
Elevation gain: 1,400 to 2,220 feet
Highest point: 9,720 feet
Time: 5 1/2 hours to 2 days
Difficulty: moderate to strenuous
Maps: USGS topographic: Mulkey Bar, Red Hills, Short Creek, Massacre Mountain; Forest Service: Challis National Forest
Information: Lost River Ranger District
Getting there: Follow directions under the Dry Creek Trail to drive to the trailhead below the old Dry Creek Dam. Then walk to the end of the Long Lost Creek Road 5.8 miles from the trailhead at a campsite marked by a large boulder.

Shadow Lakes are milky turquoise tarns in gray talus and ledges softened by grass, moss, larkspur and giant pale green blossoms of elk thistle. An immense cliff of swirling vertical stripes overhangs the lakes. To the left of it the ends of slanting rock layers form pinnacles on the ridge. To the right of the swirled cliff, the layers are horizontal. Small waterfalls splash in chimneys, and snow cornices garland the top of the cliffs. A short side trip up a discontinued trail leads to a divide with a view into the canyon of Big Creek and often a view of deer, elk or mountain goat.

From the end of the road, follow the trail along the right side of the creek to the ford to the left (east) side of Long Lost Creek at 6.6 miles. Beyond the ford, continue up Long Lost Creek to the Shadow Lakes Junction at 6.8 miles. From this junction, the trail to the lakes turns up Hell Canyon on the left side of its creek, NOT the right side as shown on the topographic map.

The trail climbs steeply along the side of a rocky slope patched with subalpine fir and whitebark pine. The rock layers on the mountain across the canyon are so bent and curved that they resemble layers of rope. After crossing a tiny side stream the trail goes along grassy talus below tilted rock layers that have eroded into pinnacles. Below, the creek meanders in a rocky trench. At 7.8 miles the trail tread stops in a grassy basin at timberline. Beyond here rock cairns mark the way.

Switchbacks of an old trail (the Wet Creek-Long Lost Trail) into Big Creek appear ahead to the left going up ledges to a divide. To reach the lakes, ignore the switchbacks and follow the stream up between ledges and over turf to the first lake at 8.5 miles. To reach the upper lake at 8.6 miles, go around the lower one on the right and climb carefully up the ledges.

To reach the divide instead, from the base of the switchbacks climb carefully up them. On several the corners are slid away, making the footing treacherous. There are plans to renovate the trail. It is .5 mile and an 800-foot climb to the top of the divide. For a better view of the other side, follow rock cairns for .5 mile along the left side of the 10,535-foot flat summit northeast of the divide. From this summit you can see the trail descending an intermittent stream flowing into Big Creek east of the flat summit.

Lemhi Range – West Side

22. NORTH FORK OF BIG CREEK

Round trip: 13 miles to the junction with the Park Fork Trail
Elevation gain: 1,100 feet
Elevation loss: 40 feet
Highest point: 7,660 feet
Time: 8 1/2 hours
Difficulty: Strenuous
Maps: USGS topographic: Big Creek Peak, Yellow Peak; Forest Service: Challis National Forest
Information: Challis Ranger District
Getting there: On U.S. Highway 93, 19 miles northeast of Challis at the Ellis post office turn right (south) onto the paved road signed May and Patterson. The road passes a turnoff for May at 10.7 miles and one for the Patterson school at 22.6 miles. Turn left (east) onto the Big Creek Road (097) at 29.8 miles, just after a bridge over Big Creek. Drive to the end of this dirt road at 33.3 miles, passing the

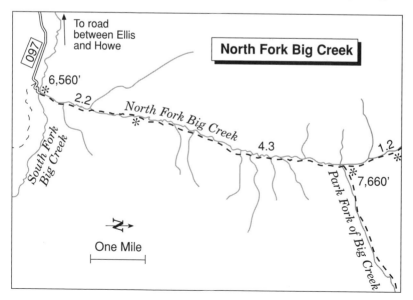

beginning of the South Fork of Big Creek trail at 33.1 miles. There is ample parking at the South Fork trailhead, but the North Fork trailhead across a bridge over the South Fork has limited parking. The .2 mile between the two trailheads is steep and rocky.

This trail leads from the Douglas fir and mountain mahogany growing on the cliffs of the narrow entrance to the canyon into a wider canyon of forest, talus, willows and raspberries. By the time it reaches the Park Fork the walls are again lined with cliffs and ears of rock, but the forest has changed to lodgepole pine and aspen. The lower part of the trail makes a pleasant day hike, especially in early summer when wildflowers are at their height. The trail received a lot of work in 2000, including rerouting around boggy areas. Because the access road is better than the road to Timber Creek Reservoir on the east side of the range, this route to Yellow Lake is easier for horse parties.

As you approach the access road from the north, you pass near the villages of May and Patterson. May was named by the postmaster's wife because the application for a post office was made in the month of May. Patterson was named for Joe Patterson, who found a silver ledge there in 1879. In 1903 tungsten was discovered on Patterson Creek and it was mined from 1911 to 1958.

The trail up the North Fork of Big Creek starts out through willows below talus and ledges, then climbs above the creek in Douglas fir and mountain mahogany. At .6 mile, it crosses a side creek on rocks. The way continues along steep, grassy and forested hillsides.

At 1.2 miles, just beyond the confluence of the West Fork and the North Fork, the trail fords to the left (west) side of the creek. From the ford, blazes lead upstream to a log footbridge. Now on the west side of the creek, the trail goes along the base of a talus slope then into Douglas fir. At another ford at 2.2 miles, take a blazed path through the willows 150 yards to a log footbridge leading back to the (right) east side of the creek. The footbridge path rejoins the main trail at 2.3 miles at a cairn.

The trail goes through willows and Douglas firs and then climbs away from the creek. At 3 miles it hops a side creek, then comes out on a grassy hillside where brown cliffs are across the creek. At 3.7 miles the trail climbs a knoll with a view of the canyon. At 4 miles it crosses the first of three talus slopes just above thick shrubs. Many of these are berry bushes, so watch for bears.

At 4.4 miles the trail enters a lodgepole forest that burned in the 1990 Big Creek Fire. Be cautious here, for dead trees may fall, especially on windy days. At 4.7 miles is a large campsite in a grassy flat.

Next, the trail goes along level in grass and Douglas fir opposite two rocky knolls. At 5 miles and 5.2 miles the trail fords side streams, then edges the creek and heads away from it over outcrops and boulders, and through alders and aspens. At 6 miles you can look across the creek to a high cliff. At 6.4 miles the trail crosses the Park Fork in two sections on rocks or downstream logs. Beyond a jumble of avalanched logs the trail turns up the Park Fork to the junction with the Park Fork Trail at 6.5 miles. This trail gives access to Yellow Lake in 6 miles and to the Big Timber Creek Trail.

23. DEVILS BASIN AND THE PARK FORK LOOP FROM YELLOW LAKE

Round trip: 26.5 miles
This section (loop trip from Yellow Lake): 12.1 miles
Total elevation gain: 5,780 feet
Elevation gain for loop: 3,230 feet
Highest point: 10,250 feet
Time: 10 1/2 hours
Difficulty: Expert
Maps: USGS topographic: Yellow Peak; Forest Service: Salmon National Forest
Information: Challis Ranger District
Getting there: Using the directions under Yellow Lake from the Middle Fork of Timber Creek, hike to Yellow Lake. Or use part of this description and the preceding description to reach Yellow Lake via the North Fork of Big Creek.

This loop trip on little-used trails and one cross-country stretch gives hikers a thorough view of the Lemhi Range. The highlight is a wildflower meadow at the

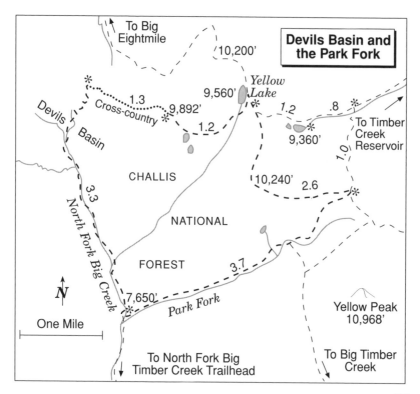

65

base of a 800-foot prow of rock in Devils Basin.

To begin the loop from Yellow Lake, hike down to the pond below the lake, ford the outlet and find a trail at the base of cliffs and follow it to the left (southwest). It disappears at times, but at 1 mile can be found climbing a gully northwest to a 9,892-foot divide. South of the trail about 200 yards from where it begins to climb are two tiny unmapped lakes at 9,493 feet. They can be seen from the divide.

North of the divide is the canyon of Big Eightmile Creek with a trail coming up it that leads to Yellow Lake. There is a sketchy trail from the divide down into Big Eightmile Creek Canyon, but there is no trail at present from Big Eightmile Creek into Devils Basin even though one is shown on the map.

Therefore, to reach the basin from the divide you must go west cross country to a saddle between Big Eightmile Creek and Devils Basin. To do this, descend the trail towards Big Eightmile Creek 200 vertical feet. Then leave the trail and climb left (west) over big boulders to a high grassy shelf at 9,800 feet at 1.5 miles. Go west across the shelf to a stream at 2 miles. From here, follow a game trail northwest up the ridge ahead to the 9,600-foot divide at 2.5 miles. A few yards west of the divide, the constructed trail down to Devils Basin appears just left (east) of the center of the little canyon that leads to the divide.

Follow this trail down through the woods to the meadow with the view and the wildflowers at the lower end of Devils Basin. Here the tread disappears. From the lower end of the meadow the trail has been rerouted from what is shown on the map. It fords the creek to the right (west) bank just below the meadow at 3.5 miles, rather than .2 mile below the meadow as the map shows. The route descends the right side of the creek through lodgepoles, rocks and a couple of side streams to a ford to the left (east) bank at 4.5 miles. The trail continues though grass and willows, disappears briefly now and then, and crosses back and forth over the creek, ending up on the east bank at 4.8 miles. At 5.2 miles it fords a side creek called the

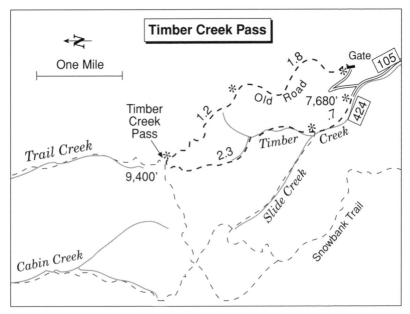

Lake Fork. This ford may be difficult in early summer.

The trail descends the Lake Fork a few feet, then continues down the main North Fork to a junction with the Park Fork Trail at 5.8 miles. The junction is 2.3 miles below Devils Basin and 6.5 miles above the North Fork of Big Creek trailhead.

From here on the distances are measured from the junction for the convenience of those going to Yellow Lake from the North Fork of Big Creek trailhead. It is 6.3 more miles from this junction to Yellow Lake.

The trail up the Park Fork switchbacks up the canyon wall at the edge of a gorge. At 1 mile it becomes less steep and there are rocks and avalanche debris. At 1.8 miles below a meadow the creek runs in a ravine. After a second meadow, the trail climbs away from the creek and at 2.6 miles crosses the outlet of a little lake known as Park Fork Lake. The route crosses to the right (east) bank of the main creek, then at a crossing not shown on the topographic map at 2.8 miles it returns to the left bank. Now the tread disappears from time to time, but it stays on the north side of the creek.

Continue straight ahead for 150 yards on a faint track, watching for blazes. At a curve to the right, an apparent path goes straight ahead uphill, but this is not the trail. Take the path that curves right. From here until the Middle Fork of Timber Creek Divide, the trails and their junctions are confusing. They are even more confusing because they are not correct on the topographic map. At 2.6 miles the route meets a trail that runs south over a divide to Big Timber Creek. This signed junction is on the north side of the creek at the lower end of a sloping, half-mile-long meadow.

To continue to Yellow Lake or the Middle Fork of Timber Creek from this junction, turn left (north) and look up the meadow 200 yards to a blaze on a big tree. There is no tread, but this is the trail. To find it, follow widely spaced blazes and metal posts. At the upper end of the meadow, trail tread appears again, and it leads to the Middle Fork of Timber Creek Divide at 3.5 miles. The junction of the trail to the Middle Fork of Timber Creek and the trail to Rocky Creek with the trail to Yellow Lake are at the 9,520-foot divide rather than .5 mile southeast of it as the map shows. At the junction on the divide, turn left (west) on the Yellow Lake Trail which curves north over the ridge at 10,240 feet as shown on the map and drops 700 feet to the lake at 6 miles. The loop from Yellow Lake is 3.5 miles to Devils Basin, 2.3 more miles to the Park Fork junction and 6 more miles back to the lake, for a total of 12.1 miles.

24. TIMBER CREEK PASS

Loop trip: 6.8 miles
Elevation gain: 1,640 feet
Highest point: 9,400 feet
Time: 6 1/2 hours
Difficulty: moderate
Maps: USGS topographic: Iron Creek Point; Forest Service: Salmon National Forest
Information: Lost River Ranger District
Getting there: From Howe, 23 miles northeast of Arco on Idaho Highway 22-33, go north on the road between Howe and Ellis for 38.5 miles to the Sawmill

Canyon Road (101). (Only part of the last 9 miles is paved.) Turn right (north) on the improved Sawmill Canyon Road, passing the Fairview Guard Station at 46.8 miles. Ignoring several side roads, keep on Road 101 to the 50-mile point. Here turn left (west) on Road 105 up Timber Creek, passing Road 422 to Timber Creek Campground. Continue on 105, passing a turnoff for the Redrock Creek Road at 54.5 miles. At 55.6 miles, the road splits. Road 462 turns to the right uphill, Road 105 goes straight, and Road 424 turns left. Roads 424 and 105 are closed to motor vehicles at 200 yards. Both of these roads turn into trails, and a loop hike to Timber Creek Pass can be made by going up one and down the other.

As seen from Timber Creek Pass, Yellow Peak forms a butterscotch face with a pleased smirk and three eyes, two of them winking. Below to the north, the canyon of Timber Creek curves northeast between reddish-gray cliffs. Below to the southwest sprawls Bear Creek Point like a cinnamon-colored bear covered with the claw marks of avalanche chutes. To the south is Sawmill Canyon and the hazy green valley of the Little Lost River.

To reach the trailhead, follow the access directions above.

This hike is described as a loop, going up the trail beginning at the end of Road 424 and down the trail leading to Road 105 because the trail from Road 424 is more shaded.

From the motor vehicle barrier, walk along Road 424 between sagebrush and forest. The road curves to the creek at .7 mile and ends. Here the Slide Creek Trail turns off to the left across the creek. This trail goes 2.5 miles in a 1,380-foot climb to another pass to Timber Creek at the head of Cabin Creek.

Go straight ahead here on the unsigned Timber Creek Trail.

In lodgepoles and subalpine firs, the trail soon crosses the creek to the left side and back, then climbs a steep bank. At 1.2 miles is a flat meadow, with a view of a black cliff shaped like a slice of bread.

At 1.5 miles the trail crosses a tiny side stream and an open area below a sagebrush slope. After more forest and a long meadow, the trail crosses the creek over and back twice, returning to the right side at 2.3 miles. From here the route climbs through a subalpine fir forest, switching back to the left above a hidden creek that isn't on the map.

At 2.5 miles the trail zigzags up a grassy hillside dotted with whitebark pines and subalpine firs, then climbs straight up over steep gravel. From here you can see the great bell of Bell Mountain to the south. At 2.9 miles an unmarked path comes in from the left and a path signed "Trail" comes in from the right from Road 105. Go straight ahead to the top of the pass at 3 miles. From the pass a trail leads north across the grass and down Trail Creek, but there is no tread for the first 50 yards. A trail also goes west along the crest of the range. It is called the Snowbank Trail. It meets the Cabin Creek Trail that comes up from Big Timber Creek and then goes south toward Iron Creek Point and southeast down to the Bull Creek Road. It is about 13 miles from Timber Creek Pass down to Bull Creek on this trail with a 1,700-foot elevation gain and 4,260-foot elevation loss.

To return by the other trail and Road 105, go back to the "Trail" sign just below the pass and turn east on that trail. It goes along the side of a ridge, passing above a pebbly outcrop at 3.5 miles. At 4 miles, the trail crosses the top of a knoll and below a gravel bank at 4.2 miles it reaches the end of Road 105.

The rest of the hike is down this road, which is closed to motor vehicles to protect wildlife. At 4.4 miles on the crest of a ridge, go east a few yards off the trail for a view of the Meadow Lake Divide and the gray fuzz of an old burn.

68

At 4.6 miles a side road leads to a mining claim. Beyond this side road only one of the switchbacks on the map exists. At 6 miles the road is gated. Beyond the gate it crosses a stream and descends it back to the junction with Road 424 at 6.5 miles. From here you can complete your loop by walking .3 mile back up Road 424 to the motor vehicle barrier at 6.8 miles.

25. MILL CREEK LAKE

Round trip: 5 miles
Elevation gain: 880 feet
Highest point: 8,120 feet
Time: 3 1/2 hours
Difficulty: Easy
Maps: USGS topographic: Big Windy Peak, Gilmore; Forest Service: Challis National Forest
Information: Lost River Ranger District
Getting there: From the road between Ellis and Howe in the Little Lost River Valley, turn northeast on the gravel and then dirt Sawmill Canyon Road (101) 38.5 miles north of Howe. Drive 10.4 miles to the primitive Mill Creek Road (171). Turn right (northeast) and go .8 mile to the end of the road where there is a small campground.

Mill Creek Lake is set in a double ring, the inside one of pale orange talus and the outside one of dark green subalpine fir and whitebark pine. Above, a sandy ridge leads toward the lake from a double-humped peak. Two inlets flow through grass and shrubs into the north side of the lake. The lake's outlet comes at the bot-

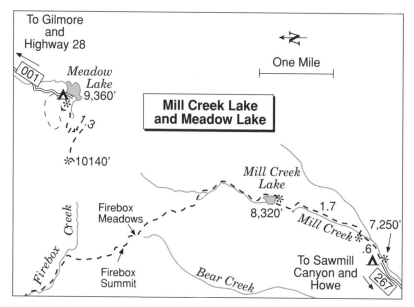

tom of a natural rock dam.

From the trailhead, the trail leads up the left (northwest) side of a small creek not shown on the map, then crosses it on logs to the right at .2 mile. The way goes up through three open areas of sagebrush, then crosses Mill Creek to the right (east) side on a foot bridge at .8 mile.

The trail now climbs among scattered Douglas firs above a 100-foot gorge, then goes over talus. At 1.9 miles the path switchbacks left (west) across the side of a knoll and the creek disappears in the talus below.

At 2.1 miles the trail curves right (north) above a tiny green pond. At 2.2 miles is a meadow with a stream meandering from two springs at the base of the natural dam that holds in the lake. At 2.5 miles the path climbs over this ridge to the lake. Paths go both ways around the lake. There are campsites at the edge of the forest at the north end. In recent years Arctic grayling have been stocked in the lake. Trout have also been stocked from time to time.

You can make a loop hike or bike ride by continuing beyond the lake over Firebox Summit. The trail follows the stream through a meadow for another 1.3 miles and leaves the stream at a set of springs. It continues to Firebox Meadows and Firebox Summit at 5 miles. Then the trail descends Firebox Creek and the Main Fork of the Little Lost River to Forest Road 101 (the main road up Sawmill Canyon) at 8.5 miles. From there it is about 5 miles south by road back to the Mill Creek Lake trailhead. To save effort, you can either set up a car shuttle or stash a mountain bike at the Little Lost River trailhead.

Lemhi Range – East Side

26. BEAR VALLEY LAKES AND BUCK LAKES

Round trip: 12.4 miles for largest Bear Valley lake, 2.4 miles more to see upper Bear Valley lakes; 9.8 miles to see Buck Lake alone, 4.4 miles extra if Buck Lake is only a side trip.
Elevation gain: 2,360 feet to largest Bear Valley Lake, 600 feet additional to see lakes in north canyon also; 1,674 feet for Buck Lake alone, 960 feet additional if Buck Lake is only a side trip.
Highest point: 9,240 feet

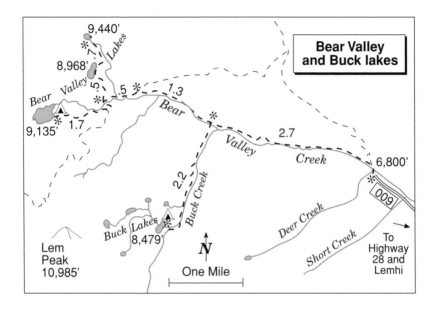

Bear Valley and Buck lakes

Time: 9 hours for largest lake alone; 7 1/2 hours for Buck Lake alone; to see upper lakes and Buck Lake as well as Bear Valley Lakes requires two days
Difficulty: Strenuous
Maps: USGS topographic: Hayden Creek, Lem Peak; Forest Service: Salmon National Forest
Information: Leadore Ranger District
Getting there: Turn west off Idaho Highway 28, 26.3 miles south of Salmon onto the Hayden Creek Road. At 3.3 miles the pavement ends where the Basin Creek Road turns off to the right. Keep straight ahead and at 8.4 miles turn right onto the Bear Valley Creek Road. At 9.7 miles, at a sign for Ford Creek, keep on the main road, which turns right sharply. The trailhead is at 13.2 miles, at Deer Creek, but the last part of the road is not shown on the topographic map.

Above the largest Bear Valley lake, one peak resembles a Tyrolean hat; another, a fence made of rock. Near the lower end of the lake an inlet runs through wildflowers into a bay enclosed by a rocky peninsula. This lake has an unusual flower: pale pink mountain heather that is a hybrid between red and cream-colored species. Shallow green Buck Lake is ringed with golden pebbles below 400-foot gray cliffs that are shaped like a bird in flight. These lakes boast good fishing.

One mile before the trailhead, a new campground designed for equestrians has recently been constructed with a water trough, hitching racks, and parking for horse trailers. A one-mile trail leads from the campground to the trailhead. Horse riders should leave horse trailers at the campground where there is space for them and ride this trail to the trailhead. Hikers can still park at the trailhead.

The trail begins by crossing where the Basin Creek High Trail turns off. Another branch of this trail takes off 4 miles up Bear Valley Creek. The two branches meet and continue to a four-wheel-drive road at the forest boundary gate just off Basin Creek Road.

71

At the Bear Valley Creek trailhead, keep left (west) at the junction just across the bridge. Take the Bear Valley Trail along the creek in sagebrush and Douglas fir. After the first half-mile it enters thick fir forest, a real plus on hot days. Soon the canyon becomes several hundred feet deep. At 2.7 miles, 720 feet above the trailhead, the unmarked trail for Buck Lake turns left (south) downhill across Bear Valley Creek.

Keep straight ahead, crossing small mossy streams among lodgepoles and sub-alpine firs. At 4 miles the second branch of the Basin Creek High Trail turns off to the right at a sharp angle. The main trail climbs away from the creek, crosses a side stream, then returns to the creek. At 4.5 miles the trail to the Upper Bear Valley Lakes turns off to the right.

Just beyond this junction the main trail crosses the creek to the left (south) side. Then it turns east, climbs above the creek, and gradually curves back to the west. It comes to a junction with the Allison Creek–Bear Valley Trail at 5 miles. (This trail goes over the divide for 3 miles to meet a jeep trail in the Allison Creek drainage at 9,400 feet.)

At a round meadow at 5.4 miles the trail curves left as the creek curves right. At 5.5 miles a shortcut to the Allison Creek Trail turns off. The trail climbs rolling ground among whitebark pines and patches of red, white, cream and pink heather to the lake at 6.2 miles.

To see the upper lakes, back at the junction at 4.2 miles take the side trail north. It climbs a lodgepole-covered hillside into a rocky meadow and disappears. A blaze on the right side of the meadow shows where the path continues along a small ridge. It reaches the first of the upper lakes in the woods at 5 miles. It is another .7 mile and 250 feet of climbing to the smaller, higher lake, which is sur-rounded by talus. From here a trail goes on over the divide and down to the North Fork of McKim Creek Road.

To reach Buck Lake, turn off the main trail 2.7 miles from the Bear Valley Creek trailhead. The trail to Buck Lake is an official Forest Service trail but is not on the topographic map. First it crosses two sections of Bear Valley Creek on logs. Then the trail climbs the canyon on the right (west) side of Buck Creek through a lodgepole-subalpine fir forest and small bogs. At 1.3 miles opposite a talus slope the trail leaps a side stream that is the outlet of a pond. At 1.6 miles the path fords Buck Creek to the left (east) side and goes along a small ridge between Buck Creek and a side stream that parallels the creek on the east. At 2 miles the path returns to the right side of Buck Creek and goes between it and the lake's outlet to the lake at 2.2 miles. Higher lakes may be reached by strenuous cross-country trav-el through downed timber.

27. MILL LAKE

Round trip: 8 miles
Elevation gain: 1,400 feet
Highest point: 8,840 feet
Time: 6 1/2 hours
Difficulty: Moderate
Maps: USGS topographic: Stroud Creek, Mogg Mountain; Forest Service: Salmon National Forest
Information: Leadore Ranger District

72

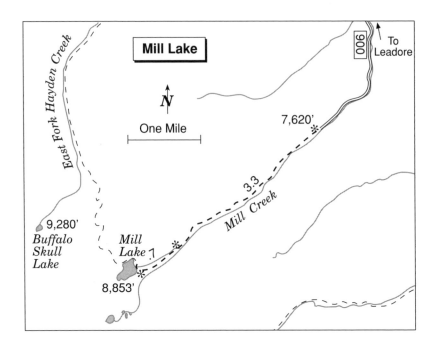

Mill Lake

East Fork Hayden Creek

To
Leadore

006

N

One Mile

7,620'

3.3

Mill Creek

9,280'
Buffalo
Skull
Lake

Mill
Lake

8,853'

Getting there: Drive 47 miles south of Salmon on Idaho Highway 28 to Leadore. The town was named for the ore that led to its settlement in 1904. Turn west (right) on the paved Timber Creek–Big Eightmile Road. At 5.4 miles at the Big Eightmile Creek junction, turn right (north) toward Mill Creek. The pavement ends at 10.4 miles. At 12.8 miles turn left on the Mill Creek Road (006). This rough dirt road reaches the forest boundary at 14.1 miles. At 14.5 miles, at the junction of the Mill Lake and Hayden Creek roads, turn left (south) and stay on Road 006, which becomes primitive and goes into the timber. At 15 miles the Little Mill Creek Road turns off to the right. Keep straight ahead. At 16.1 miles is an open grassy area. At 16.4 miles a gated jeep trail goes off to the right. Keep on the main road, but it is best to park here unless you have four-wheel drive because the road ahead can be very muddy where streams run over it.

Mill Lake is a big blue-green lake with an artificial dam made of white rocks at the lower end. The rounded solid-rock face of the peak on the west side is fluted by slanting chimneys. On the southwest, rock layers split into an open book in the center of a mountain.

From the jeep trail that turns off at 16.4 miles, walk up the main road through a lodgepole-grouse whortleberry forest. The road has ruts and puddles and even runs along the middle of a stream for 100 yards. At 1 mile gray ledges and cliffs can be seen across the canyon, and at 1.8 miles you pass the site of an avalanche that threw trees clear across the canyon. The road becomes rockier and at 2.3 miles crosses blocks of talus from a talus slope on the right.

The track curves uphill to the right away from the creek then, opposite a rock tower, returns to the creek. At 3.3 miles Mill Creek runs in a badlands of gravel.

Here the road fords the creek to the left (south) side.

The track now climbs away from the main creek and runs between the two parallel creeks. At 4 miles it reaches the dam at the lower end of Mill Lake. Although the dam detracts from the lake's beauty, the rugged mountain walls make up for it.

On the far (north) end of the dam the East Fork of Hayden Creek trail, which is not shown on the topographic map, climbs up talus and over a saddle and down to the East Fork of Hayden Creek Road, 6.6 miles from Mill Lake. Near the head of the canyon, it gives access by cross-country travel to Buffalo Skull Lake.

28. STROUD LAKE

Round trip: 6 miles, (3 miles with four-wheel drive)
Elevation gain: 1,230 feet
Highest point: 8,751 feet
Time: 5 1/2 hours
Difficulty: moderate
Maps: USGS topographic: Stroud Creek; Forest Service: Salmon National Forest
Information: Leadore Ranger District

Stroud Lake in the Lemhi Range.

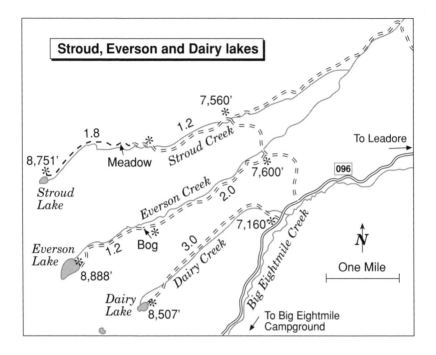

Stroud, Everson and Dairy lakes

7,560'

1.8   1.2   Stroud Creek

8,751'   Meadow

Stroud Lake

Everson Creek   2.0   7,600'   096   To Leadore

Everson Lake   1.2   Bog   3.0   7,160'

8,888'   Dairy Creek   Big Eightmile Creek

N

One Mile

Dairy Lake   8,507'

To Big Eightmile Campground

Getting there: At Leadore 47 miles south of Salmon on Idaho Highway 28, turn west onto the Timber Creek–Big Eightmile Road. Keep straight ahead where the Timber Creek Road turns off at .9 mile. At 5.4 miles where the Mill Creek Road turns right (north), go straight ahead on the Big Eightmile Road (096). At 6.6 miles the pavement ends, and the road curves left and forks. Keep straight ahead. At 9.3 miles it enters the Salmon National Forest and at 11.4 miles reaches the Stroud Creek–Everson Creek Road. Turn right (north) on this road up a sagebrush hillside and around the end of it at 12.7 miles. The unsigned Everson Lake jeep trail is at 13.4 miles and the signed Stroud Lake jeep trail at 14.3 miles.

Stroud Lake is a small blue-green lake surrounded by sand and a complex of rugged peach-colored peaks. Above its upper end, two triangular summits resemble the ears of a fox because they are blackened with lichen. From these peaks a knife-edged ridge runs left to black and orange humps resembling a dinosaur and an elephant. The narrow earthen dam that holds in the lake is so well covered with grass and lodgepole pines that it looks natural except for a culvert in the outlet.

At low water, two-wheel-drive vehicles can drive the first 1.2 miles of the road. At .2 mile the road fords the creek to the left (south) bank, then climbs through a Douglas fir forest to a steeper, rockier ford at 1.2 miles. Beside it grow bluebells, wild geraniums and pink-flowered dwarf willowweed. Park before this second ford unless your vehicle has four-wheel drive.

On the other side of the ford, the jeep trail climbs the right (north) side of the creek in grass and lodgepole pines. At 1.5 miles it descends into a flat, 200-yard meadow and disappears. At the far end of the meadow the track reappears, turns right and narrows. Park four-wheel-drive vehicles here because beyond this point

75

trees make the track too narrow for a vehicle.

The track climbs steeply over rose and white quartzite rocks. At 2 miles it runs above a 20-foot gorge with a view of pointed peaks ahead. Soon it reaches a wet meadow, which is across the canyon from a black and orange face.

Beyond here the track splits. The right (north) branch climbs to an old log cabin with earth and flowers covering its shingles. The left branch fords the creek to the left (south) side and follows the gorge in a lodgepole forest pitted with prospect holes. At 3 miles, the trail descends a few feet from a knoll to the lake.

29. EVERSON LAKE

Round trip: 6.4 miles; about 2.4 miles with four-wheel drive
Elevation gain: 1,280 feet
Highest point: 8,880 feet
Time: 5 1/2 hours
Difficulty: Moderate
Maps: USGS topographic: Stroud Creek; Forest Service: Salmon National Forest
Information: Leadore Ranger District
Getting there: At Leadore, 47 miles south of Salmon on Idaho Highway 28, turn west onto the Timber Creek–Big Eightmile Road. Keep straight ahead where the Timber Creek Road turns off at .9 mile. At 5.4 miles where the Mill Creek Road turns right (north), go straight ahead on the Big Eightmile Road (096). At 6.6 miles the pavement ends, and the road curves left and forks. Keep straight ahead. At 9.3 miles it enters the Salmon National Forest and at 11.4 miles reaches the Stroud Creek–Everson Creek Road. Turn right (north) on this road up a sagebrush hillside and around the end of it at 12.7 miles. At 13.4 miles the track bridges Everson Creek and passes an unsigned road on the left that begins in a logged area. You will probably want to park at the beginning of this road unless you have four-wheel drive. The upper section of this jeep trail is so rough that it is best traveled on foot even if your car has four-wheel drive.

Above Everson Lake dark cliffs form a picket fence of six pointed towers. Across the lake, cliffs with scalloped tops descend a ridge from a prominent scallop that resembles a head. White, pink, apricot and lavender rocks line the shores. Some are pocked with holes like Swiss cheese.

The road begins by climbing a steep hill through logging slash on the left (south) side of Everson Creek. After 200 yards it enters forest, and the surface has big rocks. At .3 mile the track crosses an open flat, then returns to forest and is often blocked by downed timber. At about 1.5 miles an old logging road goes off to the right, and at 2 miles the road has been rerouted around a boggy meadow that used to stop even four-wheel-drive vehicles.

Beyond here the track is rocky and climbs steeply, then goes downhill to cross a boggy side creek that is not on the map. Cliffs now appear behind the trees on the left. The track climbs up on a little ridge, then turns right and drops to ford another side creek with rocks and logs for hikers. The surface becomes even rockier. Soon the trail passes the ruins of a log cabin. Here the route curves left and climbs a rocky hillside below cliffs. The road ends on a bench above the lake at 3.2 miles. Several paths lead 50 yards to the shore of the lake.

76

30. DAIRY LAKE

Round trip: 6 miles; four-wheel-drive vehicles can drive entire road
Elevation gain: 1,230 feet
Highest point: 8,751 feet
Time: 5 1/2 hours
Difficulty: moderate
Maps: USGS topographic: Stroud Creek, Yellow Peak; Forest Service: Salmon National Forest
Information: Leadore Ranger District
Getting there: At Leadore, 47 miles south of Salmon on Idaho Highway 28, turn west onto the Timber Creek–Big Eightmile Road. Continue straight ahead where the Timber Creek Road turns off at 0.9 mile. At 5.4 miles where the Mill Creek Road turns right (north), go straight ahead on the Big Eightmile Road (096). At 6.6 miles the pavement ends, and the road curves left and forks. Keep straight ahead. At 9.3 miles it enters the Salmon National Forest and at 11.4 miles reaches the Stroud Creek–Everson Creek Road. Stay on the Big Eightmile Road. At 11.8 miles is the Dairy Lake jeep trail. Those without four-wheel drive should park here.

Above Dairy Lake loom black and orange cliffs indented with small caves. To the left of them, an avalanche chute filled with tiny trees separates the cliffs from a wooded ridge. To the right of the cliffs a tiny meadow rises to rocky peaks. A round wooded island appears to float on the green water below the cliffs. At the lower end of the lake is a low earthen dam.

One of the main attractions at Dairy Lake is the fine trout fishing.

From the Big Eightmile Road, the Dairy Lake jeep trail climbs along the left side of the creek beside spruce, alder and monkeyflower. The first 200 yards are the rockiest and most difficult of the whole road. At .4 mile the track crosses the creek to the right (north) bank on an old wooden bridge. Just before the bridge a blocked-off road goes uphill to the left. Beyond here, the jeep trail to the lake does not follow the route shown on the topographic map. Across the bridge the Dairy Lake road continues through a gate. It enters a Douglas fir forest, then climbs above the creek, which is in a ravine.

At 2 miles is an open sagebrush area. At 2.5 miles the track fords the creek back to the left (south) side. It climbs in forest away from the creek to the lake at 3 miles.

31. BIG EIGHTMILE CREEK

Round trip: 10 miles to meadows near upper end of trail; 13 miles to Yellow Lake
Elevation gain: 1,960 feet for high meadows; 2,880 feet for Yellow Lake
Highest point: 9,320 feet at the high meadows; 10,200 feet on ridge above Yellow Lake
Time: 8 hours for meadows; two days for Yellow Lake
Difficulty: strenuous

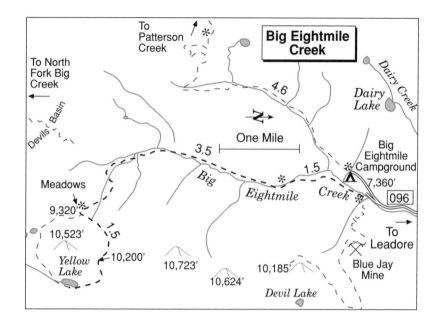

Maps: USGS topographic map: Yellow Peak; Forest Service: Salmon National Forest

Information: Leadore Ranger District

Getting there: At Leadore, 47 miles south of Salmon on Idaho Highway 28, turn west onto the Timber Creek–Big Eightmile Road. Keep straight ahead where the Timber Creek Road turns off at .9 mile. At 5.4 miles, where the Mill Creek Road turns right (north), go straight ahead on Big Eightmile Road (096). At 6.6 miles the pavement ends, and the road curves left and forks. Keep straight ahead. At 9.3 miles it enters the Salmon National Forest and at 11.4 miles passes the turnoff for the Stroud Creek-Everson Creek Road. At 11.8 miles the Dairy Lake Road turns off to the right. Keep straight ahead. At 13.4 miles the road forks again. The right fork goes 1 mile farther to Big Eightmile campground. Park and take the left fork, which goes across an old bridge over the creek that is closed to motor vehicles.

The problem with the Lemhi Range is that it's so far away from towns and cities. But that is probably why it remains one of the better-kept secrets in Idaho. You may see only one other party on the trail in a day, even on the Fourth of July weekend.

The Lemhis are big. Most of the crest of the range tops 10,000 feet. Several peaks are well above 11,000 feet. Many of the lakes boast fantastic fishing, even the kind where you catch a fish with each cast. If they were closer to a population center the Lemhis would become as popular as the Tetons.

The Big Eightmile Creek trail, just west of Leadore, is great for hiking, horseback riding and mountain biking. The road to the trail features a few side roads, so it pays to bring along a Salmon Forest map to help figure things out. Once inside

78

the national forest boundary, there are several informal campsites just off the road. The canyon soon leaves the desert valley and becomes heavily forested and lush with growth, especially in spring and early summer.

About 7 miles from the pavement is the Big Eightmile campground, a small campsite with water and a pit toilet. The road to the Big Eightmile Trail turns off to the left about a mile before the campground.

The hike starts at the old bridge over Big Eightmile Creek, and the trail mileage is measured from this point. On the other side of it, the road forks again. The left fork climbs to the closed Blue Jay Mine on the east side of the canyon and provides access by cross-country travel to Devils Lake. Take the right fork up the left (east) side of the creek to the former trailhead at the end of the old road 1.5 miles from the bridge.

Immediately past the trailhead sign-in, the trail crosses the creek on fallen logs to the right (west) side. For the next mile it still looks like an old road. About a mile past the sign-in is a collapsed log cabin once used by miners.

The trail continues to parallel the creek before crossing it again 3 miles from the bridge. At this point it steepens and heads for the crest of the Lemhis. Look for some pretty cascading falls at the creek crossing.

The trail climbs steeply; at 5 miles it levels off in high mountain meadows accented with a variety of wildflowers. The crest of the Lemhis is less than a half-mile away. There are some nice campsites in this relatively flat area. Beyond the meadows the trail winds 1.5 miles over a pass to Yellow Lake on the other side of the crest. The lake is too shallow to support fish. It is nearly surrounded by peaks, and drains down the west side of the range into the North Fork of Big Creek.

If you continue up the main road past the turnoff for the Big Eightmile Creek Trail, there is another trail that begins at the campground. It is the Patterson Creek Trail, which winds 4.6 miles to the crest of the Lemhis. From there this trail descends the East Fork of Patterson Creek 5.5 miles to the Patterson Creek Road, which can be reached from the road between Ellis and Howe. North of this summit .5 mile off trail is a small lake called Big Eightmile Lake, at 9,028 feet.

An .8-mile trail to this lake has recently been constructed. It begins one mile east of the summit of the Patterson Creek Trail and contours around to a point 200 yards before the lake. Also a scenic trail linking Patterson Creek and Big Eight-mile trails along the Lemhi Crest has been constructed. Where it drops to connect with the Big Eightmile Trail, the track is suitable only for foot travel.

32. NORTH FORK OF LITTLE TIMBER CREEK LAKE

Round trip: 10 miles (6 miles with four-wheel drive)
Elevation gain: 1,060 to 1,500 feet
Highest point: 8,420 feet
Time: 5 to 7 1/2 hours
Difficulty: easy to moderate
Maps: USGS topographic: Sheephorn Peak, Yellow Peak; Forest Service: Salmon National Forest
Information: Leadore Ranger District
Getting there: There are two ways to reach the trailhead. The signed route by

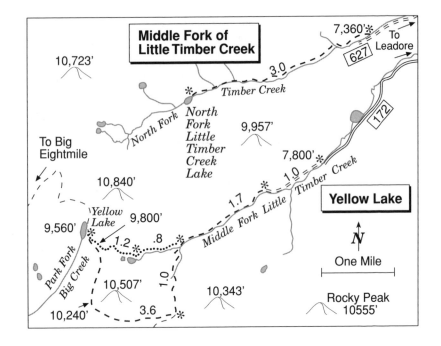

Middle Fork of Little Timber Creek

Yellow Lake

way of a primitive road requires fording four irrigation ditches and a creek, and opening and closing five gates. An alternative four-wheel-drive route is shorter, fords only a creek, and has fewer gates.

To reach the trailhead, turn west off Idaho Highway 28 at Leadore, 47 miles south of Salmon, onto the paved Timber Creek–Big Eightmile Road. At .9 mile turn left (south) on the road to Timber Creek Reservoir. To take the signed route, at 4.6 miles go straight ahead on the North Fork Timber Creek Road 106. At 5.1 miles take the right branch of the road, which fords ditches at 5.5 and 5.8 miles. Just beyond the second ditch, turn left and go through a gate. Avoid a road at 6.3 miles that cuts over to the reservoir road. Just beyond it is another gate, and at 6.6 miles two more ditches. At 7.6 miles is another gate. Then at 8 miles the road goes close to the North Fork, and at 8.4 miles the road fords it to the south (left) side. Four-wheel drive is needed for this ford, and the road beyond it. On the south side of the ford, a four-wheel-drive road from the reservoir road provides an alternate access.

A much simpler way to reach the trailhead is to ignore the North Fork of Timber Creek Road at 4.6 miles and continue on the Timber Creek Reservoir Road, passing by roads leading south to Swan Basin at 7.7 miles and Big Timber Creek at 8.3 miles. About .1 mile past the Big Timber Creek turnoff an unsigned two-wheel track turns right (north). (It is shown on the topographic map as a four-wheel-drive trail but not on the forest map.) Hike or drive in four-wheel drive along this road, which fords the Middle Fork of Timber Creek in .2 mile. It is 1.2 miles to where it meets the other route at the North Fork ford, which you don't have to cross on this route until after the trail begins. Beyond where the routes join, a gate marks the forest boundary. From the gate the road goes next to the creek just

80

beyond a mudhole at .5 mile and continues up the very rocky and rutted road to the trailhead .8 mile above the gate. From the gate to the trailhead requires four-wheel drive. Since there are two ways to reach the trailhead, the trail mileage starts at the trailhead, even though both access routes require some four-wheel drive.

A natural dam of white rocks holds in this little green lake in a canyon marked by pleated cliffs and a big orange tooth. Beside the orange tooth the banded summit of Gunsight Peak looks down the avalanche trough that feeds the dam. The lake is shallow with marsh grass at the upper end, forest on one side, and bluebells on the other. Two other small lakes and a tiny pond can be reached by climbing cross-country to high benches on the north canyon wall.

From the trailhead, the trail skirts a wet meadow, goes over to the north bank of the creek on logs, and climbs a sagebrush knoll. Next it curves into a side canyon and crosses a mossy creek on rocks at .7 mile. The tread disappears here, but cairns show the way. At 1 mile the route climbs a bluff covered with grasses and Rocky Mountain iris.

Cairns mark the way down to a tiny reed-filled pond, where the trail enters the woods, and once again has a tread and blazes. It goes along in rocks and lodgepole pines past a miniature gorge. At 2 miles the trail descends onto a grassy flat beside the creek. After climbing up and down over rocky ground, the trail returns to the creek and crosses two small side streams in a wet meadow at 2.2 miles.

The trail climbs along at varying distances from the creek in white rocks that extend up the canyon wall. At 2.5 miles under the orange tooth, the trail crosses another side stream at a wildflower flat. At 2.8 miles it climbs the white rock dam and ends. To reach the shore at 3 miles you have to climb down through boulders.

33. MIDDLE FORK OF LITTLE TIMBER CREEK AND YELLOW LAKE

Round trip: 14 miles to Yellow Lake (9.4 miles for shortcut)
Elevation gain: 2,550 feet (2,100 for shortcut)
Elevation loss (return climb): 700 feet (250 feet for shortcut)
Highest point: 10,250 feet
Time: 2 days
Difficulty: Strenuous
Maps: USGS topographic: Sheephorn Peak, Yellow Peak; Forest Service: Salmon National Forest
Information: Leadore Ranger District
Getting there: At Leadore, 47 miles south of Salmon on Idaho Highway 28, turn right (west) onto the paved Timber Creek Road. Turn left (south) at .9 mile onto a gravel road. At 4.3 miles pass a turnoff for the North Fork of Timber Creek. At 7.7 miles where the road to Swan Basin goes straight ahead, turn right onto the road for Stone Reservoir and the Middle Fork of Timber Creek. At 8.3 miles a road to Big Timber Creek turns left. Keep straight ahead to the reservoir and continue above its left side on a forested ridge. At 10.1 miles the reservoir appears below, and the road drops to the upper end at 10.4 miles where there are undeveloped campsites. From the shore of the aquamarine reservoir there is a view ahead of a splintered face scored with chimneys. Keep going beyond the reservoir. At a ford

North Fork of Little Timber Creek Lake in the Lemhi Range.

of the Middle Fork of Timber Creek at 11.1 miles, a side hill and boulders on the
far side stop most vehicles, even those with four-wheel drive.

In its grassy basin, the blue-green sliver of water called Yellow Lake resembles a water hazard on a golf course. On the west side, cliffs stairstep 800 feet
down to the water. To the south, Yellow Peak, for which the lake is named, is hidden by ridges.

A shortcut to Yellow Lake by way of a non-system trail and some cross-country travel passes an unnamed lake at the head of the Middle Fork of Timber Creek.
The edges of this pale green lake in the woods are lined with amber-colored
stones. Opposite the trail, cliffs zigzagged with cracks and chimneys overhang the
lake.

After crossing to the right (north) side of the ford on a downstream foot log,
walk along the road up and down over little wooded hills. At a register box at 1
mile, the road becomes a trail. It crosses a side stream here, then climbs along the
main creek. For the first mile the trail has been widened to allow ATVs. At 2.4
miles it leaps another side creek, then skirts a small meadow of lodgepoles at 2.6
miles. At 2.7 miles a nonsystem trail (the shortcut to Yellow Lake) turns right up
the creek 50 yards before the main trail curves left and fords the creek to the left
(south) side.

To reach Yellow Lake by the main trail, a route that is safer for average hikers,
ford the creek here or cross it on small logs. The trail switchbacks up the canyon
wall on the right (west) side of a side stream in lodgepoles and grouse whortleberry. At 3.2 miles it crosses the stream to the east side, and at 3.5 miles comes out

into a rolling meadow below short cliffs. The path climbs over a grassy divide at 3.7 miles. (This is 2.7 miles from the official trailhead.) Here, the trails on the map differ from those on the ground.

The four-way trail junction is at the divide, not down in the canyon as is shown on the topographic map. Only the trail straight ahead shows tread, and it disappears in a few yards. Experts can follow it down into the canyon to a junction with trails to Big Timber Creek and the Park Fork of Big Creek. To the left at the divide a sign points to the little-used Rocky Creek trail; blazes for that trail can be found in the trees to the southeast. To the right (due west) of the divide blazes appear in the trees in a few yards for the trail to Yellow Lake.

Take this trail along the side of the ridge among whitebark pines. After a half mile it curves northwest and steepens. At 5 miles a little wooded lake appears below on the south. It is informally called Park Fork Lake. At 6.4 miles the path runs along a rocky slope and at 6.5 miles reaches the crest of a 10,250-foot divide. To the southeast now you can see Yellow Peak, which on the east side looks as though the rock has been bulldozed away. On that side the peak is yellow-orange and topped with cliffs and rock needles.

From the divide, the trail descends talus to the timber and disappears in the grass. Instead of curving down to the pond below the lake as shown on the map, it continues straight north until it is just west of the divide between Yellow Lake and the unnamed lake and then descends through timber to the lake near its lower end. There are several campsites under whitebark pines back from the shore, especially at the upper end.

To reach Yellow Lake by the shortcut instead of the main trail, back at the unsigned junction at 2.7 miles turn right (west) upstream on the non-system trail. This trail is plain to "No Name" Lake, but sketchy beyond it. It goes along the right (north) side of the creek, wandering through forest, boggy places and downed timber, and splitting at times to avoid obstacles. At 3.2 miles this path crosses a side creek, then steepens in lodgepoles at a distance from the creek. It soon crosses another side creek not shown on the map. A short climb up the center of a lodgepole ridge leads to the lake at 3.5 miles. There are several campsites.

Do not go up the meadows above the tiny pond at the head of the lake because they are boggy and full of hidden rocks. Instead, circle the meadows on the right, then cross them to the left (south) side just above the pond. Now climb toward the head of the canyon, finding a faint path from time to time. Near the headwall, this path aims to the right (northwest) toward a C-shaped tongue of talus that is to the right (north) of the divide. Beyond this talus, the path is easier to find as it switches back to the left (southwest) and heads for short cliffs on the skyline. However, the footing is treacherous. At the divide at 4.3 miles the trail tread disappears. The main trail is a few yards to the northwest. This trail plunges to the lake at 4.7 miles.

34. BIG TIMBER CREEK

Round trip: 15 miles to Falls Creek; 4 miles additional for Flatiron Mountain loop; 22 miles to the Park Fork of Big Creek

Elevation gain: 800 feet to Falls Creek, 2,160 feet for Flatiron Mountain loop, 2,460 feet for Park Fork of Big Creek

Elevation loss (return climb): 560 feet

Highest point: 8,040 feet at Falls Creek, 9,400 feet on Flatiron Mountain loop,

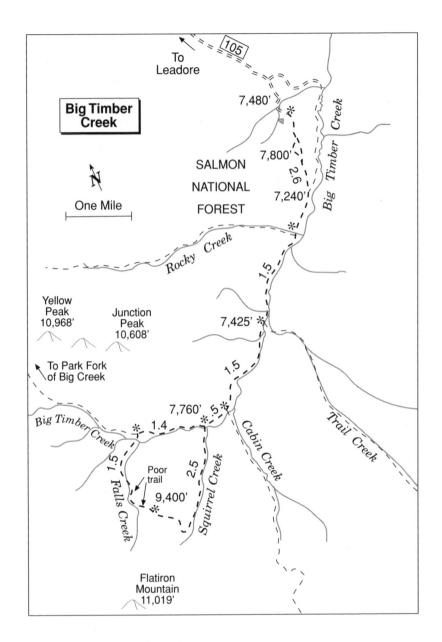

9,702 feet for the Park Fork

Time: 9 1/2 hours for the mouth of Falls Creek; two days to include the Flatiron Mountain loop or the Park Fork of Big Creek

Difficulty: moderate to the mouth of Falls Creek except for the distance and the steep downgrade at the beginning; expert for the Flatiron Mountain loop because of route-finding

Maps: USGS topographic maps: Sheephorn Peak, Iron Creek Point, Big Creek Peak, Yellow Peak; Forest Service: Salmon National Forest

Information: Leadore Ranger District

Getting there: Take Idaho Highway 28 to Leadore, 47 miles south of Salmon. Turn west onto the Big Eightmile–Timber Creek road. After .9 mile turn left (south) onto the Big Timber Creek Road. At the turnoff at 4.4 miles for the North Fork of Timber Creek, keep left. At 7.7 miles the road forks again. Take the right fork toward Timber Creek Reservoir. At 8.3 miles turn left on Road 105 for Big Timber Creek. Stay on this bumpy and rocky road until it ends at a trailhead at 12.8 miles. You will probably want to park .2 mile before the trailhead, where there are big dips and humps in the road.

The canyon of Big Timber Creek is a pleasant surprise because it is a giant canyon, like an entire valley. It is also surprising how flat most of the trail is. You begin by dropping into the canyon from its rim. Once in the canyon the trail follows its wide, flat bottom for the next several miles. The canyon's other attractions include a beautiful waterfall hidden several hundred yards off trail and some comfortable campsites in a large meadow 6 miles up the trail. Except for the first half-mile of steep downhill, the trail is perfect for mountain bikers. The canyon attracts fishermen in summer and hunters in fall, so in fall be sure to wear blaze orange.

The first few miles there are remnants of jeep roads, and ATVs are allowed the first couple of miles, but only trail bikes after that. The side trails up Rocky and Cabin creeks are open to motorized use, but the other side trails are not. The canyon is heavily grazed by cattle. The trail passes through a few gates separating grazing allotments.

The trail starts as a jeep road along the north canyon rim, with the creek 250 feet below on your left. After .5 mile notice a footpath on the left. Take this path, which parallels Big Timber Creek. The footpath is a shortcut that saves about 150 feet of elevation gain. It reconnects with the jeep trail after another .3 mile. Beyond it, the trail drops steeply to the bottom of the canyon. Once down, the trail remains mostly flat for the next 5 miles.

Because the canyon is as much as two football fields wide in some places, the trail is often far from the creek. On the southeast, Sheephorn Peak, 10,465 feet, dominates this section of the canyon. The vegetation on the northwest side of the canyon is patchy firs, aspens and brush, while the southeast side is a deep forest of firs. Along the creek are a mix of willows, aspens and some firs.

A half-mile up the canyon you come to a gated fence that spans the canyon. The trail passes through two more gates farther up the canyon. Remember to shut all gates that were shut when you opened them to pass through.

At 2.6 miles the trail crosses Rocky Creek. This creek runs year-round but is fairly shallow and can easily be crossed on steppingstones. In late spring and early summer you may have to take your boots off.

Immediately beyond the creek is a junction with the Rocky Creek trail. This trail heads west and after 5 miles connects with the Park Fork of Big Creek and Middle Fork of Timber Creek trails. The Rocky Creek Trail has been rerouted and improved in the upper section.

Just above where Rocky Creek joins Big Timber Creek are beaver dams. Now the trail begins to follow Big Timber Creek more closely. In midsummer Big Timber Creek is knee-deep and 12 to 15 feet wide here. Occasionally the trail winds through thick willows, where you may meet cows.

85

Near the fourth mile is a junction with the Trail Creek Trail. This trail immediately crosses Big Timber Creek and follows Trail Creek south for 4 miles up to Timber Creek Pass on the crest of the Lemhis.

Big Timber Creek Trail enters a wide brushy area and climbs gently for the next half-mile. At about 5.5 miles is a junction with Cabin Creek Trail. The Cabin Creek trail goes south across Big Timber Creek, then it goes up Cabin Creek for 3 miles where it crosses the crest of the Lemhis and intersects with the Snowbank Trail.

About .3 mile beyond the Cabin Creek junction, the Big Timber Creek Trail enters Squirrel Creek Meadows. This huge meadow and Squirrel Creek are 6 miles from the trailhead. The area has a few nice campsites near the creek.

There are two good possibilities for further exploration. One is to take the Flatiron Mountain loop trail. It goes up Squirrel Creek and comes back down Falls Creek. This route takes you to the base of Flatiron and Pahsimeroi mountains, which are both over 11,000 feet.

After hiking the long, flat Big Timber Creek trail, this loop trail is a rude return to the reality of mountain hiking. The 4-mile loop trail gains and loses 1,000 feet per mile. The Squirrel Creek section is a little gentler and so it is probably best to climb it and descend Falls Creek. The Squirrel Creek Trail is much fainter than the Big Timber trail and at times disappears. A few cairns and tree blazes mark the route where this happens. It switchbacks to the top of the long, steep ridge that separates the two canyons.

The top of the ridge provides some super views of the mountains surrounding Big Timber Creek. Snow lingers all year on some of these summits.

You can skip the strenuous loop hike and just go hunting for the waterfall. The falls are about 50 to 60 feet high and splash down to a couple of small drops and pools. They're tricky to find and tough to photograph because of the rugged terrain and thick timber, but worth the struggle.

The best approach is to continue up Big Timber Creek beyond Squirrel Meadows and take a left on the Falls Creek trail. When you can see or hear the creek on your left, leave the trail and bushwhack upstream. The falls are about .2 mile upstream from Big Timber Creek.

If you're interested a longer pack trip, there are a couple of loop trails that take you over the crest of the Lemhis. The most difficult is to go up the Rocky Creek trail from the junction with the Big Timber Creek Trail. It is difficult because the trail in the upper parts of Rocky Creek is rugged, but has been improved recently. The second loop route is to go up Trail Creek to Timber Creek Pass, head west to connect with the Cabin Creek Trail, then decend. Both these trails offer fine views of the Lemhis, but are strenuous because of the elevation gain.

35. NEZ PERCE LAKE

Round trip: 5.4 miles (4.4 miles with four-wheel drive)
Elevation gain: 1,460 feet from trailhead; 1,760 feet from spring
Highest point: 8,880 feet
Time: 5 to 6 hours
Difficulty: Moderate, except for one steep, slippery stretch
Maps: USGS topographic: Purcell Spring, Sheephorn Peak; Forest Service: Salmon National Forest

Nez Perce Lake in the Lemhi Range.

Information: Leadore Ranger District

Getting there: Turn right (west) on the Cold Springs–Timber Creek Road (212) from Idaho Highway 28, 6 miles south of Leadore. At 3.6 miles, 300 yards before a cluster of farm buildings, turn right on a two-wheel track. At 4.6 miles at a scummy green pond (Purcell Spring) the road gets much rougher, and in early season the mud may require four-wheel drive or be impassable. At 5.9 miles take the right-hand road at a Y in the sagebrush. At 6.4 miles a gate marks the Salmon Forest boundary. Beyond the gate the road is covered with grass and occasional rocks. At 7.1 miles a log corral encloses the Nez Perce rifle pits at Nez Perce Spring. These holes in the dirt were used by Chief Joseph's riflemen as the band fled down the Birch Creek Valley after the battle of the Big Hole in the 1877 Nez Perce War. From this campsite Chief Joseph sent out scouting parties to ensure the band's safety. South of here, near Lone Pine, one of the scouting parties killed all of a party of freighters except for one driver and two Chinese, who escaped while gathering wood.

Beyond Nez Perce Spring the road becomes a four-wheel-drive road. Therefore, the hike mileage begins at the spring. It is .5 mile more to the trailhead.

A band of dark gray and sage green rock softened by plants surrounds this narrow green lake in the woods. Across the lake from the trail, a waterfall braids a white net down a meadow of bluebells. (The inlet shown on the map as coming in at the north end of the lake is often dry by July.) To the right of both streams behind an orange talus hill, a ridge of cliffs sweeps up to a gray triangular peak, which is Sheephorn Peak, 10,465 feet. On the way to the lake the trail passes through three or four acres entirely covered with bluebells.

From Nez Perce Spring, walk up the road to the signed trailhead. Beyond the trailhead, the trail still looks like a jeep track, but there are blazes. It begins by climbing a very steep, slippery hillside with no switchbacks. On the return, a walk-

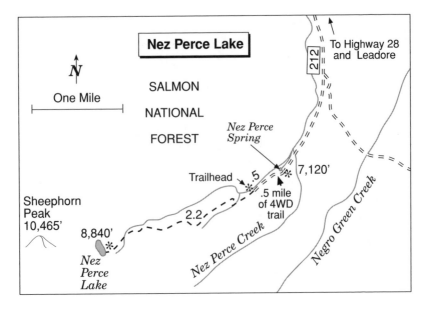

ing stick is recommended here, or taking the alternate switchback route, which reconnects with the main trail.

Soon the grade lessens and follows a little ridge to the left of the creek in a Douglas fir forest. At 1 mile the trail turns right for 200 yards and then back to the left and continues up the ridge. The stream that the topographic map shows the trail crossing in this section is usually dry.

In lodgepoles at 1.5 miles it becomes less steep. The next part of the trail goes along the right (north) side of a larger ridge. At 2 miles the trail comes within 100 feet of the creek, but continues on the left side with talus and a rocky ridge glimpsed to the left. At 2.3 miles is the big meadow of bluebells. The trail is marked with cairns through the meadow. You cross the creek here at a wide place on stepping stones. Be careful of the stinging nettles on both sides of the trail near the creek crossing.

The trail then goes along the right edge of the meadow and back into the forest. It climbs steeply up on a rocky ridge through subalpine fir and lodgepole, to the right of talus hills. At 2.5 miles the trail turns to the right (west) at signs for the lake. Here you turn left on a path and drop to the lake at 2.7 miles (2.2 miles from the trailhead). There are possible campsites up in the trees before the trail drops to the lake.

The largest Arctic grayling ever caught in the state was caught here, but the grayling here are hard to catch.

The outlet doesn't flow over the glacial moraine holding in the lake. Instead, it emerges from the ground a few hundred yards below.

36. MEADOW LAKE TRAIL

(MAP ON PAGE 69)

Round trip: 2.6 miles
Elevation gain: 1,040 feet
Highest point: 10,200 feet
Time: 3 1/2 hours
Difficulty: Moderate
Maps: USGS topographic: Gilmore; Forest Service: Salmon National Forest
Information: Leadore Ranger District
Getting there: From Idaho Highway 28, 17 miles south of Leadore, turn west on the gravel road (008) to the ghost town of Gilmore and the Meadow Lake campground. After climbing 2,200 feet in 7 miles the road reaches the campground. The unsigned Meadow Lake trail begins at the far end of the campground loop by going 200 yards up a new 1-mile loop trail. There is limited parking at the trailhead, so if you plan this as a day hike you may need to park before reaching the campground and walk through it for .3 mile.

The fractured cliffs of an unnamed peak rise 1,200 feet above blue-green Meadow Lake, which is surrounded by whitebark pines and white metamorphic rocks. The trail begins in a flower garden of bluebells, pink mimulus, yellow cinquefoil and red paintbrush. Under a sawtoothed wall, it passes an aqua tarn that is edged with orange pebbles and white-flowered Labrador tea. Above jut the gray cliffs of the peak that dominates Meadow Lake. Above the tarn, the trail climbs to a divide with an excellent view of the Lemhi, Beaverhead and Lost River ranges.

The access to Meadow Lake is from near Gilmore Summit, the divide between the drainages of Birch Creek to the south and the Lemhi River to the north. This divide was originally called Days Defile after a member of the Wilson Price Hunt expedition who died there while trapping. His will, made the day before he died, was the first probated in Idaho.The lead and silver mines at Gilmore were first organized into a mining district in 1880. Lack of transportation to markets that were at least 85 miles away hampered mining development. One investor, F.G. Laver, tried using steam engines with wide wheels to pull the ore wagons along the road in 1902, but the road was so rough the wheels wore out right away.

Before long, Pittsburgh investors bought the claims, and in 1910 built a railroad from the Northern Pacific Line at Armistead, Montana, over Bannock Pass to Leadore. They extended one branch to Salmon and the other to Gilmore and called it the Gilmore and Pittsburgh Railroad. Mining continued at Gilmore until the power plant exploded in 1929 and the Depression prevented rebuilding. Twenty-five of the original 500 residents still lived there in 1942.

The trail to the divide above Meadow Lake takes off from the new 1-mile handicap-accessible loop trail that starts at the upper end of the campground and ends at the lower end. The trail to the divide turns off the loop trail about 200 yards above the upper end of the campground and goes up the right side of the inlet, passing a tarn at .3 mile. (In the future, the trail will be rerouted to begin at the highest point of the loop trail and will go above the tarn.)

From the tarn, the trail leads northwest along its inlet between a talus hill and forest. At .5 mile the trail turns left (south) up a talus hill. From here, follow cairns to the left (southeast) through the talus and over outcrops to the place where the trail begins to angle up the ridge at .6 mile. The trail makes three switchbacks though white, peach, and purple talus up the side of the ridge. At .9 mile it switchbacks right (northwest) toward the pass and continues straight toward it. This stretch was recently improved by digging trail tread and adding a retaining wall.

From this section there is a view of a pond north of the tarn. At 1.3 miles the trail reaches the divide. The ground here is sprinkled with alpine plants such as the magenta-flowered Least Lewisia. The view includes the wide brown face of Iron Creek Point across Sawmill Canyon to the southeast, the blue snow-streaked peaks of the Lost River Range to the west, high peaks of the Lemhis to the north, and Meadow Lake and the tarn below.

37. BELL MOUNTAIN CANYON

Round trip: 6 miles
Elevation gain: 1,000 feet
Elevation loss (return climb): 80 feet
Highest point: 8,440 feet
Time: 5 hours
Difficulty: easy
Maps: USGS topographic: Coal Kiln Canyon; Forest Service: Targhee National Forest
Information: Dubois Ranger District
Getting there: From Idaho Highway 28 turn west 13.3 miles north of the Lone Pine Store and Cafe onto the Charcoal Kilns road. At 4.9 miles turn left (south) onto a dirt track toward Mammoth Canyon. At a junction at 5.3 miles, just past a gate that must be opened and shut, keep straight ahead on Road 183. At 6.3 miles is another gate, and at 6.4 miles the road drops into Mammoth Canyon. Park before the drop unless your car has four-wheel drive. The hike description starts here.

This hike up an old jeep trail gives a closeup view of the umbrella tent of Bell Mountain. From farther north and from the west it does resemble a bell, even though it wasn't named for its shape but for a former state mine inspector, Robert Bell. The route leads beside an unnamed gray and orange peak with a face of triangles. In June and July the open slopes along the trail are covered with cream-colored sego lily and umbrella plant, bright yellow stonecrop, and pale green Fras-

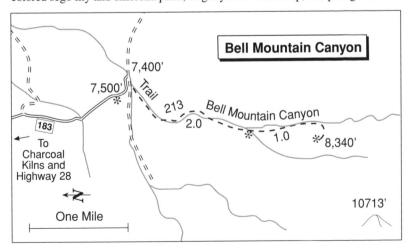

er's gentian.

On the way to this hike you come close to the charcoal kilns that produced charcoal for the Nicholia smelter across the valley from 1882 to 1889. Only four of the 16 twenty-foot kilns are standing, but they are well worth the short side trip. Each one held 40 to 50 cords of wood, and the fire in it was controlled by opening and closing small draft doors.

From the top of the descent into Mammoth Canyon, walk down the road and cross the canyon. Avoid the road to the right (west) that goes up Mammoth Canyon. Instead, turn left on a jeep trail that winds southwest up Bell Mountain Canyon. At .5 mile, the trail goes through a slot between eight-foot cliffs made of naturally cemented pebbles. At 1 mile the track curves left (southeast) in a grassy flat and then back south again. The creek in the canyon is dry by early summer and there is no shade except for one grove of Douglas firs.

At 1.8 miles, where the canyon forks, the road is closed to motor vehicles. Camping at this spot would be lumpy. The track jogs uphill to the right here and climbs along an open ridge of sagebrush and grass with a view of the Beaverhead Mountains to the east.

As the trail continues along the side of the ridge in the sagebrush, Bell Mountain disappears below the woods on top of the ridge. At 2.7 miles the track splits and each branch goes .3 mile farther. Turn right (west) and follow the road to a saddle at 3 miles. For a view of Bell Mountain and the peak of triangles, turn north of the track and climb the ridge for about 200 yards.

38. ROCKY CANYON

Round trip: 11 miles to the fork of the canyon
Elevation gain: 1,800 feet
Elevation loss (return climb): 380 feet
Highest point: 8,000 feet
Time: 7 1/2 hours
Difficulty: strenuous
Maps: USGS topographic: Nicholia, Diamond Peak; Forest Service: Targhee National Forest, Dubois and Island Park Ranger Districts
Information: Dubois Ranger District
Getting there: On Idaho Highway 28, 34.5 miles south of Leadore turn left (west) on a rocky, gravel road toward a radio relay station. (The turn is 7.5 miles north of the Lone Pine Store.) The Forest Service map shows this road as a dead end, but it really continues by way of a two-wheel track to meet the road that has come up Rocky Canyon from the highway. Just before the relay station at 2.4 miles, turn right onto the two-wheel track. At 3.7 miles the road that has come up Rocky Canyon comes in from the left, and at 4.1 miles the road splits. Keep left here and drive to the top of a hill. Passenger cars should be left before the hill. The steepness of the track on the other side of the hill makes it best to leave even four-wheel-drive vehicles on the hilltop.

Rocky Canyon lives up to its name with cliffs, alcoves, teeth and towers from the beginning of the trail clear to the forks of the canyon. The best display is from 4 to 5 miles where rust, gray, cream and brown towers decorate the peaks of the canyon walls like a parade of dinosaurs. The bottom of the canyon holds a series

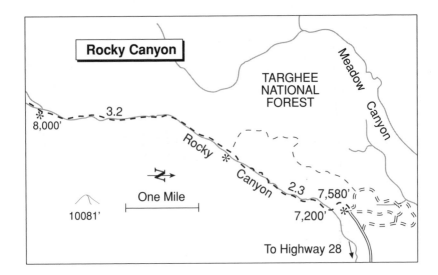

of long narrow meadows sprinkled with blue gentians, white yarrow, yellow cinquefoil, rose-colored avens, red and yellow columbine, purple lupine, and lavender aster. In addition, yellow and pink monkeyflower grow along the creek.

Three miles south of the access road, 21 springs give birth to Birch Creek. Some of them can be seen by stopping at the Kaufman Recreation Area about 4 miles north of the Lone Pine Store.

To begin the hike, walk down the other side of the hill 100 yards to where the track splits. Take the left branch and then turn off it onto a path that drops into a meadow at the bottom of the canyon at .5 mile and disappears. At .8 mile, at the far end of the meadow, the trail reappears in a shady glen under outcrops, Douglas firs, and 50-foot cliffs. At 1.5 miles the glen opens up into a meadow, and a side creek comes in from the left. Here one of the inner canyon peaks looms ahead and the creek crossings begin. From here on, the trail crosses back and forth over the three-foot-wide creek dozens of times, partly because the trail tread is maintained more by cattle than by humans.

After passing through a short defile, the trail enters a larger meadow, where a four-wheel-drive road descends into the canyon from the right (west) at 2.3 miles. Beyond here the meadows narrow and the sagebrush hills are replaced by forested ones. At 3.2 miles the trail crosses the creek from left to right and goes along the west side of a shady ravine. By midsummer instead of water, the creek contains only moss-covered boulders. Next, the trail climbs along in the trees below talus slopes, with orange cliffs to the right. At 3.5 miles it comes out on a .2-mile-long meadow which has aspen groves.

On the other side of a grassy knoll, the trail reaches a meadow that is twice as long as the previous one. Here, at 4 miles, a gray tower with a flat orange top appears on the right, and on the left rise three brown teeth and red, white and rust cliffs. This section of the canyon is the most beautiful.

The trail continues through rolling grassy meadows. At 4.7 miles is the largest, a .8-mile-long and .2-mile-wide meadow. Here the trail disappears in grass. At the far end of this meadow the canyon forks. Bits of trail continue straight ahead up

92

Rocky Canyon in the Lemhi Range.

the Left Fork to an elevation of 8,700 feet below a shoulder of Diamond Peak.

39. PASS CREEK LAKE

Round trip: 5.2 miles
Elevation gain: 1,160 feet
Elevation loss (return climb): 400 feet
Highest point: 8,000 feet
Time: 5 hours
Difficulty: moderate, with some slippery footing
Maps: USGS topographic: Eightmile Canyon, Fallert Springs; Forest Service: Targhee National Forest
Information: Dubois Ranger District
Getting there: On Idaho Highway 28, 8.3 miles south of the Lone Pine Store and Cafe, there are two roads a mile apart. The northern one of these fords Birch Creek one mile from the highway. This ford is often still 18 inches deep or deeper in mid-August. Even high-clearance four-wheel-drive vehicles can have their engines stalled here. To avoid the ford, continue south on Highway 28 for 1.1 miles. Then turn west on a dirt road that is not on the Forest Service map, but is signed Eightmile Canyon. It is just south of the canal that diverts Birch Creek across the highway. Drive along this road along the left (south) side of the canal.

At 1.7 miles the road crosses the dry bed of Birch Creek. Once across, turn right on a gravel two-wheel track and follow it north along the left (west) side of Birch Creek to intersect the Eightmile Canyon Road on the far (west) side of the

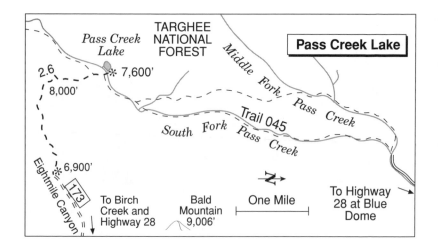

ford at 3.3 miles.

Turn left on that road and continue to the trailhead for the North Fork of Eight-mile Canyon Trail (026) at 9.3 miles. Mud holes at 8 and 8.7 miles may be a problem for passenger cars. There are two other trails to Pass Creek Lake, reached by the Pass Creek Road. One (045) goes up the south and the other up the middle fork of Pass Creek. They are both more than 5 miles one-way and have no shade.

Still another trail begins on the west side of the Lemhis on the Uncle Ike Creek Road 8 miles from the Pahsimeroi Highway. It is 7.5 miles and a 2,260-foot elevation gain to the lake by this route.

At first the trail up the North Fork of Pass Creek runs in a narrow gorge lined with 150-foot cliffs pitted with caves. From the trail's high point two peaks with slanting layers of rock rise across Pass Creek. The green lake is set between peninsulas of grass under hills of aspen and sagebrush. Below the lake the canyon wall holds a forest of rock blades and turrets.

At the junction of the Eightmile Canyon Road with Highway 28, the hills on the east are pitted with caves for several miles in both directions. The caves were prehistoric dwellings and shelters, and Idaho State University has conducted major archaeological digs in some of them.

From the trailhead, the trail climbs steeply up the gorge of the North Fork, crossing back and forth over it. ATVs have widened the trail to a two-wheel track. In places, it is slippery with loose gravel over hard-packed dirt. You may need to zigzag across it.

The gorge is filled with Douglas fir and riparian shrubs along the usually dry creek. By .8 mile the cliffs have receded to high on the wall. Where the trail splits into a path and an ATV track, keep close to the creek on the path for easier walking.

At 1.3 miles is a grassy basin with the ruins of two log cabins. Here, take the main trail when it turns right (west) up a side canyon toward a saddle as shown on the topographic map. Avoid an ATV track that climbs the ridge to the left and then cuts over to the main trail because it is longer and steeper.

At 1.6 miles, the trail crests the saddle, which has a view of high peaks. At the top of the saddle, you must go through a gate. Signs of cattle soon appear. The trail heads down to a spring and tiny pond in a meadow at 2 miles.

Because the lake can't be seen from the main trail and the ATV tracks are confusing, a topographic map is needed to find it. There is no sign of the trail up the South Fork of Pass Creek at 2.3 miles, just various ATV tracks. Continue down the main trail to near the lower end of the lake. At about 2.5 miles turn left onto a signed side trail that fords the outlet and climbs 50 feet to the lake at 2.6 miles. This trail turns off where the main trail makes a right turn.

Salmon River Mountains
-North of Challis

40. CHALLIS CREEK LAKES

Round trip: 13.8 miles, (11 miles with four-wheel drive), 1.8 miles more for upper lakes
Elevation gain: 1,860 feet, 60 feet more for upper lakes
Highest point: 8,980 feet
Time: 8 1/2 to 10 hours
Difficulty: Strenuous
Maps: USGS topographic: Twin Peaks, Challis Creek Lakes; Forest Service: Challis National Forest
Information: Challis Ranger District
Getting there: From U.S. Highway 93 at Challis, turn north on the main street, and just beyond the high school turn right (east) on the Challis Creek Road. Take this road, which is paved for 9.3 miles, to a junction at 10.4 miles. Here turn left on the Mosquito Flat Road (080) keeping straight ahead at a junction with the Pine Summit Road at 16.7 miles. At 17 miles, at the reservoir and picnic area in sagebrush, the road becomes primitive. Continue around the side of the reservoir, avoiding a road to the right to a corral. There is a mud hole at 18 miles, another at 18.5 miles with a detour of it to the right, then a ford of a side creek at 18.9 miles. Those without four-wheel drive should park before these obstacles. A larger mud hole at 19.2 miles, a ford of Challis Creek at 19.4 miles, and big rocks and side hills farther up will stop many four-wheel-drive vehicles. Because drivers will stop

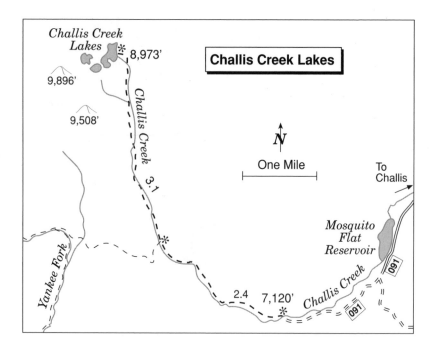

at different places on the road, the hike mileage starts at the ford of Challis Creek at 19.4 miles. From the first mud hole the hike will be 1.6 miles longer one way.

Challis Creek Lakes sprawl in a rocky basin sprinkled with whitebark pines. The largest lake has been dammed. On its west side rises a gray talus ridge with black knobs on its summit and black cliffs and ledges on its side. The middle lake hugs this wall, and at the highest lake a curved avalanche trough shaped like a backwards S splits the cliffs. In late summer the waterline of the lakes creeps down, revealing beaches of sharp stones. The country is rugged and reminds some people of the description fur trapper John Work wrote of the country around Challis in 1830: "From the top of the mountain there is nothing to be seen but mountains and deep narrow ravines as far as the eye can reach . . ."

From the ford to the right (north) side of Challis Creek at 19.4 miles, the jeep trail starts out in sagebrush and clumps of Douglas fir, and at 1 mile begins to curve to the right. Just beyond a side creek at 1.8 miles it crosses talus that would be difficult for vehicles. At 2.2 miles is a junction with a foot trail west to the Yankee Fork. Here you can look up the canyon to a bare rounded mountain. Otherwise there are no landmarks. At 2.8 miles the jeep trail crosses the creek to the left (west) side and at 3.3 miles returns to the east and climbs in woods. At 3.8 miles it crosses once again to the left (west) bank of the creek.

In the next 1.7 miles the track climbs 770 feet over rocks, often in the sun. At 4.5 miles it leaps a side stream, and at 5.1 miles returns to the right (east) bank of Challis Creek. At 5.5 miles the road comes out on the dam of the lowest lake. Because of rocks the only good campsites are at the north end of the lake.

To reach the upper lakes, go south along the lake on a fisherman's path. Then, using the topographic map, walk cross-country to the second lake at 6.1 miles and the highest at 6.4 miles. This hike is best for early summer when the lakes are full and wildflowers and snowbanks soften the rocks, but at that time the mud holes and creek crossings will be deeper.

41. OPAL LAKE

Round trip: 2 miles
Elevation gain: 520 feet
Highest point: 7,540 feet
Time: 2 hours
Difficulty: Easy
Maps: USGS topographic: Opal Lake; Forest Service: Salmon National Forest
Information: Salmon/Cobalt Ranger District
Getting there: From Challis drive east on U.S. Highway 93 for 9 miles and turn left (north) at a sign for Cobalt on Road 055, the Morgan Creek Road. Drive over the Morgan Creek Summit at 19.2 miles and at 24.1 miles, turn right (east) on the Opal Lake Road (252). It crosses the creek to the north side at 24.6 miles. When it splits at 25.3 miles take the right branch, which fords the creek back to the south side. Then drive to the end of the road at 25.5 (1.4 miles from the Morgan Creek Road). Early in the summer the fords will require four-wheel drive.

The blue-green teardrop of Opal Lake gleams in a basin of pink quartzite rocks. The lake occupies a groove between wooded ridges, with a bare headwall up the canyon leading to the rounded gray peak of Taylor Mountain. A meadow at

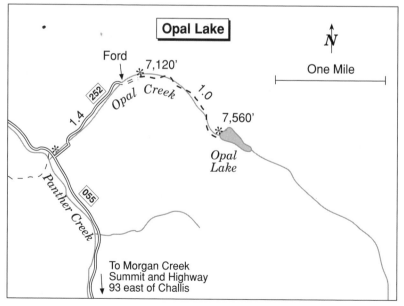

the upper end and aspens at the lower end soften the pink rock.

From the end of the road, a trail that used to be a road leads up the right (south) side of the creek. After .3 mile it crosses to the left bank. The trail is different from the jeep track shown on the topographic map; sections of the old jeep trail are visible too. The trail continues along the left (northeast) side of the creek, climbs above it and crosses a talus slope. At .8 mile the path hops back over to the southeast side of the creek, which disappears just beyond this. At 1 mile the trail comes out above the lake on top of a rocky knoll that is dotted with white sego lilies in July.

Salmon River Mountains - North and West of Salmon

42. HAT CREEK LAKES

Round trip: 6 miles, 2 miles additional for off-trail lakes
Elevation gain: 432 feet, 100 feet more for off-trail lakes
Elevation loss (return climb): 972 feet
Highest point: 9,238 feet
Time: 5 1/2 to 6 1/2 hours
Difficulty: Easy to moderate
Maps: USGS topographic: Taylor Mountain, Wards Butte; Forest Service: Salmon National Forest
Information: Salmon/Cobalt Ranger District
Getting there: Turn north off U.S. Highway 93 at the Shoup Bridge, 5.2 miles south of Idaho Highway 28 in Salmon and 54.7 miles northwest of Challis. Turn left (south) at 1 mile and at 2.5 miles keep straight ahead toward Iron Lake, on the Williams Creek Road (021). (Do not turn south toward Williams Lake.) The pavement ends at 4 miles. At 5 miles is the forest boundary and at 7 miles another turnoff (028) to the left to Williams Lake. Keep straight ahead. The Cougar Point Campground is at 10.5 miles.

At 13.8 miles, at Williams Summit, turn left (south) on the signed dirt road

98

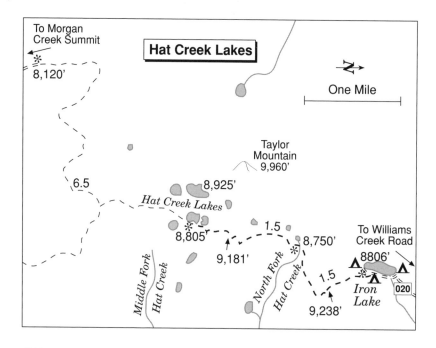

To Morgan Creek Summit

Hat Creek Lakes

One Mile

8,120'

6.5

Taylor Mountain 9,960'

Hat Creek Lakes

8,925'

1.5

8,805'

8,750'

To Williams Creek Road

9,181'

8806'

1.5

Middle Fork Hat Creek

North Fork Hat Creek

9,238'

Iron Lake

020

(020) toward Iron Lake. This road is rocky and rough in places and not suitable for passenger cars. The road passes the site of the Lake Mountain Fire at 22 miles. China Springs and the upper trailhead for the Old Thunder Mountain Trail are at 22.3 miles. Here the pinkish towers of the Bighorn Crags appear to the north. Just beyond China Springs, Road 020 turns off to the right. Make this turn. The road comes to the first campground at Iron Lake at 32.5 miles. The Hat Creek Lakes trail takes off to the left at the Iron Lake Campground fee area sign.

The five Hat Creek Lakes accent dark green forest with a brighter green below the pale gray talus and fractured cliffs of Taylor Mountain. The largest lake, set under cliffs on the west side of the basin, glows with a brilliant aqua-green color. The trail begins beside the green oval of Iron Lake, which is set between talus ridges sprinkled with whitebark pines. Because of crowds, this hike is best for midweek and after Labor Day but before hunting season.

From the Iron Lake Campground the trail climbs through lodgepole pines and grouse whortleberry to a flat saddle at .5 mile, high enough for subalpine fir and whitebark pine. The route switchbacks down to the left and then back to the right below a talus slope at 1.2 miles. At the bottom of the canyon, at 1.4 miles, is a junction with the North Fork of Hat Creek Trail. At 1.5 miles the main trail crosses Hat Creek to the south side on a bridge. Then it goes up and down through woods and across mossy bogs on puncheon bridges before climbing through thick forest onto an open talus ridge at 2 miles. Ahead is the summit of Taylor Mountain, and below are two unnamed lakes. Switchbacks across talus lead to the top of the ridge at 2.5 miles.

The path zigzags down to an intermittent pond in a bowl of rocks and wanders through the trees past paths to the first two lakes at 3 miles. They are 50 feet to the

99

right (west) of the main trail. A short cross-country hike from the first lake takes you to the largest lake. Continuing south on the trail puts you in reach of the two southern lakes, which are also off-trail. Seeing the largest lake and the two to the south will add 2 miles to the round trip and 100 feet of elevation gain. Campsites are plentiful. The trail continues south and west 6.5 miles to the Challis Forest trailhead for Hat Creek Lakes at Morgan Creek Summit, which is a longer but much less crowded hike.

43. OLD THUNDER MOUNTAIN TRAIL

Round trip: 9.4 miles
Elevation gain: 3,100 feet
Highest point: 8,959 feet
Map: Lake Mountain
Time: 4 to 7 hours
Difficulty: strenuous, steep
Information: Salmon/Cobalt Ranger District
Getting there: On U.S. Highway 93 at the Shoup Bridge, 6 miles south of Salmon, turn west onto the Williams Creek Road (021). At 1 mile turn left (south), and at 2.5 miles turn left (south) again onto the Lake Creek Road (028). The pavement ends at 4.6 miles. Continue to a junction at 9.6 miles. Turn right (north) past a BLM campground, Forest Service boat dock, and the south shore trailhead. Continue up a grade, passing Tin Cup Creek, to a loading chute at a fork of Lake Creek at 14.2 miles. This loading chute is on private land. When parking do not block access to the loading chute or adjacent gates.

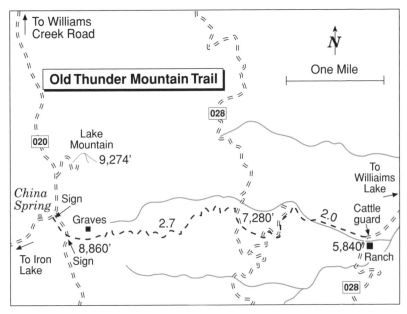

Near the Clipper Bullion Mill in the Salmon River mountains.

The Salmon-Challis National Forest has relocated, marked, and reconstructed this historic trail that originally connected Salmon with the Thunder Mountain mines at the head of Monumental and Marble Creeks above the Middle Fork of the Salmon. This trail was one of four to Thunder Mountain from different directions. The blazes on the trees are so old the bark has grown over them, making them look like splashes of black paint. The lowest three miles of the trail from the loading chute to where the trail crosses Forest Road 028 has a view of the Salmon River canyon and blue-green Williams Lake set in pinkish-gray cliffs. The upper section of the trail ends at China Springs on Forest Road 020, the road between Williams Creek Summit and Iron Lake. From the open ridge here you can see the Bighorn Crags in the distance. China Springs commemorates three Chinese killed here for their gold dust. It is a much easier hike if you start at China Springs and go downhill to Williams Lake with the help of a car shuttle than it is to start at Williams Lake and go uphill.

From the trailhead, the trail starts out through a gate that requires strength to open. Please don't climb over it, as climbing gates and fences damages them. The first section climbs a grass and sagebrush hillside as it follows the creek. At .8 mile the trail turns left into Douglas firs over a small hill. Then it climbs along next to the creek and crosses it to the left side. At 1.25 miles the trail switchbacks to the left and crosses the end of a ridge. The path comes out in the sun among scattered trees and the trail goes straight uphill through arrowleaf balsamroot with a view into a deep canyon on the left. It angles to the left of the center of the ridge as it climbs.

At 1.6 miles the trail intersects an old logging road, which you follow to the left. It switchbacks right for 200 yards with a view of Williams Lake, then left for 50 yards and right again. In 50 yards a sign points to the trail leading uphill from the road.

Now the trail goes up the left side of a ridge in open sagebrush. This part of this trail may have difficult footing. The path contours left and passes a view of

Williams Lake. At 1.4 miles it turns up a sagebrush slope with gray outcrops on the right. Across the canyon to the west a road can be seen. At 2 miles the trail comes to Forest Road 028 at a grassy flat.

The upper part of the trail leaves this road .2 mile to the right (north). From here the trail mostly climbs along the top of a ridge spur, reaching an open summit at 8,567 feet at 3.7 miles. After a steep 200-foot climb up a bench, the trail meanders through the woods to the trailhead at China Springs on the Ridge Road (020), (also called the Salmon River Mountain Road) at 4.7 miles.

44. PINE CREEK RIDGE TRAIL AND THE CLIPPER BULLION MILL

Round trip: 3 miles for the mill and view of Shoup; 10 miles one way to a spur of the Moose Creek Road (061)
Highest point: 3,700 feet at viewpoint
Elevation gain: 400 feet; about 5,000 feet to a spur of the Moose Creek Road
Time: 3 hours for mill and viewpoint
Difficulty: Easy, but poor trail
Maps: USGS topographic: Pine Creek Rapids, Shoup; Forest Service: Salmon

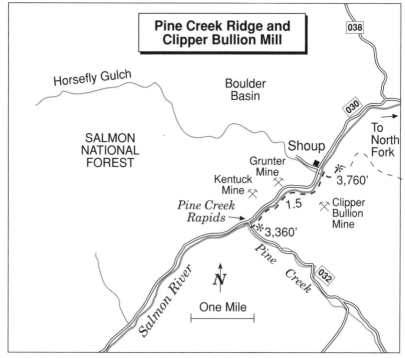

National Forest
Information: North Fork Ranger District
Getting there: Turn west off U.S. Highway 93 at North Fork and drive 20 miles along the Salmon River to the Pine Creek Bridge and park at the far (south) end of the bridge.

This easy hike to the ruins of a historic stamp mill, the Clipper Bullion, lets hikers see the rusty stamps and cam shafts of the mill and the ore buckets on an old tramway. Cliffs and ledges of buff-colored Idaho batholith rock covered with black lichens line the walls of the Salmon River Canyon. In between the outcrops Douglas fir, ponderosa pine, mountain mahogany, currant and squawbrush soften the canyon walls. From the bridge at the beginning of the trail, you can look downstream at the white water tumbling in a jade green trough down Pine Creek Rapids. These are the rapids that stopped Lewis and Clark from attempting to go by boat to the Columbia.

William Clark and 11 men explored along the river to see if it could be floated, even though the Indians had told him it was impossible. Of this trip along the river, he wrote, "The River from the place I left my party to this Creek is almost one continued rapid, five very considerable rapids . . ."

Climbing up the canyon wall beyond the mill to a viewpoint on the trail up Pine Creek Ridge gives a view of the river and of the log house, false front store and board-and-batten cabins of Shoup. This is a hike for history rather than solitude for the trail parallels the road on the other side of the river.

The town of Shoup (pronounced "Shoop") began in 1881 when Pat O'Hara and Samuel James discovered the Grunter lode. James soon discovered the Kentuck lode and enlisted the help of investors. The town, which was named for Idaho's first governor, George L. Shoup, a merchant in Salmon, grew up to serve the mines and the village of Pine Creek two miles downriver. By 1889, 300 lodes had been discovered near Shoup. One of the stamp mills that served the mines was the Clipper Bullion.

To begin the hike, at the south end of the Pine Creek bridge look around for the trail, which starts out overgrown by shrubs. While traveling this trail watch for rattlesnakes. They are less likely to appear in spring or fall when nights are below freezing, or on a rainy summer day. The trail follows the river about 20 feet above it. After .5 mile it passes small cabins right across the river from the old mine which is open for tours. Here the trail tread disappears, but is soon found again to the left of the cabins. Avoid the path that goes behind the cabins to a mine tunnel.

The trail continues above the thickets of the river bank and under big granite boulders. At a corner at .8 mile, the river flows around an island at low water. At 1 mile the path descends into a flat with the mill ruins ahead. To avoid a fall, look at and photograph the ruins from a distance.

To reach the viewpoint continue along the next flat past a little cabin, watching for poison ivy. From the flat you can look up the canyon of Boulder Creek across the river behind Shoup. At 1.3 miles the trail switchbacks up the canyon wall. Hike up it 400 vertical feet to an open grassy hillside with the best view at about 1.5 miles. Shoup can be seen for about a mile on this part of the trail.

The trail continues on up China Gulch, connecting with Road 60023 approximately 4.5 miles from the river with a 3,400-foot elevation gain. From there the trail continues climbing another 2 miles up to Stormy Peak Lookout with a 1,500-foot elevation gain.

103

45. DIVIDE TRAIL FROM THE SPRING CREEK ROAD

Round trip: 7.6 miles to a viewpoint (to Lost Trail Pass 55 miles roundtrip)
Elevation gain: 720 feet
Elevation loss: 960 feet
Highest point: 8,640 feet
Time: 5 to 6 hours
Difficulty: moderate
Maps: USGS topographic: Shoup; Forest Service: Salmon National Forest
Information: North Fork Ranger District
Getting there: From U.S. 93 at North Fork drive 17.5 miles west on the paved and gravel Salmon River Road (030). Then go 10.4 miles up the dirt Spring Creek Road (038) to the trailhead.

From this trail, the Bitterroots gleam white to the north over blued ridges. To the south, wooded hills drop into the hazy blue gulf of the Salmon River canyon.

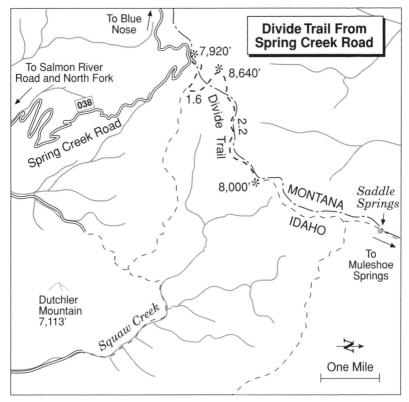

104

Beyond it rise the blades and scallops of the Bighorn Crags. To the east, logging roads wind across the canyon walls above Indian Creek. To the west, the silvered trees of the 1985 Long Tom Fire cover the hills with a gray mist. Along the trail, wolf lichen feathers some of the whitebark pine trunks with brilliant chartreuse filaments. The Divide Trail continues for 28 miles to Lost Trail Pass, so a through trip of several days can be made with a car shuttle. You can also access the trail at several points along it, such as from the Allan Lake trail.

From the Spring Creek Road, the Divide Trail heads downhill 100 yards through beargrass and a lodgepole-subalpine fir forest, then starts climbing. After a couple of switchbacks it comes out on sagebrush and lupine and heads southeast. At 1 mile the trail switches back to the northwest. At this switchback, a path goes off down a ridge above Squaw Creek.

Just beyond the switchback is a mossy spring edged in yellow and pink monkeyflower. The trail goes back into the timber, then passes a view to the west of Blue Nose and Salmon Mountain. Next it turns northeast to an open grassy area at 1.6 miles with a view north of the Bitterroots. The path goes downhill along the north side of the ridge and then climbs east to its crest at 2 miles. On the crest, the trail comes out of the subalpine firs and whitebark pines onto a long stretch of sagebrush with a view of ledges and cliffs.

Now the trail returns to the timber and climbs up and down. At another big open area at 3 miles you can look east over the canyon of Indian Creek to the Continental Divide and south to the Bighorn Crags and Salmon River. The trail returns to the trees, then descends to a saddle at 3.3 miles. This saddle makes a good destination for a day hike as does the crest of the ridge just beyond it at 3.8 miles, 400 feet higher. From this point there is an excellent view of the Salmon River canyon.

46. ALLAN LAKE

Round trip: 7.4 miles
Elevation gain: 1,690 feet
Highest point: 7,802 feet
Time: 6 hours
Difficulty: moderate
Maps: USGS topographic: Allan Mountain; Forest Service: Salmon National Forest
Information: North Fork Ranger District
Getting there: From Salmon, drive 20 miles north on U.S. 93 to the village of North Fork. Continue north on 93 for 6 miles and turn left (west) on the Hughes Creek Road (Forest Road 091). Drive 2.5 miles and turn right (north) on Road 089. There should be signs to Allan Lake. Drive 4 miles, sticking to Road 089 until you come to a gate. There is a trail sign up off the road and a parking area just before the gate.

Allan Lake has two major claims to fame. One is great rainbow trout fishing. The other is its subalpine larch trees, which grow in only a few places in Idaho. The larches are at their most southeastern range at Allan Lake.

On top of these features, this is just a beautiful area to visit. Beyond the lake, the trail continues for another 3 miles where it connects with the Idaho-Montana Divide Trail. (The Continental Divide Trail enters Idaho farther north at Lost Trail Pass on U.S. 93 and goes southeast from it along the crest of the Beaverhead

105

Allan Lake in the Salmon National Forest

Mountains.)

Lost Trail Pass was probably crossed by Lewis and Clark on their way north to Lolo Pass. It was certainly crossed by Alexander Ross in March 1825 after 50 men and 240 horses had spent 21 days making a road in the snow over it from the north. Because he let some trappers from another company use the road, too, his reward for his heroic effort was being fired from his trapping company.

Along the access road up Hughes Creek, mines were discovered in the 1880s that helped make the roller mill and five stamp mills profitable at the nearby town of Gibbonsville until 1899.

Allan Lake sits about 13 miles as the crow flies north of the tiny town of North Fork. The trail to the lake takes you up into the Bitterroot Range in the Salmon National Forest.

The mountains around Allan Lake are mostly covered in deep forest. There are several different kinds of trees in this forest: fir, juniper, whitebark pine, spruce and aspen. The canopy is high and covered, which makes summer hikes much cooler.

Finding the trailhead is not difficult once you get on the right road. Signs help. Eventually you come to a parking area just before a locked gate that marks the end of the road. The sign says 4 miles to the lake, but the trail is closer to 3.7 miles.

The route is your basic follow-the-creek trail, in this case Ditch Creek, all the way to the lake. Most of the trail is uphill, but the last mile is a real workout. There are a few side streams to cross, but nothing serious by midsummer.

The trail also has a few boulder fields. The rocky sections offer good chances to view the surrounding mountains, but be careful where you step. The trail passes near Rocky Mountain, 8,691 feet, at about 2.5 miles. Look northeast for occasional glimpses of the highest peaks at the top of the canyon.

Just before 3 miles the trail begins to switchback up steeply. In this section you can hear a cascading waterfall on the west side of the trail. To see it you'll have to go off the trail 100 yards.

106

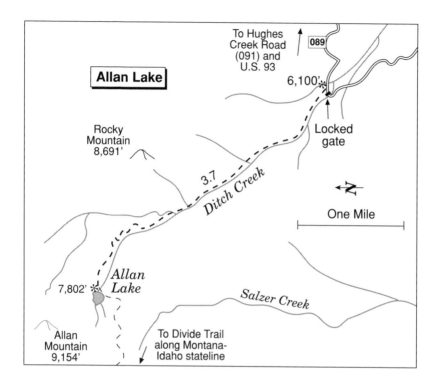

Just when the trail stops climbing you are at the lake. It crosses the outlet on steppingstones and continues around the south side of the lake. There are some nice campsites along it. In another 200 yards, a trail sign says it is 3 miles to the Idaho-Montana Divide.

A couple of small inlets feed the lake on its north side. Several springs also feed the lake at various points. There are quite a few small fish.

If you're looking for a longer hike, there are several possibilities. Most will require a car shuttle or a stashed mountain bike. One trip is to continue up the trail toward the divide for about 2.2 miles to a fork. Here, the right fork goes to the divide. To make a loop trip, take the left fork. It heads southwest to Ax Park on a trail known as Ax Park Way. From Ax Park you can hike down to the Hughes Creek Road at Salzer Bar.

If you take the right fork instead, you will reach the Divide in 1 mile. Here there is another junction. To the right the Divide Trail heads northeast along the Idaho-Montana border to Lost Trail Pass, passing tiny Frog Pond Lake on the way. A car shuttle will allow a two- or three-day trip along this trail.

If you go left on the Divide Trail from the junction for 1 mile you'll pass another trail to Ax Park. Three more miles brings you to a junction at Bare Springs, where a trail turns off to go south along Butcherknife Ridge to the West Fork of Hughes Creek Road.

Beaverhead Mountains

47. LEWIS AND CLARK TRAIL AT LEMHI PASS

Round trip: 5 miles
Elevation loss (return climb): 1,230 feet
Highest point: 7,730 feet
Time: 4 to 5 hours; 2 1/2 hours for a through trip with two cars
Difficulty: Expert, due to difficult footing and lack of trail tread
Maps: USGS topographic: Lemhi Pass; Forest Service: Salmon National Forest
Information: Leadore Ranger District
Getting there: From Idaho Highway 28, turn left at Tendoy, 19 miles south of Salmon onto the improved Agency Creek Road (013). Take a right turn at .2 mile at a sign for Lemhi Pass. At .4 mile make a left turn and drive up Agency Creek, avoiding side roads. At 10.1 miles a sign for the Lewis & Clark Trail marks where it crosses the road. Continue up the steep road to Lemhi Pass at 12.1 miles.

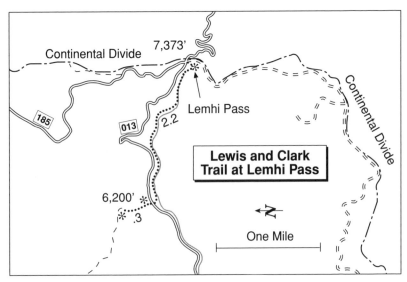

The grass, sagebrush, and fir-covered hills near the pass are prettier in early summer when the grass is green, the flowers are out, and snow still caps the Lemhis across the valley. Since Lewis and Clark crossed the pass in the month of August, the first Europeans to do so, hiking the trail then in the dry grass is more authentic. From the pass you can look west to peaks of forest and rock in the Lemhis and east to similar ranges in Montana.

Several changes are planned in time for the Lewis and Clark Bicentennial in 2005. They include a new interpretive site at Lemhi Pass, a new campground on the Montana side near the Sacajawea Monument, and an overlook and interpretive trail near the Warm Springs Road north of the pass. In addition, access to the Continental Divide Trail leading south is being moved away from the pass to the new campground.

A short distance down the Montana side of the pass is the Sacajawea Monument. Sacajawea was the young Shoshone wife of the Lewis and Clark guide, Toussaint Charbonneau. She gave birth to a son on the journey, and cared for her son and acted as interpreter for the expedition. She had been kidnapped and sold as a child, and on the Lemhi River beyond the pass she found the village of her people.

Meriwether Lewis and three of his men crossed the Continental Divide here at Lemhi Pass on August 12, 1805, on an Indian trail. Of that day he said he "Proceeded on to the top of the dividing ridge from which I discovered an immense range of high mountains still to the West of us."

Near the road up Lemhi Pass, the Mormons under Thomas Smith established a mission in a mud fort on the Lemhi River in 1855. It lasted three years before it was abandoned after an Indian raid. About 2 miles up the pass is a sign for a turnoff to Chief Tendoy's grave. He was chief when Ulysses S. Grant gave the Lemhi Indians their own reservation here in 1875. After Tendoy's death, the Lemhis were forced to move to the Fort Hall Reservation. Today the Lemhis are trying to get their reservation land back.

Farther up, near the summit of the pass, are the largest deposits of the rare earth thorium in the United States. It is used in metal alloys and can also be processed to produce uranium.

For the easiest hiking of a section of the Lewis and Clark Trail near the pass, bring two cars and leave one where the road crosses the trail below the pass. To begin the hike, walk down the Agency Creek Road from the pass a few yards to the Lewis and Clark trail markers. The trail is not shown on the topographic map. (Avoid any tracks leading south along a ridge from the pass.) Wear boots, because except for the first .5 mile there is no trail tread, and the ground is steep and lumpy.

From the first markers, follow an old wagon road downhill to the west. Where this road makes a switchback at .1 mile, turn off it and follow a path down to a register box in the grass. From it, descend the ravine and its stream to the northwest on a path, following the markers, which are about 100 yards apart. Each marker can't be seen from the preceding one and must be searched for.

At .5 mile the path you are on splits into cow paths at a bog full of yellow monkeyflower. Here cross the stream to the right (north) side and climb up the steep sagebrush hillside to find the next marker. Continue along above the ravine in the sagebrush. At 1 mile the route crosses a side creek that may be dry and reaches the next marker near a big tree. Follow the path to a ford of Horseshoe Bend Creek at 1.5 miles, just above its confluence with Agency Creek. The trail continues beside the river bottom vegetation down a gentle slope. The path is sketchy in a flat area with aspens and firs that leads to a parking area at 2.2 miles. Here the trail turns north across the Agency Creek Road and follows an overgrown track (not open to motor vehicles) in the open among grass and sagebrush hills for about .3 mile.

48. GILMORE AND PITTSBURGH RAILROAD GRADE

Round trip: 5.2 miles
Elevation loss (return climb): 343 feet
Highest point: 7,485 feet
Time: 4 hours
Difficulty: Expert (requires route finding)
Maps: USGS topographic: Deadmans Pass, Bannock Pass; Forest Service: Salmon National Forest
Information: Leadore Ranger District
Getting there: From Idaho Highway 28 at Leadore turn east on Highway 29 toward Dillon, Mont., which becomes Road 089 when it enters the forest. The pavement ends at 4 miles; drive up the gravel road to 13 miles, .4 mile before Bannock Pass. Park near where the sagebrush-covered railroad grade crosses the road.

From the road up Bannock Pass this old railroad grade goes east to a tunnel and west to two switchbacks. The switchbacks were a spur track leading off the main track at a bend and attached to it by short tracks that made a triangle. A train went forward into the switchback, then backed out onto the main track and into the next switchback. When it pulled back onto the main track it was going forward

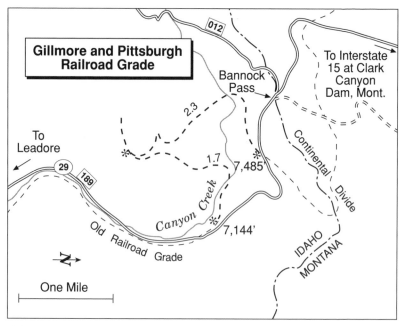

again. Going up the grade they used the spurs in reverse order. The spurs allowed the track to have a sharper switchback here than a train could otherwise negotiate without derailing. Because many of the old ties are still in place, it's easy to imagine the trains traveling to and from the mining town of Gilmore, which is now a ghost town. It is a good place to see wildflowers in spring and wildlife all year. The Forest Service has proposed the railroad grade for a Rails-to-Trails trail.

In 1907 the Northern Pacific Railroad started the Gilmore and Pittsburgh Railroad, using that name to confuse any competitors. It ran from Armistead, Montana, to Leadore, Idaho, with a branch north to Salmon and south to the mining town of Gilmore. Construction began in 1909. Although it ran only until the Depression, the company had planned to extend it down the Salmon River to the Snake.

To hike out to the switchbacks, crawl under a barbed-wire fence on the left side of the highway, being careful not to damage the fence, and follow the grade to the west. At .3 mile the grade goes through a road cut, then crosses a section of fill. It continues alternating cuts and fills. At Canyon Creek at 1 mile the railroad grade has eroded away, so hikers must climb down to the creek and ford it.

Past Canyon Creek it is easier walking to detour off the grade now and then to avoid the sagebrush jungle on the railroad bed. At 1.5 miles the grade passes a scummy pond, and at 1.9 miles two spur tracks meet the main one at an angle, forming the triangle of track mentioned earlier. At 2.3 miles is the long straight spur. From it, the railroad bed descends mostly on fill to the Bannock Pass road and crosses it at 4.5 miles. It is easier to cut over a few yards to the road at 4 miles rather than follow the bed parallel to the highway for a half mile. From the 4-mile point, walk back up the road to the upper crossing at 5.2 miles. If you choose to hike 1 mile to the tunnel from this crossing, remember that it is more than 90 years old. Don't enter it.

49. HAWLEY CREEK, THE CONTINENTAL DIVIDE, AND MORRISON LAKE

Round trip: 6 miles for the Continental Divide, 10 miles for Morrison Lake
Elevation gain: 1,280 feet
Elevation loss (return climb): 700 feet for Morrison Lake
Highest point: 8,880 feet
Time: 5 hours for the Continental Divide; 8 hours for Morrison Lake
Difficulty: moderate
Maps: USGS topographic: Reservoir Creek, Tepee Mountain, Morrison Lake; Forest Service: Salmon National Forest
Information: Leadore Ranger District
Getting there: From Idaho Highway 28 at Leadore turn east on Highway 29, which goes up Railroad Canyon. At .3 mile turn right on a gravel road at a sign for Eighteenmile and Hawley creeks. At a four-way intersection at 4.3 miles, turn left toward Hawley Creek. At 7.6 miles is another four-way intersection. Turn left here onto Road 275, which goes up the canyon ahead as a two-wheel track. At 9.6 miles is a small campground. At 10.1 miles the road splits and the right branch crosses the creek on a bridge. On the south side of the bridge, to the right, is another small campground. Take the road to the left, still 275. It becomes dirt and continues up the canyon of Hawley Creek. At 11.4 miles an unsigned rocky road goes off to the

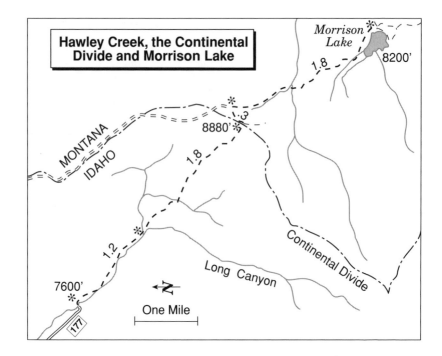

Hawley Creek, the Continental Divide and Morrison Lake

Morrison Lake 8200'

1.8

8880'

1.8

MONTANA IDAHO

1.2

Continental Divide

Long Canyon

7600'

N

One Mile

177

right, Road 177 goes straight ahead up Big Bear Creek, and the Reservoir Creek Road (275) goes off to the left.

Take Road 177 up Big Bear Creek. A high-clearance vehicle is essential, and four-wheel drive is advisable. At 12.6 miles the road fords the creek to the north side in a crossing that may require four-wheel drive. The track fords the small streams of Poison, Bog, and Meadow creeks at 13.7, 14.3, and 14.9 miles. Bog Creek and the area beyond it will be muddy in early summer. At 15.3 miles the road fords to the south side of Big Bear Creek, which is by then small. At 16.4 miles the track drops 30 feet and returns to the north side of the creek. Only high-clearance four-wheel-drive vehicles should be taken across this ford. The hike mileage has been figured from here. The Forest Service is evaluating whether to improve the ford.

At the head of Big Bear Creek, the Continental Divide is covered with short grasses and sagebrush and dotted with clumps of whitebark pine and subalpine fir. In early summer it is awash in wildflowers. From here the Continental Divide Trail goes north along the road and south down to Morrison Lake. To the south are high talus peaks, which drop away on the Montana side into a cirque of wrinkled cliffs. Below the cirque stretches the blue sheet of Morrison Lake.

From the ford of Big Bear Creek at 16.4 miles, the jeep trail climbs over small rocky knolls and through sagebrush. At 1 mile it climbs a rocky hogback and then drops to ford Horsethief Creek at 1.2 miles, where there is a signed trailhead. Most four-wheel-drive vehicles should be left here to avoid damage, even though the road is maintained as a four-wheel-drive road all the way to the Continental Divide. That's because the next part of the road climbs 300 feet in .3 mile over prickly outcrops and loose, sharp rocks. Once past the steep section, the road improves.

The track climbs to a sagebrush ridge at 1.7 miles, then switchbacks down into a flat dry meadow and crosses it to a forest at 2 miles. It climbs in the woods to a meadow and small spring at 2.5 miles. Beyond the meadow the track curves left, goes through a gate (leave it the way you find it), and reaches the Continental Divide at 3 miles. From the divide at the head of Big Bear Creek an old road goes south .5 mile to a fenced spring, campsite, and view of Morrison Lake.

The track leading north from this divide is the Continental Divide Trail. It is open to four-wheel-drive vehicles for several miles to Tepee Creek. From Tepee to Deadhorse creeks over Elk Mountain, 7.2 miles of trail tread has recently been constructed for foot and horse travel. (All new construction for the Continental Divide Trail is for non-motorized use.)

The Continental Divide Trail leading south turns off to the southeast to Morrison Lake .2 mile north of where the trail up Big Bear Creek reaches the divide. Follow this trail down a branch of Indian Creek past a spring to Morrison Lake at 5 miles. The access on the Montana side to the lake is better than it is from Idaho via Big Bear Creek.

50. DIVIDE CREEK LAKE

Round trip: 12.6 miles
Elevation gain: 1,400 feet
Highest point: 8,800 feet
Time: 8 hours dayhiking or 1.5 days backpacking
Difficulty: Strenuous
Maps: USGS topographic: Deadman Lake; Forest Service: Caribou-Targhee National Forest, Dubois Ranger District
Information: Dubois Ranger District
Getting there: From Idaho Highway 22, 6 miles west of Dubois turn right (north) onto the paved Medicine Lodge Road, which makes four 90-degree turns in the first 10 miles: west at 3 miles, north at 4.5 miles at the village of Small, west at 8.3 miles, and west across Indian Creek at 10.3 miles. Here the road enters a canyon of lava cliffs, and at 15 miles the pavement ends. At 22.4 miles is the turnoff for Webber Creek Campground. Beyond the turnoff for Fritz Creek at 28.8 miles, the road becomes primitive and is signed Road 280. It follows an electric transmission line. At 34 miles turn left (west) on the Divide Creek Road (300). (The main road continues over Bannack Pass into Montana.) At 34.5 miles on the Divide Creek Road is an old cabin and corral, referred to on trail signs as Cow Camp. The road beyond Cow Camp to a campsite and the trailhead at 35.5 miles requires four-wheel drive because of a muddy ford and a steep stretch just beyond it.

On the west side of this round green lake, a grassy ridge with dark gray outcrops marks the Continental Divide. Behind the ridge rises a grassy mountain where mountain goats graze. To the left of this in the distance stands a steep-sided peak like a Tyrolean hat. Below the lake at its northwest corner, small caves punch holes in a wall of 400-foot buff and gray cliffs. Medicine Lodge Creek, which the access road follows, is named for the large number of Indian sweat lodges once found here. The road follows the route of an old Indian trail into Montana.

Because the road from Cow Camp to the trailhead requires four-wheel drive, the trail mileage for this hike starts at Cow Camp. Walk up the road to the trailhead at 1 mile, passing an undeveloped campsite about halfway along. From the trailhead, the trail goes along between a big willowy meadow and a Douglas fir forest above, gradually going up into the forest a little and staying above the creek. At 1.5 miles it crosses a stream coming down a canyon from the south, and the main canyon narrows. At 2.7 miles the canyon widens in meadows and the trail crosses the creek to the right (west) side. At 3.2 miles the path goes over to the left side for 50 yards before returning to the right bank. Soon the creek sneaks through a narrow slot between 20-foot cliffs. At 3.5 miles the creek splits, and the trail climbs the left (east) fork on its right (west) side.

This creek flows down a miniature gorge of dark volcanic rock. The trail climbs well above the gorge, then drops back down to the creek. At 4 miles the track crosses to the left side of the creek for 300 yards. Now the canyon is grassy and sprinkled with sagebrush and Douglas firs. The trail climbs a hill and goes along on a steep hillside above the right side of the creek. Here a ridge ahead on the left resembles the end of a loaf of bread. The trail drops into a narrow canyon and at 4.7 miles crosses the creek to the left side, and at 5 miles crosses back. Here you may see the large cream-colored columbine, which is a close relative of the blue and white Colorado ones. The route now climbs a steep forested hill and then returns to the open. The last three creek crossings shown on the topographic map before the lake no longer exist. Beginning at 5.5 miles, the trail has been rerouted away from the creek toward the right (west) as it climbs the last 300 feet to the lake at 6.3 miles. To protect the lakeshore, please camp at the camping area above and to the north of the lake.

51. DIVIDE CREEK LAKE TO WEBBER CREEK

Round trip: 18.6 miles (16.6 miles with four-wheel drive)
Elevation gain: 2,240 feet
Elevation loss (return climb): 760 feet
This section one way (from north): 3 miles, 840 feet gain, 760 feet loss (return climb)
Highest point: 9,440 feet
Time: 2 days
Difficulty: Strenuous
Maps: USGS topographic: Deadman Lake, Scott Peak; Forest Service: Caribou-Targhee National Forest, Dubois Ranger District
Information: Dubois Ranger District
Getting there: Hike to Divide Creek Lake, following directions in that hike description (Hike 50).

This trail section has a view of the rolling grassy hills, alpine wildflowers, and plentiful wildlife typical of the Continental Divide in Idaho. It crosses the divide twice. In addition, from the hill above Divide Creek Lake you can look south up the canyon of Deadman Creek to gray cliffs with semicircular layers.

Beginning at Divide Creek Lake, the trail crosses a bridge over the outlet and goes around the left (east) side of the lake past a junction with a route to Deadman

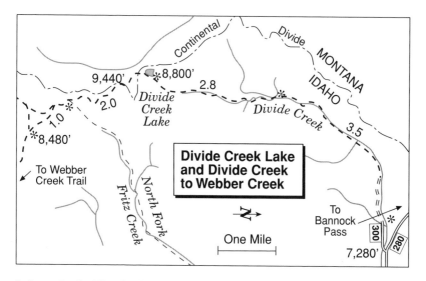

Lake at .2 mile. Then it climbs a grassy slope to the Montana line and Continental Divide. (Montana is on the west and Idaho on the east here.) The next section follows grassy ridges and is marked by cairns and poles. It climbs over two little sagebrush hills, then curves to the right past a pond at .8 mile.

Beyond the pond, the trail curves left (east) up into the trees and climbs steeply up an open ridge. On top of this ridge at 1 mile the trail crosses back into Idaho. The trail continues along the left (east) side of a talus ridge ahead, still climbing. From here you can see the main road to Bannock Pass. After a couple of little hills, the trail comes out on top of a flat grassy shelf with a deep canyon just ahead. At 1.8 miles the trail drops 120 feet into the head of the canyon of the North Fork of Fritz Creek. Then it contours along another shelf and climbs to the top of a narrow east-west grassy ridge at 2.1 miles. Just before it, at 2 miles, is a junction with the North Fork of Fritz Creek Trail to the northwest.

From the grassy ridge the trail drops into a side canyon of Webber Creek without much tread, but with posts marking it. Just before the canyon steepens at 2.2 miles (9,200 feet) a signed side trail cuts over to meet the Webber Lakes trail .3 mile below the first lake. The main trail continues down the grassy canyon to meet the Webber Lakes trail at 3 miles. From here to the lakes the trail is open to motorcycles. It is 1 mile up to the first lake from this junction. The trails are not shown correctly on the topographic map. The main trail goes directly up Webber Creek rather than climbing up the side canyon 200 feet and coming back down.

52. WEBBER LAKES

Round trip: 18 miles
Elevation gain: 2,680 feet
Highest point: 9,560 feet

Time: 2 days
Difficulty: Strenuous
Maps: USGS topographic: Heart Mountain, Scott Peak; Forest Service: Caribou-Targhee National Forest, Dubois Ranger District
Information: Dubois Ranger District
Getting there: From Idaho Highway 22, 6 miles west of Dubois turn right (north) onto the paved Medicine Lodge Road, which makes four 90-degree turns in the first 10 miles: west at 3 miles, north at 4.5 miles at Small, west at 8.3 miles, and west across Indian Creek at 10.3 miles. Here the road (280) enters a canyon of lava cliffs, and at 15 miles the pavement ends. At 22.4 miles turn left (west) on the primitive Webber Creek Road (196) and drive to the end of the road at 27.2 miles.

The three aquamarine Webber Lakes nestle under 1,200- to 1,500-foot cliffs of layered rock that is bent into curves. Above the grassy basin of the first lake, buff-colored rock layers curve up at each end, forming ears. The eared peak also forms a backdrop for the second lake, which sprawls in a talus basin that has only a few trees. The highest lake has even more rock around it. Above it, layered cliffs drop from a flat-topped peak most of the way to the milky blue water. To the right of this peak, rock layers encircle a hollow, forming an eye.

From the campground, the trail stays on the right side of the creek. At 1 mile is a small meadow, and at 2 miles a grass and sagebrush flat with log cabin ruins. From the flat, the trail runs along a steep hillside in a Douglas fir forest. At 2.9 miles in another sagebrush flat, it fords a side creek that may be dry. The trail continues through willows, Douglas firs, sagebrush, and talus.

At 3.8 miles is a junction with a trail down the South Fork of Webber Creek. It is called the Myers Creek Trail (113) because it goes 5.5 miles to the Myers Creek Road (191).

Beyond the junction is nearly a mile of willows and beaver lodges. At 5 miles

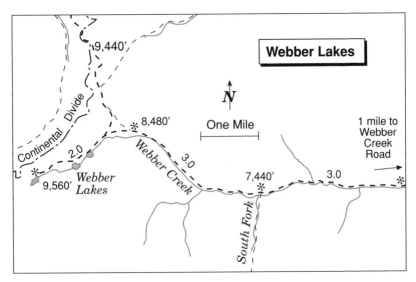

the route switchbacks up onto a hill of pines. At 5.5 miles it skirts the base of a talus slope above narrow meadows of columbine and bluebells. At 6.7 miles the trail leaves the creek and climbs to the junction with the Divide Creek trail at 6.9 miles, near the ruins of several log cabins.

The ascent continues to be steep until the trail meets the shortcut from the Divide Creek trail at 7.5 miles. At 7.9 miles is the first lake, with undeveloped campsites at the lower and upper ends.

The path circles the right (north) side of the lake at a distance from it and climbs through trees to the second lake at 8.1 miles. There are some possible campsites between the trail and the lake.

The trail to the upper lake heads up a timbered hill towards the cliffs of the wall on the right. At 8.6 miles the grade slackens and the trail edges talus, way above the creek, and becomes faint. The route goes between two outcrops to the edge of the creek's ravine at 8.8 miles. From here, walk between rock benches and over grassy flats to the lake at 9 miles. There are no campsites because all the ground is rocky.

Centennial Mountains

53. SALAMANDER LAKES

Loop trip: 7.3 miles
Elevation gain: 1,400 feet
Highest point: 8,440 feet
Time: 6 hours
Difficulty: moderate
Maps: USGS topographic: Winslow Creek; national forest map: Caribou-Targhee National Forest, Dubois Ranger District
Information: Dubois Ranger District
Getting there: Drive 49 miles north of Idaho Falls on Interstate 15 and take the Dubois exit, heading east. Stay on the main road and head northeast 27.4 miles to Kilgore. At the T-intersection at 28.3 miles just beyond Kilgore, turn left (west) and drive .5 mile. Turn right (north) on Forest Road 026 and drive 4.3 miles to where the road splits. Here Road 026 goes both straight ahead and to the left. Keep straight ahead and go about 1.5 miles to the junction with Road 027, just past Cottonwood Creek. At the junction, Road 027 turns off to the right. Take the left

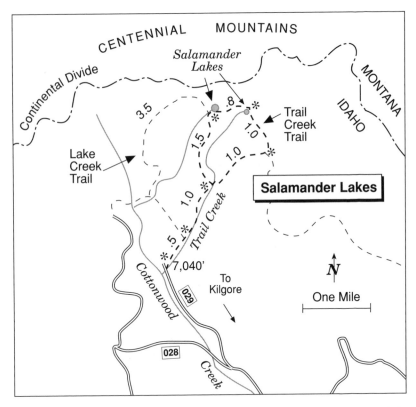

(west) branch, which is still Road 026 and go .8 mile to Road 029. Turn right (north) on 029 and go about 2 more miles to the trailhead at the end of the road. The trailhead is on the right, but the parking area is just before it on the left.

The trail up Trail Creek to miniature Salamander Lake goes into the heart of the Centennial Range along the Idaho-Montana border just east of Interstate 15. This is prime backpacking, horsepacking and day-hiking country, with opportunities to hike the Continental Divide and check out a fun fishing lake. You'll find thick forest and feisty streams and trails that are mostly in good shape. This beautiful country is usually visited from mid-summer to early fall only by locals on weekends and by sheepherders.

The Trail Creek trail is about 8 miles as the crow flies north of the tiny town of Kilgore. Kilgore sits just south of the Centennials in the middle of flat rangeland. As you drive north to the mountains, the road seems to pass a line at the Targhee National Forest boundary. On the north is forest and on the south is grass.

The trailhead at the end of Road 029 is well-marked. There is plenty of parking for several cars and horse trailers. The trail is closed to motorized vehicles except snowmobiles. It is too rough and steep for mountain bikes.

The trail begins near where Trail Creek joins the larger Cottonwood Creek, and follows the west side of Trail Creek. The forest here is fir and pine with a sprinkling of aspen and willow.

118

A half-mile from the trailhead is a junction. The trail to the left here is the Lake Creek Trail. This trail goes 1 mile northwest to a crossing of Salamander Creek, which is the outlet of Salamander Lake. It then turns north for about 2 miles before hooking east for 1 mile, where it rejoins the Trail Creek trail just south of Salamander Lake. In the high meadows near the lake, the Lake Creek Trail has little tread, so it is hard to find.

From its first junction with the Lake Creek Trail .5 mile from the trailhead, the Trail Creek Trail continues to follow the creek. About 1.5 miles from the trailhead, the trail forks again to form a loop. Beyond this point, either side of the loop is steep and strenuous. If you go to the right, the trail immediately crosses Trail Creek to the east side and begins to climb out of the canyon. Occasionally the forest opens up into sloping meadows, which have a fine display of wildflowers in midsummer.

At 2.5 miles the Continental Divide Trail joins from the right from Aldous Lake with little trace except for CD signs on tall poles. As you follow the Continental Divide Trail west to Salamander Lake, it gains elevation.

At 3.5 miles the trail passes a pond. This pond feeds Trail Creek through most of the summer, but by September often has receded below its outlet. At that time it is surrounded by sunflowers.

Just beyond the pond, the trail begins to drop. In places deadfall forces a detour that is not easy to follow in the high grass.

From the pond, the trail heads due west, and at 4.3 miles comes to Salamander Lake. This tiny lake has a good population of small trout. You may catch enough to "stink up your frying pan" or see a kingfisher having good luck.

There is a campsite at the lake, but it shows overuse. Therefore, low-impact camping is especially important. Be sure not to build any new campfire rings.

About 100 yards south of Salamander Lake, the trail joins Lake Creek Trail, which has come in from the northwest. To finish your loop, turn south here. It is 1.5 miles back to the Trail Creek Trail at the second junction. From there it is 1.5 miles back to the trailhead.

54. ALDOUS AND HANCOCK LAKES

Round trip: 4.6 miles
Elevation gain: 960 feet
Highest point: 7,960 feet
Time: 4 1/2 hours
Difficulty: easy
Maps: USGS topographic: Slide Mountain; Forest Service: Caribou-Targhee National Forest, Dubois Ranger District
Information: Dubois Ranger District
Getting there: From Idaho Falls drive north on Interstate 15 to Dubois. Here, turn east on County Road A2 toward Kilgore and Island Park. At .7 mile this road turns left (north) across the railroad tracks. At 24.5 miles the road joins one that has come in from Interstate 15 through Spencer. At 27.4 miles turn left at a sign for Kilgore and proceed to a T-intersection at 28.3 miles, where the pavement ends. Turn left here toward Camas Creek for .5 mile, then turn right on Forest Road 026. At 33 miles Road 026 goes both straight ahead and to the left. Keep straight ahead. At 34.3 miles, just past Cottonwood Creek, turn right (east) on

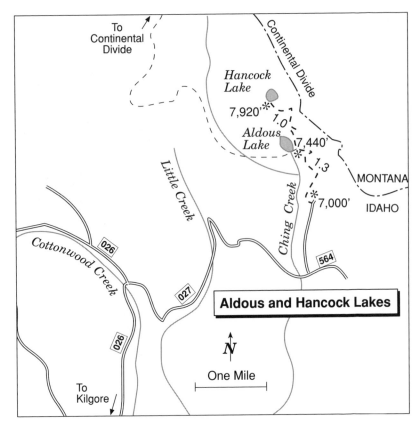

The map contains the following labels:

To Continental Divide

Continental Divide

Hancock Lake

7,920'

1.0

Aldous Lake

7,440'

1.3

Little Creek

Ching Creek

MONTANA

7,000'

IDAHO

Cottonwood Creek

026

027

026

564

Aldous and Hancock Lakes

N

One Mile

To Kilgore

Road 027. In about 3.5 miles, the road switchbacks up a hill. At 39.8 miles, where a road goes off to the right, keep straight ahead on Road 027 to the trailhead at 40.8 miles.

This hike is on an easy shaded trail that is especially pretty in late June or early July when the mountain bluebells and yellow and magenta monkeyflowers are in bloom. Small green Aldous Lake nestles in the woods below a pink ridge scratched with avalanche chutes. In late summer, Hancock Lake dwindles to a green pool in a rocky basin below the pink ridge and a shoulder of Slide Mountain. The trail as far as Aldous Lake is part of the Continental Divide Trail.

This hike is a good introduction to the Centennial Mountains, which run east and west along the Continental Divide. They are one of only two ranges in the West that don't go north and south. This range connects the Beaverhead Mountains on the west with the Henry's Lake Mountains on the east.

The access road passes by Camas Meadows, where Chief Joseph's band in their 1877 flight stole many of General Howard's mules by mistake in the middle of the night. They had thought they were the cavalry horses.

The trail begins as a section of the Continental Divide Trail. It crosses a small creek on a plank bridge, then climbs through lodgepoles and subalpine firs with

120

Blair Lake, just north of the Idaho-Montana border in the Centennial Mountains

wild geraniums underfoot. A second plank bridge and a short climb leads to a ravine containing Ching Creek, at .7 mile, but the trail doesn't cross this creek. It continues over boggy areas on planks and then switchbacks a few times. At 1.3 miles is the outlet of Aldous Lake, 400 feet above the trailhead.

Trails go around both sides of the lake through grouse whortleberry, thimble-berry, and lodgepole pine, passing several campsites. On the west side of the lake, the Continental Divide Trail turns west toward Salamander Lake (see Hike 53).

From the cow parsnips at the upper end of Aldous Lake, the trail to Hancock Lake climbs an open grassy slope dotted with Douglas firs. Then it follows a gul-ly, turns to the right, and climbs to a shelf. A couple of steep pitches lead to the crest of a hill. The trail then drops 40 feet to the lake at 2.3 miles. A few campsites are west of the inlet, across the lake from the trail. Because of the short distance and easy grade, either of these lakes make good day hikes or overnights for Boy Scouts, families, or beginning backpackers. This is also a good mountain biking trail. Aldous Lake boasts a good trout population.

55. BLAIR AND LILLIAN LAKES

Round trip: 4 miles to Blair Lake from the Road Closed sign, 14 miles from the Yale-Kilgore Road; 6.4 miles to Lillian Lake from gate.
Elevation gain: 540 feet for Blair Lake; 900 feet for Lillian Lake
Elevation loss (return climb): 550 feet for Blair Lake; 380 feet for Lillian Lake
Highest point: 8,640 feet for Blair Lake; 8,100 feet for Lillian Lake
Time: 2 hours for Blair Lake and 4 hours for Lillian Lake if you can drive clear to the Road Closed sign or gate

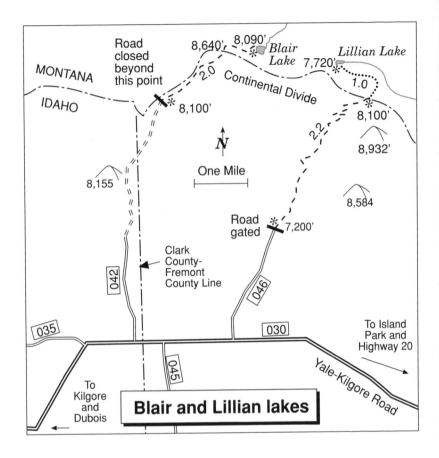

Blair and Lillian lakes

Difficulty: Moderate to expert because of the need for route finding
Maps: USGS topographic: Mount Jefferson; National Forest: Caribou-Targhee National Forest, Island Park, Ashton Districts.
Information: Island Park Ranger District
Getting there: From Ashton drive north on U.S. Highway 20 for 29 miles to the Yale-Kilgore Road, about 3 miles north of Ponds Lodge. Turn left (west) on this road (Road 030) and drive 14 miles to the Clark County-Fremont County line sign. The access road for Lillian Lake (046) is the last right turn before (east of) the county line. The access road for Blair Lake is the next dirt road to the right (042), also known as the Keg Springs Road. It is west of the county line. It becomes a high-clearance vehicle road after about 2 miles. This road climbs from 6,600 feet to 8,100 feet in 5 miles. It is rocky in places, and when it is wet or snowy drivers need four-wheel drive.

What is surprising about crossing the Continental Divide to visit Blair Lake in the Centennial Mountains is the beauty. In August the wildflowers are usually still in bloom and grasses are green. In fact, the access road to Blair Lake from Keg Springs to the divide has one of the best wildflower displays in the state. In late

July a quilt of red paintbrush and blue penstemon and lupine spreads over the grassy hills. Blair Lake lies on the Montana side of the 20-mile-long Centennial Range. From the crest of the range, which is also the Continental Divide, you can see much of the Island Park area in Idaho, the Tetons in Wyoming, and the Red Rock Lakes National Wildlife Refuge in Montana.

Beautiful 15-acre Blair Lake is surrounded by forest on the north, east and south and by grass and wildflowers on the west. There are usually rising trout and often ducks, elk, moose, deer and even an osprey. Remember that fishing in the lake requires a Montana license. Because of the ruggedness of the mountains and canyons on the Montana side, the best way to get to Blair Lake is from Idaho.

However, the access road is rough. You can drive a high clearance vehicle up it or ride a mountain bike. From the Road Closed sign on a grassy saddle below the divide, the trail climbs 540 feet before descending to the lake. Because people will vary in where they want to leave their vehicles, the trail mileage starts at the Road Closed sign.

If you take a mountain bike up the road from the Yale-Kilgore Road, you will find there are downhill as well as uphill stretches. The worst parts are the rocky areas, but most of them are short. The first mile of road gains elevation slowly and passes through thick forest. The second mile climbs to a ridge. Several areas in the next two miles have been clear-cut. The rest is dominated by subalpine fir. As the road nears the top of a ridge, it becomes very rocky for 200 yards. Along this ridge you get good views of Shotgun Valley below and the Teton Mountains to the southeast.

In the next few miles the road climbs through patchy timber and levels off in grassy areas. It stops near a corral at a large sign marking the state line and the Continental Divide and the closure to vehicles.

Beyond the sign, walk up the road as it follows the divide for .7 mile, climbing 500 feet. The trail to Blair Lake follows the Continental Divide Trail. The route and divide part ways and cross again on a high, flat grassy area after another .2 mile. From here the divide continues southeast, and the road heads northeast another .5 mile. It enters thick forest and soon forks. Both routes take you toward the lake, but the right fork brings you to a view of it sooner and makes the lake easier to find.

Soon after the fork in the road, the route drops dramatically. Bicyclists may want to park here and walk the rest of the way. The road continues another .2 mile, crosses an intermittent stream in a gully and quits at a campsite. To reach the lake, recross the gully at the campsite and follow a faint trail north. Blair Lake is still 120 feet below in a deep bowl. The trail winds down steeply and crosses a small stream. Here the trail can be easily lost in deadfall and game trails. Use your compass to head southeast after crossing the small stream.

Lillian Lake is about 1.5 miles east of Blair Lake and is also on the Montana side of the Continental Divide. To reach Lillian Lake, drive or bike up Road 046 to the gate at 2.2 miles. From the gate you can hike or bike 2.2 miles to the Divide, where the road ends. From this ridge look northwest down the canyon to a small lake, which is Lillian Lake. There is no trail, and reaching the lake requires bushwhacking down a wet but beautiful canyon and detouring around a marsh.

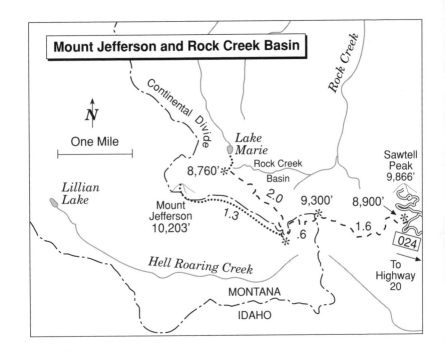

Mount Jefferson and Rock Creek Basin

N

One Mile

Continental Divide

Rock Creek

Lake Marie

Rock Creek Basin

Sawtell Peak 9,866'

8,760'

Lillian Lake

Mount Jefferson 10,203'

1.3

2.0

9,300'

8,900'

1.6

.6

024

Hell Roaring Creek

To Highway 20

MONTANA

IDAHO

56. MOUNT JEFFERSON AND ROCK CREEK BASIN

Round trip: 7 miles to Mount Jefferson; 8 miles to Lake Marie
Elevation gain: 1,440 feet for peak; 560 feet for lake
Elevation loss (return climb): 360 feet for peak, 1,000 feet for lake
Highest point: 10,203 feet
Time: 8 hours
Difficulty: strenuous
Maps: USGS topographic: Sawtell Peak, Mt. Jefferson; Forest Service: Caribou-Targhee National Forest, Island Park District
Information: Island Park Ranger District
Getting there: From Ashton, drive north on U.S. Highway 20 about 32 miles and turn left on the signed Sawtell Peak Road (024). Drive about 12 miles up this good gravel road and park at the pullout near the trail sign.

The Island Park area is known for its world-class fishing and its beautiful campgrounds. Being neighbors with Yellowstone National Park and the famous Madison River, and having the headwaters of the famous Henry's Fork and Henry's Lake makes the area popular. There are some nice trails in the area worth skipping a day's fishing to explore. One is the Sawtell Peak trail, also known as the Rock Creek trail. Sawtell Peak is named for the first known settler in Island Park, Gilman Sawtell. He came there in 1867 and lived by trapping and by catching and selling fish from Henry's Lake.

The main attraction on this trail is the view. Most of the surrounding country is a high forested plateau. This trail takes you up into the northeast end of the Centennial Mountains. The range follows the Continental Divide and Idaho-Montana border for about 30 miles. Once on top of these mountains, there are splendid views of Henry's Lake, the Island Park Reservoir, and the Tetons. An added bonus for this trail is that you gain most of the elevation in your car.

Henry's Lake, which you see from the summit of Mount Jefferson, was named for fur trapper Andrew Henry who discovered it in 1810. That winter he and his men wintered on the north fork of the Snake River that now bears his name. It was so cold they had to eat their horses to survive.

To get to the trailhead, drive up the road (024) that winds to the top of 9,866-foot Sawtell Peak. At the top is a Federal Aviation Administration radar site. About 1.5 miles from the top is a well-marked pullout and trailhead.

The trail, which begins at 8,900 feet, starts out going downhill before climbing slowly west toward Mount Jefferson. Part of this trail follows an old jeep road that has been barricaded for years. The north-facing slopes are thick with whitebark pine and subalpine fir, while the southern slopes are covered with grasses, brush, and a few whitebark pines. At the top of the ridges, the trees are more stunted and many are twisted and turned in silent evidence of the harsh weather of this elevation.

About .5 mile from the trailhead the trail passes exposed rock. A sharp eye and a few turned stones will often turn up fossils. Most are the remains of plants and small sea animals trapped in an ancient seabed.

After 1.6 miles you come to the Continental Divide, which is also the Idaho-Montana border. In the basin to the southeast is the head of Hellroaring Creek. This is the farthest reach of the Mississippi/Missouri River system. A cairn marks the spot considered to the source. A mason jar in the cairn contains a notebook that hikers can sign and leave a short message about their impression of the area.

At 2.2 miles the trail turns sharply north toward Rock Creek Basin. To reach the summit of Mount Jefferson, leave the trail and take an obvious route up the mountain's southeast side. Stay on the ridge and follow it northwest to the summit at 3.5 miles. From this side, the peak is a walkup. At 10,203 feet, Mount Jefferson dominates all the surrounding peaks. From the top you can see Henry's Lake to the north, Island Park Reservoir to the south, and some of Yellowstone to the east.

To see Lake Marie and Rock Creek Basin on your return, pick up the trail by returning down the ridge the way you came to the sharp bend in the trail 2.2 miles from the trailhead. From here the trail descends north into the upper reaches of Rock Creek. The trail stops at the pond-size lake, 4 miles from the trailhead. It is often a destination for backpackers. The trail that used to descend Rock Creek to Road 051 on the south side of Henry's Lake is no longer maintained and is hard to find.

The Sawtell Peak trail is too steep for most mountain bikers, and horseback riders may need to park well below the trailhead to find enough space. Because of the high elevation, the trail isn't accessible until July. In the fall, there are hunters in the area, so be sure to wear blaze orange at that time of year.

Henry's Lake Mountains

57. TARGHEE CREEK AND LAKES

Round trip: 13 miles; 2.6 miles more for upper two lakes
Elevation gain: 2,040 feet; 500 feet more for upper lakes
Highest point: 9,000 feet; 9,500 feet at upper lakes
Time: 9 1/2 hours
Difficulty: Strenuous to expert
Maps: USGS topographic: Targhee Pass, Targhee Peak; Forest Service: Caribou-Targhee National Forest, Island Park District
Information: Island Park Ranger District
Getting there: Go north of the Island Park Ranger Station on U.S Highway 20 for 16 miles. Just .8 mile south of Targhee Pass at the Montana border, turn left (west) onto the dirt Targhee Creek Road (057) and drive 2.7 miles to the Targhee Creek trailhead.

This trail leads past cliffs and towers up a canyon full of wildlife. Its goal is six small lakes set in high grassy hills. The white towers on the canyon wall vary from Grecian columns to stacks of pancakes. Higher up, peach-colored cliffs descend to orange ribs resembling chenille fabric. Whitebark pines and wildflowers sprinkle the hills. Moose, elk, and grizzlies are found here, so it is a good idea to talk or make noise while hiking. Special food storage regulations are in effect. Contact the local ranger station for information on food storage. The trail follows Targhee Creek most of the way to the Continental Divide Trail, although that trail is still partly on the drawing board.

The Targhee Creek Trail begins on rolling hills in grass, aspens, and Douglas firs. At .7 mile it comes out on a meadow edged in aspens then returns to the woods. In a second small meadow at .9 mile a sign points to the left (west) to the Dry Fork Cutoff trail, which goes about 1.5 miles to the Dry Fork Trail. You can return down the Dry Fork to make a loop trip. It is 6.5 miles to the divide on the Dry Fork Trail and 2.5 miles along it to connect with the Targhee Creek Trail on top of the Divide.

Beyond the Dry Fork Cutoff, the Targhee Creek Trail travels another meadow, where an old road joins it at 1 mile. The route now goes along the old road in forest, willows, and grassy clearings beside beaver ponds. At 1.7 miles the trail goes up into forest. At 2.2 miles avalanche areas are on the opposite canyon wall. The trail crosses a bridge to the left (west) side of the creek at 2.4 miles.

Now it climbs sagebrush and grass hillsides, above the meandering creek.

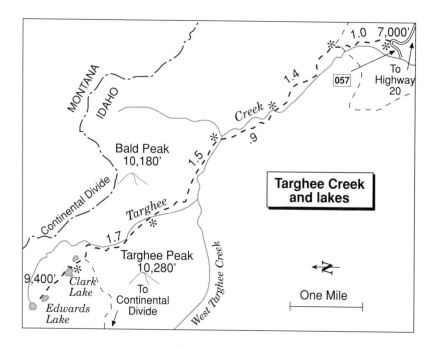

There is a beaver pond on the creek at 2.7 miles. The route treads a marshy area on bog bridges and climbs through forest. At 3.3 miles it returns to the creek and fords it to the right (northeast) side.

Above here the trail squeezes between two immense boulders and then returns to the creek at the base of an open hillside at 3.4 miles. Then it climbs away from the creek in woods and crosses an avalanche area. At 3.9 miles it skirts an open area below 200-foot cliffs. Here you can look up the West Fork of Targhee Creek at 800-foot layered cliffs. At 4.2 miles the trail climbs steeply on an open hillside, gradually turning right (north) up the main creek. At 4.8 miles it crosses the creek to the left (west) side in two 6-foot wide sections.

The trail continues uphill in forest, makes a couple of short switchbacks, and goes along small open areas. Then it turns left over sagebrush knolls, climbing away from the creek along the side of a ravine. At 5.7 miles the path crosses a large side creek that is dry in late summer and comes out onto a 150-yard open area where the cliffs across the creek resemble pancakes.

At 5.9 miles the trail turns 90 degrees left (west) and heads up open grassy hills dotted with whitebark pines. Cairns mark the route. A big cairn and sign mark the junction of the Targhee Creek Trail with the Continental Divide Trail. New trail was constructed in 1995 from here to the Continental Divide. It is 1.5 miles from here to the top of the divide. From the top the Continental Divide Trail heads northwest down Mile Creek Canyon in Montana. The Dry Fork Trail turns southeast down the West Fork and Dry Fork of Targhee Creek back to the Targhee Creek trailhead.

To reach the lakes from the junction back at the cairn, turn to the right (north) on the path. It leads over a low saddle to a viewpoint of the unnamed lowest lake at 6.3 miles. This milky blue lake, rimmed in trees except on the south side, has a lowered water line in late summer. To reach the second lake, Clark Lake, go around the left (west) side of the lowest lake and then head west .2 mile until another lake appears. It is sometimes dry by late summer. The other three lakes, including the largest, Coffin Lake, can be reached by cross-country travel. Edwards Lake is at 7 miles, an unnamed lake at 7.2 miles, and Coffin Lake at 7.8 miles (9,500 feet. A trip to the upper lakes will add 2.6 miles to the round trip and 500 feet of elevation gain.

58. TYGEE CREEK BASIN

Through trip: 7 miles from basin to Reas Pass; additional .6 mile to go north to the Continental Divide Trail from .5 mile before the end of the road
Elevation gain: 1,000 feet
Elevation loss (return climb): 1,400 feet
Highest point: 8,200 feet
Time: 6 hours
Difficulty: moderate
Maps: USGS: Targhee Pass, Big Springs, Reas Pass, and Madison Arm

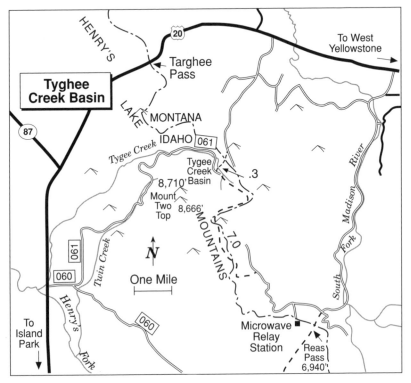

(Wyoming); Forest Service: Caribou-Targhee National Forest, Island Park District

Information: Island Park Ranger District

Getting there: From Island Park drive 12 miles north on U.S. Highway 20 and turn right (east) on Forest Road 060. This road is 2 miles south of the turnoff to Henry's Lake State Park. Drive east on Road 060. Where it forks at 1 mile at the national forest boundary, turn left (north) on Road 061. Drive up it for 7 miles to Tygee Basin.

This trail offers a pleasant hike mostly along the Continental Divide over forested mountaintops and meadows near the Two Top Mountain area of Island Park. It begins in Tygee Basin and goes to Reas Pass, which is covered under the Warm River Rail Trail.

From the Continental Divide above Tygee Basin you get views of the South Fork of the Madison River and the Madison Plateau. In addition, the road to Tygee Basin makes a fine mountain bike ride, and trout dart around in the deeper holes of Tygee Creek.

A half-mile before the road ends, a trail turns off to the left that crosses Tygee Creek and leads to the Continental Divide Trail in .3 mile. From this junction, the Continental Divide Trail goes north down the Buttermilk Creek Road to U.S. 20 about two miles east of Targhee Pass. Here it's funny to see signs posted twice as high as normal reading "Speed Limit 50 mph" when you're having a hard time negotiating the trail at 6 mph on a bike. The reason for the signs is that this trail is mainly used by snowmobilers. If you decide to ride down Buttermilk Creek, be cautious because the trail is steep for a mile. Take care to stay in control.

Going south, the Continental Divide Trail follows the road to Tygee Basin to its end, where it becomes a trail again. The trail leads south across the basin to a sign for the Continental Divide Trail in a half-mile. Tygee Creek Basin has recently been put under road closures to protect the marsh and meadow, but the trail passes right through the marshy meadows. If on a bike, leave it or walk it through the meadows.

The Continental Divide Trail goes southeast over rolling wooded hills broken by occasional grassy areas. These openings allow you to look out toward Yellowstone. After 4.5 miles the trail joins a jeep road. After 2 miles on this road you come to a microwave relay station. A half-mile east of it the Continental Divide Trail intersects with the Warm River Rail Trail at Reas Pass. From Reas Pass the Continental Divide Trail descends along the railroad trail to the Black Canyon road and follows that road southeast for several miles. You can set up a car shuttle by driving up the South Fork of Madison River Road, which begins 2 miles west of West Yellowstone on U.S. Highway 20.

If you decide to bike up the road up Twin Creek to Tygee Basin instead of driving, the road follows the edge of the forest, which is the national forest boundary. On your left is pasture and the Henry's Lake flats and on the right is thick forest. After 1.5 miles the road heads east and begins to gain elevation. It gains about 1,000 feet between the road fork and Tygee Basin. Two miles from the fork the road enters a canyon and follows Twin Creek for the next 2.2 miles. Lodgepole pine is the predominant tree, with a few fir and aspen. After leaving Twin Creek, the road makes a mile-long winding S, bending northwest, south, and then north before it reaches Tygee Creek. The road follows Tygee Creek for the next 2 miles to its end in the basin. As it does so, it levels off in beautiful meadows. Along the creek you can see beaver dams and even a beaver lodge as well as many willows.

59. COFFEE POT RAPIDS

Round trip: 3.6 to 5 miles
Elevation gain: 50 feet
Elevation loss (return climb): 120 to 160 feet
Highest point: 6,360 feet
Time: 3 to 4 hours
Difficulty: easy, except for rocky footing
Maps: USGS topographic: Island Park, Island Park Dam; U.S. Forest Service: Caribou-Targhee National Forest, Island Park District
Information: Island Park Ranger District
Getting there: On U.S. 20 two miles north of Island Park, turn left (west) on the Yale-Kilgore Road. At 1.2 miles turn right (north) on Forest Road 130 and go 3.5 miles to Upper Coffee Pot Campground. Park at the fisherman's parking lot just outside the campground.

This hike along the Henry's Fork of the Snake River samples the birds and wildlife of the river in a tranquil stretch. The river flows so gently here that algae make the water green. Because the trail is shaded, the hike is pleasant on a hot day. The destination, Coffee Pot Rapids, sprays white water in a dark, narrow section of the canyon. The rapids came by their name many years ago when fur trapper, rancher, and scout George Rea was canoeing along the Henry's Fork. After several miles of calm water, he came to a bend in the river and a set of nasty rapids and boulders rushed out ahead of him. His canoe overturned and all he managed to salvage was his coffee pot. Rea first came to the Henry's Fork in 1865, and was the first to file for a homestead in the Island Park area.

The trail begins at the west end of the campground loop and goes along beside the river in lodgepole pine and subalpine fir. At 1 mile in an open area an old road closed to motor vehicles comes in from the south. Watch for roots and rocks from here on. Next, as the trail climbs a wooded hillside, a stream in willows, talus and

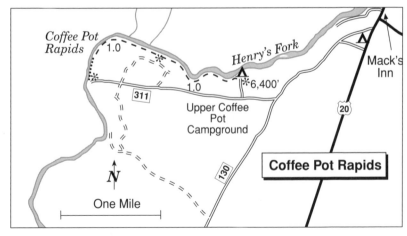

130

rock knolls appear on the far side of the river.

At 1.5 miles the channel narrows and the river begins to cascade between gray boulders. Side paths lead to fishing rocks and the trail itself descends to the water. Soon the river bends, and the rapids begin. The trail continues in a dense lodgepole and subalpine fir forest to a landslide of boulders at 1.8 miles. A sketchy path continues through the boulders, which have been polished by the river and are therefore slippery. A path continues to a private lodge at 2.5 miles, but it is safer to stop at the boulders. If you continue through the boulders .2 mile and climb up the bank you will be on Forest Road 311, which you can follow back to the campground. The footbridges shown on the topographic map do not exist. Across from the campground, there is also a path along the other side of the river partly in private land.

60. GOLDEN LAKE

Round trip: 4.3 miles
Elevation gain: 30 feet
Highest point: 6,150 feet
Time: 3 hours
Difficulty: easy
Maps: USGS topographic: Last Chance; Forest Service: Caribou-Targhee National Forest, Island Park and Ashton Districts
Information: Harriman State Park
Getting there: On U.S Highway 20, 19 miles north of Ashton, turn left (west) into Harriman State Park and go 1.5 miles to the park headquarters by following the park signs.

This easy hike leads through the wildflower meadows of Harriman State Park beside crystal ponds, creeks, and lakes that reflect the sky and clouds. Golden Lake nestles in lodgepole pine-covered hills, marsh grass and meadows with a view of the blue crags of the Tetons in the distance, like mountains in a dream. It is just a sample of the 21 miles of trails in this state park. They take you along the Henry's Fork of the Snake River, around beautiful Silver Lake, along forested ridges, and into the Harriman Wildlife Refuge. Most are nearly flat, except for the Ridge Loop trail which gains 400 feet in its 7 miles.

The park was formerly the property of the Railroad Ranch. It was called that because it was started by owners of the Oregon Shortline Railroad. When Union Pacific bought the railroad, the early owners sold the ranch to E.H. Harriman, a major stockholder in Union Pacific. Harriman added to the ranch by buying others around it. At the same time they used it as a hunting preserve as well as a working cattle ranch. When E.H. Harriman died, he left the ranch to his sons, Averell and Roland. Roland and his wife eventually donated the ranch to the state for a park.

Today 27 of the original Railroad Ranch buildings, from the cookhouse to the horse barn, are still intact, furnished, and carefully maintained. The park is day use only unless you rent one of these cabins. Reservations are taken beginning each October 1 for the following year. In winter many of the trails beginning at park headquarters are groomed for cross-country skiing

To reach Golden Lake from the parking area, walk .3 mile on the Main Access

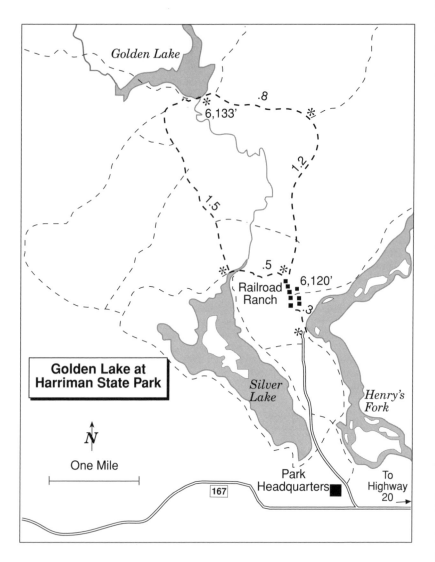

Golden Lake

6,133'

.8

1.2

1.5

.5

6,120'

Railroad
Ranch

.3

**Golden Lake at
Harriman State Park**

Silver
Lake

Henry's
Fork

N

One Mile

Park
Headquarters

167

To
Highway
20

Trail to the log ranch buildings. Here you can take a guided tour on the history of
the ranch if you wish. To go to Golden Lake, continue past the buildings to a four-
way trail intersection at two barns. Turn left toward Thurman Creek and the Silver
Lake loop. The trail passes a pond in a meadow, then crosses Thurman Creek on a
bridge at .8 mile at the north end of Silver Lake.

Across the bridge at a junction with the Silver Lake loop take the Ridge Trail
to the right (north). It goes along the edge of wet meadows, and at 1.5 miles climbs
a small hill with a view of the Tetons to the east and Golden Lake ahead. On the
other side of the hill, the trail turns 90 degrees to the left and goes along between
the base of the hills and a marsh along Thurman Creek. At the west end of the

132

Golden Lake dam at 2 miles the trail meets an old road. This road climbs west 50 yards to the signed Ridge Trail that continues uphill to the left (southwest).

To return a different way, go east on the old road across the Golden Lake dam, and at 2.2 miles keep straight ahead on the old road when another road branches north. At 2.8 miles at a narrow pond, turn right (south). The road wanders over meadows that are colorful with wildflowers all summer. In August some of the flowers are lupine, goldenrod, yarrow, wild geranium, and aster. The old road takes you through several livestock gates and back to the junction at the north end of the ranch buildings at 4 miles. Returning to the visitors parking makes the hike total 4.3 miles.

61. WARM RIVER RAIL TRAIL

Through trip: 47.5 miles from Reas Pass to the Warm River Campground; 45 miles from the Black Canyon Road-Warm River Railroad Trail intersection to the Warm River Campground
Elevation gain or loss: 1,540 feet
Highest point: 6,840 feet at Reas Pass
Time: two full days on a bicycle; several days on foot
Difficulty: easy except for length
Maps: USGS topographic: Reas Pass, Big Springs, Island Park, Hatchery Butte, Snake River Butte, Warm River; Forest Service: Caribou-Targhee National Forest, Island Park and Ashton Ranger Districts
Information: Island Park Ranger District and Ashton Ranger District
Getting there: There are several trailheads for the trail. If you want to do the whole trail, probably the best place to start is at Reas Pass, so your trip will be all downhill. Although the railroad bed exists from Reas Pass to West Yellowstone, it hasn't been made into a trail. To begin at Reas Pass, drive on U.S. Highway 20 to a point 2 miles west of West Yellowstone. Here turn south onto the South Fork of the Madison River Road. Passenger cars can drive to Reas Pass, which is about 7 miles from the highway.

Another trailhead is at the Black Canyon Road east of Mack's Inn. To reach it, take U.S. Highway 20 to Mack's Inn, about 33 miles north of Ashton. Turn east at Mack's Inn on Forest Road 059 and follow the signs to Big Springs. At Big Springs turn north on the Black Canyon Road (Forest Road 066) and drive 6 miles. A sign marks where the road intersects the rail trail. There is parking along the road just before the intersection. From here, you can go to Reas Pass or start south toward Warm River.

The Warm River Campground is at the south end of the trail. To reach it, drive east of Ashton on Idaho Highway 47 and go north on the Mesa Falls Road for about 10 miles, following the signs for Warm River.

The trail goes by several names. The old railroad bed trail from Reas Pass to Warm River is considered by many to be one of the best long mountain biking routes in eastern Idaho, and perhaps the best in Idaho. The trail follows the old Yellowstone Special route, which carried tourists from Pocatello and Idaho Falls to Yellowstone National Park's West Entrance during the first half of the century. The old steam engines chugged through the farmland and backcountry for decades until the line was no long financially sustainable. When the tracks were torn out,

133

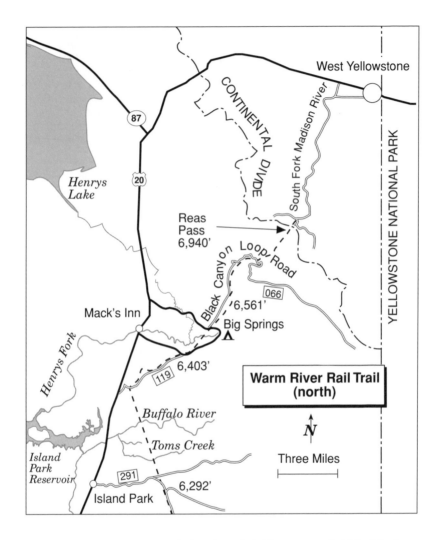

the trail that remained was graded, and trestle bridges were refurbished for horses, ATVs, motorcycles and mountain bikes in summer; and snowmobiles and skis in the winter.

Today the trail is so good that it's like riding a soft sidewalk though the backcountry, although in some sections the soft dirt can be like beach sand. About the only time the trail is rough is during the spring and early summer. During this time, trail users face downed trees across the trail and occasional boggy areas that often flood the trail. By midsummer most of the water has receded. The downfall is usually cleared away by late summer.

Because the trail is a railroad grade and so gains elevation slowly, it's a great beginner route or a good long-distance trip for those in good shape. The nice thing about this trail is that it's interesting. Just about the time you tire of the endless sea

134

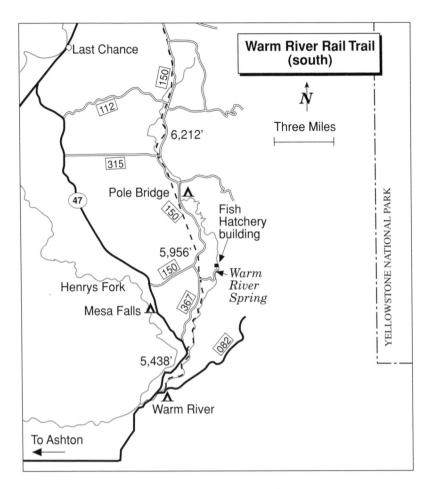

Warm River Rail Trail (south)

N

Three Miles

Last Chance

150

112

6,212'

315

47

Pole Bridge

150

Fish Hatchery building

5,956'

150

Henrys Fork

367

Warm River Spring

Mesa Falls

5,438'

082

Warm River

To Ashton

YELLOWSTONE NATIONAL PARK

of lodgepole pines, the trail crosses a trestle bridge over a creek, or the forest opens up to reveal a gorgeous view of the Island Park plateau. Places such as Big Springs, Buffalo River, and Warm River offer great opportunities for side trips, especially if you want to stop and camp and do some fishing.

Because the route is intersected by side roads, it's easy to break the trail into shorter sections. This works well if you have children along or if you want to do the entire route over a few weekends.

The entire route is about 48 miles long, which means car shuttles have to be creative. You can start at the intersection of the Black Canyon Road with the trail, or start at Reas Pass on the Idaho-Montana border. The section from Reas Pass to Black Canyon is the toughest part of the whole trail, but experienced mountain bikers will find it pretty easy. Riding down is like flying. By fall, there is only one small stream crossing the trail to slow you down. The section from Reas Pass to the Black Canyon Road is part of the Continental Divide Trail. It is 2.5 miles from the Black Canyon Road to Reas Pass.

Continuing south from the Black Canyon Road, the first 5 miles until Big Springs are scenic. The trail passes though thick forest and deep canyons. A couple of vistas open up allowing you to see most of the upper end of the Island Park plateau. There is also a glimpse of the distant Teton Range. The route descends quickly out of the Henry's Lake Mountains down to the plateau.

The first trestle bridge on the Idaho side that you cross is at Thirsty Creek, one mile north of Big Springs. These bridges have been planked to accommodate foot, bike, horse, and ATV traffic. The bridges are much wider than they were originally. Below the planks you can see the original construction.

Thirsty Creek is full of beaver activity. You will see distinct beaver trails in the soft soil and may even see where beavers have dragged aspen or willow branches over the ground. Moose, elk, and deer tracks are plentiful here.

Big Springs is a nice side trip for those with some extra time. The springs provide most of the flow for the Henry's Fork of the Snake River until it is joined by the Buffalo River. Big Springs is also a brood area for the famous cutthroat trout fishery. Just beyond the springs the trail crosses the Henry's Fork on a long trestle bridge. This section of the river is usually clear year-round because it is spring-fed.

Two miles past the Henry's Fork you cross a bridge over Moose Creek. For the next 5 miles the route generally parallels a Forest Service road. Unless a noisy truck is using it you won't notice it because of the thick forest separating the road from the rail trail.

About 5.5 miles from Big Springs the trail crosses Road 119 and soon passes through a section of private land. There are many nearby summer homes and ranches. You'll pass through locked gates with bike or ATV passages that are intended to keep vehicles out of the summer home area.

Two miles into the summer home area the route crosses the Buffalo River on another large trestle bridge. This river is also mostly spring-fed and is crystal clear nearly year-round. From the trestle you can see trout.

A mile past Buffalo River the trail passes through a huge meadow several miles square. There is usually a large herd of cows on both sides of the fenced route, but you may glimpse an elk along the fringes of the meadow.

This was the big clearing in the timber that stage drivers used to call Island Park. They called grassy clearings in the timber parks, and the one they called Island Park was on a kind of island surrounded by creeks and rivers. When the railroad came along it called their siding at the clearing Island Park. Eventually the whole area came to be known as Island Park.

About 2 miles past Buffalo River the trail crosses Tom's Creek. A mile beyond Tom's Creek the route crosses Road 291. Because this crossing is only 3 miles from the highway, it is a good place to leave a shuttle vehicle if you plan to chop the route into smaller pieces. Road 291 intersects with U.S. Highway 20, the main route through Island Park, about 2.5 miles south of Pond's Lodge.

For a mile or so past Road 291 the trail skirts the western edge of another large inholding of private land and parallels Road 150. At the beginning of this is another big meadow.

Two miles south of the private holdings the route crosses the upper reaches of the Warm River. From here the trail roughly follows the meandering river south for the next 16 miles, paralleling Road 150. It crosses this road after 2 miles. Nearby, to the west about 100 yards, Hatchery Butte Road (Road 315) intersects Road 150. Hatchery Butte Road is another good place to leave a shuttle vehicle if you'd like to bike just the lower half of the trail. This road connects with Idaho Highway 47, otherwise known as the Mesa Falls Road.

After heading south .3 mile, the trail crosses the Warm River. This is the last crossing of that river until just before the Warm River Campground. From here on the trail remains on the west side.

Two miles farther on is the Pole Bridge Campground. This Forest Service campground can be reached by riding to nearby Forest Road 150 and heading north. The Warm River passes through the campground.

Three miles from the campground, the railroad bed trail crosses Road 150 for the last time in the Cold Spring area. Just after this intersection is a half-mile of private land. A half-mile later the trail crosses Road 154, the Warm River Fish Hatchery Road. This is an interesting side trip. Up this road about one mile is a large spring that pours out of the ground and into the river at between 50 and 60 degrees. This is where the river gets its name. The old fish hatchery buildings are adjacent to the springs. The cabin is available to the public to rent year-round.

A mile from the intersection with Road 154 the trail begins to closely follow the west side of the Warm River. Within a few miles you will near the edge of the volcanic caldera, the huge plateau underlying Island Park and Yellowstone. This caldera rises from the surrounding Snake River Plain 700 to 1,000 feet. At the edge of the caldera the Warm River begins to descend much more quickly than the railroad grade trail. The canyon becomes a deep, picturesque gorge in many places. For the rest of the way the trail mostly follows the edge of this beautiful river canyon.

One highlight, especially for kids, is the railroad tunnel. About 3 miles out from the Warm River Campground the trail passes though a tunnel in the rock. It is long enough and turns enough that you can't see the other end. To get through it you may need a flashlight.

Past the tunnel, the trail begins to descend. Besides the section up and over Reas Pass on the Montana border, this is the only other serious elevation change on the entire trip. The trail drops off the edge of the caldera to the Snake River Plain at a gentle grade of 550 feet in 6 miles. An access has been developed at Bear Gulch about .2 mile south of the tunnel. There is a large parking lot, restroom and a culvert under the highway that provides access from the parking lot to the railroad grade trail.

The Warm River Campground is the end of the line. Here paved roads take over the old railroad grade. The trail comes in at the upper end of the campground. A few old pilings remain of a trestle bridge over the Warm River. Plans for planking it are under way.

There is plenty of parking outside the campground and several nice campsites with restrooms and tables in the campground.

A few miles out, the old Union Pacific railroad bed picks up again and goes from Marysville to Tetonia. There are plans to convert this route into a trail, but easements across private property must be worked out first. This route passes through mostly rolling farmland until it reaches the foothills of the Tetons. Probably the most interesting section is near Bitch Creek, where a huge trestle bridge crosses that creek's deep canyon.

Big Hole Mountains

62. BIG HOLE CREST TRAIL

Through trip: 14.2 miles
Elevation gain: 1,480 feet
Elevation loss: 2,860 feet
Highest point: 8,800 feet
Time: 10 hours to 2 days
Difficulty: strenuous, some route finding
Maps: USGS topographic: Garns Mountain, Fourth of July Peak; Forest Service: Caribou-Targhee National Forest, Palisades District
Information: Teton Basin Ranger District
Getting there: 18 miles west of Tetonia or 15 miles east of Sugar City on Idaho Highway 33 turn south on the gravel road up Canyon Creek (Forest Road 218). At 4.2 miles the road passes Green Canyon Hot Springs. At 5.2 miles, turn left onto the dirt Radio Relay Road (Road 219) and go 10.3 miles to an unsigned trailhead at the tower, 15.5 miles from the highway.

This trail follows the crest of the Big Hole Mountains, giving travelers a view across green, gold, and brown fields and pastures below the soaring Tetons. The valley between these ranges is called Teton Basin. The first European to see it was John Colter in 1808. He was a member of Lewis and Clark's party who, after the expedition, returned to the wilderness and became a fur trapper. The Basin was also called Pierre's Hole after an Iroquois fur trapper, Pierre Tevanitabon, who found the valley in 1818 and told the Hudson Bay Company about it. Two of the fur trappers' rendezvous, where trappers sold their furs to fur company representatives, were held here: in 1830 and 1832. At the 1832 rendezvous there was a battle with the Gros Ventre branch of the Blackfeet. The battle started when the Gros Ventre chief rode up with a peace pipe, and trapper Antoine Godin told one of the Flathead tribe camped there to shoot the chief, and he did. Twenty-six of the Gros Ventres, 10 Flatheads, and 3 Europeans were killed in the resulting battle. Three years later the Gros Ventres caught up with Godin and scalped him.

Wildflowers abound along the trail, especially at Elk Flat. Below dark green subalpine firs at midsummer this sloping green meadow unrolls a tapestry of purple lupine, cream-colored umbrella plant, white Queen Anne's lace, and red paintbrush below the emerald face of Garns Mountain. Farther along, the trail passes summits of red rock that contrast with the dark green firs and pines below them. Metal signs mark major junctions. When one of the authors hiked the trail a few years ago it was overgrown and hard to follow. Recently, the state motorcycle trail

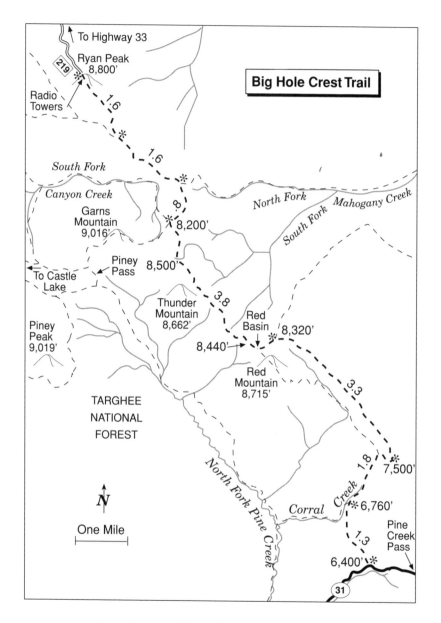

Big Hole Crest Trail

To Highway 33

Ryan Peak
8,800'

219

Radio
Towers

1.6

1.6

South Fork

Canyon Creek

Garns
Mountain
9,016'

North Fork

South Fork Mahogany Creek

8,200'

.8

8,500'

Piney
Pass

To Castle
Lake

Thunder
Mountain
8,662'

3.8

Red
Basin

8,320'

8,440'

Piney
Peak
9,019'

Red
Mountain
8,715'

3.3

TARGHEE

NATIONAL

FOREST

North Fork Pine Creek

Corral Creek

1.8

7,500'

6,760'

N

One Mile

Pine
Creek
Pass

1.3

6,400'

31

rangers and a Forest Service trail crew have worked on the trail, so it should be
much easier to find. Grasses and brush tend to overgrow this trail, so from time to
time the tread in some stretches may be indistinct.

From the radio relay station follow a rocky road along the grassy ridge top. It
is shown on the topographic map as a trail going southeast, but there is no sign.
From three tiny trees at the end of the road at .5 mile the trail goes southeast down

139

the end of the ridge through whitebark pine, sagebrush, and littleflower penstemon to a saddle at 1 mile.

On the other side of the saddle, the path climbs in a Douglas and subalpine fir forest around the right (west) side of the next section of ridge among lupine, snowbrush, and snowberry. At 1.6 miles is a metal sign for a trail down the North Fork of Canyon Creek. This sign also says it is 1.7 miles to the Garns Mountain Trail. From here the trail circles the right (southwest) side of the next section of ridge in the open. At a little saddle on the side of this ridge at 2 miles an unsigned spur trail turns off to the right a short distance.

Keep straight ahead southeast along the open side of the ridge. At 2.5 miles the path drops off the end of the ridge to a saddle at 2.8 miles, then climbs a round grassy hill between clumps of trees. Partway up, the trail curves 90 degrees to the right, then goes gently downhill to a signed junction at 3.2 miles with the North Fork of Mahogany Creek Trail, which leads east down that creek 4.5 miles to the end of Forest Road 236 in a 1,560-foot descent.

The main trail now goes south along the left side of a knoll in grasses and horsemint. It climbs onto a grassy flat full of wildflowers, turns southwest and descends into Elk Flat. Here, at 4 miles, is a junction marked Big Hole Crest Trail. The trail straight ahead to the west climbs Garns Mountain, and that to the right (northwest) descends the South Fork of Canyon Creek. The best campsites and water are .2 mile along this trail. To continue on the Big Hole Crest Trail, turn left (south). There is sometimes no trail tread here in the meadow, and from the end of the meadow on, the tread can be faint. There are also few recognizable landmarks in the next section, except for trail junctions.

The trail goes south-southeast along the meadow parallel to the woods on your left. The route curves right 4.5 miles from the relay tower, climbs in a subalpine fir forest, and flattens at a wildflower meadow with a view of a grassy hill ahead. At 4.8 miles the trail dips into a ravine and crosses a small creek that drains down Sob Canyon into the South Fork of Mahogany Creek. This is the only water on the trail between here and Corral Creek, which is 7 miles farther on. However, there are no comfortable campsites here because of grass, brush and sloping ground.

The trail goes along the center of a flat ridge and then along the right (southwest) side of it and into a little saddle that overlooks a small deep canyon to your right. The path goes along the left (northeast) side of the plant-covered sloping side of Thunder Mountain and then down into another little saddle. Here it hugs the right side of a rock rib only a few feet high and passes an unmarked trail junction to the right, which is probably a path to water at the head of Lookingglass Creek.

The main trail climbs up, crosses the rock rib, and cuts down to the left of it in a lush thicket of flowers. From here the route drops steeply down the end of the ridge, and then up the end of the next ridge. The trail circles the right side of a grassy hill that turns into a long ridge of sagebrush and grass. At the end of it is a flat grassy saddle with a grassy ridge leading left.

At this point, at 6.5 miles, the trail heads left (east) of the hill marked 8,619 on the map above the head of the steep canyon of the South Fork of Mahogany Creek. The route continues to a flat, rocky saddle with only scattered plants at 6.7 miles. From there it heads along the right (southwest) side of an open, rocky ridge of sagebrush, grass and flagged trees. The ridge narrows before a saddle at 7.1 miles where at two rock cairns the main trail turns off to the left (east) and the old Red Mountain trail to the right.

The main trail now goes along the left side of a flower-covered spur with a view of Driggs. Then it drops 400 feet off the side of the ridge to a flat. It goes left of a small knoll at 7.5 miles and drops even steeper to a saddle at 7.8 miles. To the right and uphill from the bottom of the saddle is a junction where a trail turns off to the north along Mahogany Ridge. The sign calls it the Patterson Creek Trail because it connects with a trail down that creek after 1.2 miles. It is 3.5 miles from the saddle down the Patterson Creek Trail to the end of Forest Road 237 in a 2,240-foot descent. From the junction, it is 3.5 more miles along the Big Hole crest to the Corral Creek Trail.

Now the trail goes along the south side of a hill and then along a narrow grassy ridge that appears to lead southeast for miles. This is the spot marked Government Trail Pass on the map. The trail follows the center of the ridge. At 9.6 miles the trail contours around a knob above the steep canyon of Red Creek on the right (southwest). At an overgrown flat with an old barbed wire fence at 9.9 miles the trail may disappear.

From here it goes up the left of the strip of trees that runs up the center of the hill ahead, which is Squirrel Mountain, 7,780 feet. From the summit, the route drops off the right-hand spur of the ridge heading southeast. All the hills ahead are wooded. Continue along the crest of the ridge and turn south at 10.9 miles to a distinct saddle. The saddle is just beyond (south of) a knoll marked 7,548 on the map.

Here, at 11.1 miles, there is a signed junction. The Big Hole Crest Trail goes up a wooded hill ahead to the south, and a trail goes east down Grove Creek. Because there was no tread and has no blazes for the Big Hole Crest Trail at this saddle and no water, the author took the Corral Creek Trail to the right (west) from this junction.

That trail heads downhill in thick woods to the northwest and reaches the creek, dry much of the summer, at 11.5 miles in a meadow thick with cow parsnip and coneflowers. There is no trail shown on the map turning off to Red Creek here. The main trail descends the right (west) side of Corral Creek in a jungle of plants. At 12 miles it crosses the creek to the left and returns to the right (west) side at 12.2 miles at a campsite. The trail steepens and passes a 40-foot dark gray rock covered with orange lichen. At 12.7 miles it fords to the left (east) bank.

At 12.9 miles where a side creek comes in from the left, you may want to take a shortcut that turns south. It will save 300 feet of descent and return climb but isn't shown on the topographic map. The shortcut is blazed, and from the side creek contours south through aspens back to the Corral Creek Trail after it has curved southwest. The shortcut rejoins the main trail at a flat saddle (6,840 feet) at 13.5 miles. The trail then descends though lodgepole, sagebrush and aspen to a short spur road. This road reaches the highway at 14.2 miles, 1 mile west of Pine Creek Pass.

63. MOODY SWAMP TRAIL TO THOUSAND SPRINGS VALLEY AND CASTLE LAKE

Round trip: 9 miles
Elevation gain: 680 feet
Elevation loss (return climb): 520 feet
Highest point: 7,640 feet
Time: 6 1/2 hours
Difficulty: moderate

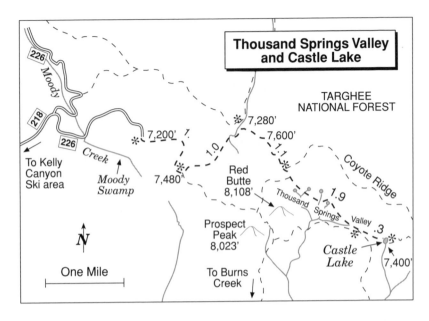

Thousand Springs Valley and Castle Lake

TARGHEE NATIONAL FOREST

226
Moody
218
226
Creek
To Kelly Canyon Ski area
Moody Swamp
7,200'
7,480'
7,280'
7,600'
1.0
1.1
Red Butte 8,108'
Coyote Ridge
Thousand Springs Valley
1.9
Prospect Peak 8,023'
.3
Castle Lake
7,400'
N
One Mile
To Burns Creek

Maps: USGS topographic: Temple Peak; Forest Service: Caribou-Targhee National Forest, Palisades Ranger District

Information: Palisades Ranger District

Getting there: From U.S. Highway 26, 14 miles east of Idaho Falls turn north and follow the signs toward Kelly Canyon Ski Area and Heise Hot Springs. One mile beyond the hot springs, turn left toward the ski area on Forest Road 218. Beyond the end of the pavement at the ski area at 6.8 miles, continue on Forest Road 218, turning left to Moody Meadows at 1.1 miles. At 18.3 miles the road passes four beaver ponds. Beyond the ponds turn right (east) on an unsigned road (226) and go to the end of it at 20.4 miles. This road follows a slightly different route than is shown on the maps: it goes around the north side of the hill labeled 7,478 rather than through Moody Swamp, although it is called the Moody Swamp Trail.

This trail has especially fine wildflowers. In mid-August they include lavender asters, bright yellow goldenrod, red paintbrush, and pink wild geranium. In Thousand Springs Valley tiny springs create green pools. Above the valley, grassy slopes contrast with the burnt red towers of Red Butte. Two miles farther on below a row of cliffs, marsh grass and aspens surround the green water of Castle Lake. On the way to the lake, the trail passes fingerlike Castle Rock. It also follows a historic stock driveway that eventually leads to Hoback Junction, Wyoming.

To reach the signed trailhead, follow the access directions above. The trail begins in huckleberries, and in 200 yards follows a new section rerouted to avoid an old jeep trail and to lessen the grade. Keep left at .8 mile where a trail turns off to go up on the side of Prospect Peak and over Red Butte to Thousand Springs Valley. The main trail descends through lodgepole forest and meadows and ends at 1.6 miles. About where Hilton Creek makes a 90-degree bend because it begins at a spring, the recently rerouted trail contours to the right (east) along the hillside, climbing to a divide at 2.2 miles.

Then the trail descends southwest into the Thousand Springs Valley. Partway down, the trail splits and rejoins in 300 yards. Red Butte appears ahead on the right and a talus ridge on the left. At 2.5 miles is an enormous meadow with aspen groves and a good view of Red Butte to the right, Coyote Ridge on the left, and Temple and Piney peaks ahead. At 2.9 miles a trail marked "sheep driveway" goes off to the left to Coyote Ridge. Just beyond this, the trail from Prospect Peak comes in from the west, having climbed over Red Butte.

Now the main trail drops 50 feet and contours southeast across the head of Thousand Springs Valley. At 3.3 miles there are small ponds above and below the trail. Beginning at 3.5 miles the trail crosses several tiny creeks from the springs. Soon it is close to Castle Rock. A junction with a trail into Burns Canyon is at 4.1 miles. There is a second junction about 200 yards farther on. To reach Castle Lake, keep straight ahead here for .3 mile. This is a side trail. The main trail goes off to the left and stays well above the lake on its north side. It climbs to Blacktail Pass at 5.3 miles then goes on to Piney Pass on the side of Garns Mountain.

64. HELL HOLE TRAIL

One-way trip: 5.5 miles
Elevation loss: 2,000 feet
Highest point: 7,200 feet
Time: 5 1/2 hours
Difficulty: moderate, but one hazardous steep stretch and 11 fords
Maps: USGS topographic: Temple Peak, Wheaton Mountain; Forest Service: Caribou-Targhee National Forest, Palisades Ranger District
Information: Palisades Ranger District
Getting there: From U.S. Highway 26, 14 miles east of Idaho Falls turn north and follow the signs for Heise Hot Springs and Kelly Canyon Ski Area. One mile beyond the hot springs turn left toward the ski area on Forest Road 218. Beyond the end of the pavement at the ski area continue on Road 218 and then turn left fol-

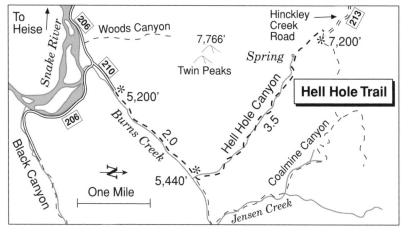

lowing the road toward Moody Meadow. Avoid unmarked side roads. At 9.3 miles from the pavement turn right (southeast) onto Road 213, the Hinckley Creek Road, which has a deeply rutted dirt surface. At 10.4 miles four-wheel drive is required even in dry weather. On top of a hill at 10.9 miles, a jeep trail turns right off the main road for 50 yards. Park here.

With a car shuttle, the Hell Hole Trail is a beautiful downhill walk through a lush green canyon of tall grasses and wildflowers, which are at their height in June and early July. The only drawbacks to the hike are an extremely steep stretch at the top and the fact that the trail fords Hell Hole Creek 11 times. At the bottom, the trail joins the Burns Creek Trail, which descends Burns Creek past limestone cliffs and towers to the Burns Canyon Road.

From the spur road at the parking spot on the Hinckley Creek Road, a path continues along the ridge, but this is not the trail. The trail plunges off to your left (southeast) only a few yards from the main road. There is no sign for the trail at the road or trailhead. The trail drops 200 feet in the first .2 mile. Here a walking stick is helpful and caution is required so as not to slip on the steep, hard-packed dirt. There is a sign for the trail at the bottom of the steep section. At .6 mile, the trail reaches Hell Hole Creek, which is only a tiny stream here. At .8 mile the path turns 90 degrees to the left (northeast) and descends through firs and rock outcrops. At .9 mile it turns 90 degrees back to the right. By this point it has already descended 800 feet.

At 1.5 miles the trail goes across the stream and back within 50 yards in the first two creek crossings. In the next .7 mile there are five more fords. Before the fifth of these the trail is on the left (northeast) side of the creek in a grove of Rocky Mountain maple. At 2.2 miles the trail crosses the creek to a grassy flat on the right (southwest) side. This flat has a view south of high cliffs up a side canyon.

Now the canyon is more open, with brush instead of trees. At 2.7 miles the trail switchbacks down to ford to the left side, and then back within .1 mile into a flat, brushy area. At 3 miles the route crosses back to the left side of the creek again and climbs well above it in sagebrush. The trail crosses back to the right side of Hell Hole Creek just before joining the Burns Creek Trail at 3.5 miles, instead of after joining it as the topographic map shows.

Turn right down the Burns Creek Trail, which at first descends the right side of Hell Hole Creek, passing under skyline cliffs that resemble hooded figures. Soon the path climbs up and down to avoid cliffs along Burns Creek. It stays on the right (northwest) side of the canyon and doesn't cross the creek as the topographic map shows. The lower canyon is open and brushy, with forest on the opposite side and tall cottonwoods along the creek. At 5.5 miles the trail reaches the dirt road up Burns Canyon. Down this road .5 mile is a gravel road (206) along the Snake River, which goes 2 miles southeast to the trailhead for the South Fork Snake River and Black Canyon trails. When setting up a car shuttle, it is easier to use the Kelly Canyon Ski Area road (218) and the Table Rock Road (217) to reach the Burns Creek trailhead than it is to drive the road along the river from Heise Hot Springs.

65. SOUTH FORK SNAKE RIVER TRAIL

Round trip: 13 miles

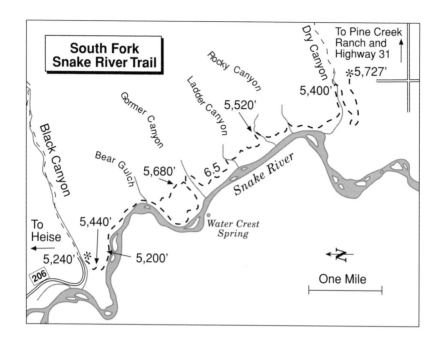

Elevation gain: 680 feet
Highest point: 5,680 feet
Time: 8 hours
Difficulty: moderate
Maps: USGS topographic: Wheaton Mountain; Forest Service: Caribou-Targhee National Forest, Palisades Ranger District
Information: Palisades Ranger District
Getting there: From U.S. Highway 26, 14 miles east of Idaho Falls turn north and follow the signs for Heise Hot Springs and Kelly Canyon Ski Area. Drive to the ski area on Forest Road 218. Then take the Table Rock Road (217) down to the Snake River. These roads are better than the one that goes from Heise Hot Springs along the river. Continue to the end of the road at Black Canyon. The trailhead is 200 yards before the Black Canyon trailhead.

Here is another trail that seems to be overshadowed by a more popular trail nearby – in this case, Black Canyon. The Snake River Trail takes you along a stretch of the gorge usually seen only by drift boaters. The trailhead is a half-mile up Black Canyon on the right. It has limited parking, but the Black Canyon trailhead 200 yards farther on has plenty of room. The trail cannot be reached from the south end at Dry Canyon because there is no public right of way at that point.

From Black Canyon the trail immediately climbs through a Douglas fir forest to the top of the gorge at .5 mile. It then drops 200 feet to the edge of the river. The trail rises and falls and dodges in and out of small side canyons for the rest of the way.

From the trail, there are opportunities for bushwhacking down to the river and testing the world-class trout waters of the Snake, which are especially productive

145

in the fall. This is gorgeous country. The bright blue-green of the river on a sunny day makes it beautiful even before you look at the cliffs and aspen groves. Wildlife is plentiful, and bald eagles and osprey are often seen in the air.

If you are looking for an extended trip you can take the trail up Dry Canyon and make a loop. It leads to the Fleming Canyon Trail and connects with the trail down Black Canyon. However, there are several unmarked junctions with other trails along the way that can be very confusing.

66. BLACK CANYON, LITTLE BURNS CREEK, AND BURNS CREEK

Loop trip: 10.3 miles (2 miles more by road to return to starting point)
Elevation gain: 2,280 feet
Highest point: 7,600 feet
Time: 8 1/2 hours
Difficulty: moderate to strenuous
Maps: USGS topographic: Wheaton Mountain, Forest Service: Caribou-Targhee National Forest, Palisades Ranger District
Information: Palisades Ranger District
Getting there: From U.S. Highway 26, 14 miles east of Idaho Falls turn north and follow the signs for Heise Hot Springs and Kelly Canyon Ski Area (Road 218). Then take the Table Rock Road (217) down to the Snake River. These roads are better than the one that goes from Heise Hot Springs along the river. Continue

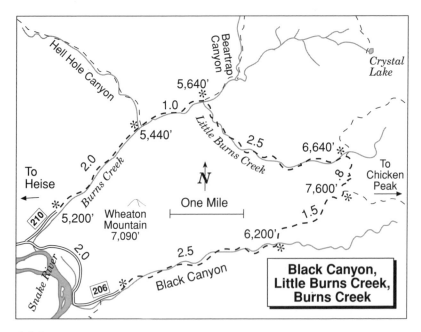

Black Canyon,
Little Burns Creek,
Burns Creek

to the end of the road at Black Canyon. The trailhead is 200 yards before the Black Canyon trailhead.

The drainage of the South Fork of the Snake River contains some of the most exciting wild land in Idaho. At present the road along the South Fork from Heise Hot Springs is mostly through private land, so access to the river and its world class fishing from that road is limited. The road is closed to public use in winter because the area is a winter range for wildlife. This area has become one of the top priorities of the Forest Service and the Idaho Department of Fish and Game for habitat protection.

In the Big Hole Mountains above the river there are many opportunities for hiking, mountain bicycling, and horseback riding in summer. The Black Canyon and Burns Creek loop is one of the better trips in the area.

The trailhead at the end of the road in Black Canyon has plenty of parking. The trail receives moderate use on summer weekends when it can be congested with trail bikes at the beginning, but at other times is not crowded.

The first 2.5 miles are along the Black Canyon, named for the black cliffs that line it. Then the trail climbs 1.5 miles over a 7,600-foot divide with a view of 8,417-foot Chicken Peak to the east. The route descends .8 mile to Little Burns Creek, and then goes down that creek for 2.5 miles to Burns Creek. From there it is 3 more miles down Burns Creek among grotesque limestone outcroppings to the Burns Creek trailhead. Then it is 2 miles by road back to the Black Canyon trailhead.

You can horseback ride the loop around to Burns Creek Canyon in one day, or hike it in one day if you're in shape (there are some tough stretches). Or you can spend the night along the way and go more slowly. The Black Canyon section of trail is not recommended for mountain biking. These trails are also good entrances and exits for longer trips into the high country of the Big Holes.

Beware of taking the loop too early in the summer. There are several stream crossings along Little Burns Creek. Also, snow often covers the upper parts of the trail into mid-June. Hikers may want to leave a car shuttle at the Burns Creek trailhead or leave a bike stashed there to avoid walking the road back to Black Canyon.

67. PACKSADDLE LAKE

Round trip: 5 miles
Elevation gain: 960 feet
Elevation loss (return climb): 414 feet
Highest point: 7,760 feet
Time: 4 1/2 hours
Difficulty: easy to moderate
Maps: USGS topographic map: Packsaddle Lake; national forest map: Targhee National Forest
Information: Teton Basin Ranger District
Getting there: From Idaho Falls drive north on U.S. Highway 20 past Rexburg and take the exit onto Idaho Highway 33 heading east. Drive about 25 miles until you come to the sign for Echo Ranch. Turn right (south) on the "Echo Ranch Road" and drive about 5 miles. Where the road makes a 90-degree turn, there is a gate with a sign behind it for Packsaddle Lake and room to park nearby. Don't block the gate or the road, since some people drive the road with four-

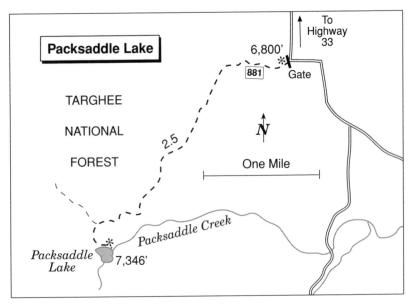

wheel-drive vehicles. Be sure to shut the gate after you go through it.

Packsaddle Lake is a beautiful landslide-created lake, surrounded on all sides by timber. You may see waterfowl and even moose. The lake's main attraction is fishing, but because it is so popular, don't count on catching anything to brag about or expect to have the lake to yourself. The entire trail is a quick but strenuous mountain bike trip. It is also popular with horseback riders and hikers looking for a short day hike.

From the gate the trail to Packsaddle Lake starts out as a jeep trail with a couple of fairly steep inclines. When the road forks, keep left. After about 2 miles a nonmotorized trail leaves the jeep road. This trail drops into a small canyon .5 mile before the lake and descends it to the lake below. Many people just take their four-wheel-drive vehicles up and walk the last half-mile. The road can be too muddy even for four-wheel drives after a heavy rainstorm. Jeeps and motorcycles have torn up some sections of the road by trying to go up when it is wet and muddy in early spring and late fall. Spring runoff adds to the erosion problems. When the road is soggy it is very slippery and dangerous. Therefore, if it is wet and muddy, walk your bike and don't take your ATV or jeep on it.

There are a couple of nice camping spots along the south end of the lake. Please use existing campsites to minimize your impact. The area is heavily hunted, so if you go there in the fall, be sure to wear blaze orange.

Snake River Mountains

68. PALISADES LAKES

Round trip: 12.4 miles to the upper lake
Elevation gain: 1,073 feet
Highest point: 6,633 feet
Time: 5 1/2 hours for lower lake; 8 hours for upper lake
Difficulty: easy to moderate
Maps: USGS topographic: Palisades Dam, Palisades Peak, Forest Service: Caribou-Targhee National Forest, Palisades Ranger District
Information: Palisades Ranger District
Getting there: Drive southeast from Swan Valley on U.S. Highway 26 to Irwin. Turn left on the Palisades Creek Road at the sign for Palisades Creek Campground. Follow this road for 1.5 miles. Just before the campground and a creek crossing is a parking area. On the other side of the creek is a horse unloading area.

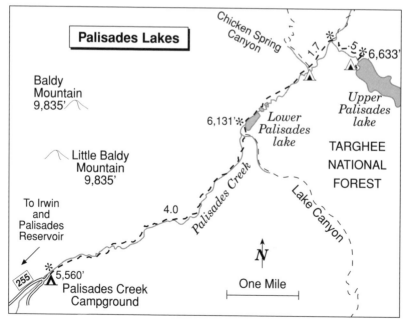

Upper Palisades Lake in the Snake River Range

The trailhead is up the creek at the end of the campground.

The trail up to the Palisades Lakes may be the most popular in eastern Idaho. There are several reason for this. The lakes offer excellent fishing, gorgeous mountain scenery, great wildlife viewing, easy hiking and a Forest Service campground at the mouth of the canyon. In addition, bridges across the creek make the route easier for bikers, hikers and horseback riders. On any summer weekend scores of people make the trek up the canyon. To avoid crowds, try to go during the week, or in spring or early fall before hunting season.

Both lakes were formed ages ago when giant landslides came down the canyon and blocked the creek. The canyon is thickly forested with fir, as well as some aspen and willow. If you scan the mountain walls you may see mountain goats. It is 4 miles to the lower end of the lower lake.

The upper lake at 6.2 miles, .5 mile from the Palisades Creek Trail, has better camping because sites at the lower lake fill up sooner.

If you're looking for a longer trip, the trail to Upper Palisades Lake continues up Waterfall Canyon and connects with the trail down Little Elk Creek. You can also continue up Palisades Creek past the turnoff for the upper lake at 5.7 miles. There aren't any bridges beyond this turnoff, so the several crossings of Palisades Creek make this part of the trail tedious for those on foot or bicycle. It's best to tackle this stretch after midsummer. It is a great way to lose the crowds, though, because few people continue beyond the lakes. If you do continue up Palisades Creek you will reach the Mosquito Creek trail, which leads into the valley of Jackson Hole.

69. WATERFALL CANYON

Round trip: 20 miles via Palisades Lakes; 14 miles via Little Elk Creek, 12.2 miles by the Sheep Creek Trail

Elevation gain: 1,440 feet via Palisades Lakes; 3,600 via Little Elk Creek;

150

Two waterfalls in Waterfall Canyon in the Snake River Range.

3,580 feet via Sheep Creek
Elevation loss (return climb): none via Palisades Lakes; 1,800 feet via Little Elk Creek; 2,080 feet via Sheep Creek
Highest point: 7,500 at the falls via Palisades Lakes; 9,160 via Little Elk Creek
Time: two or three days for either route
Difficulty: strenuous to tough
Maps: USGS topographic: Palisades Dam, Palisades Peak, Mount Baird; National Forest: Caribou-Targhee National Forest, Palisades Ranger District
Information: Palisades Ranger District
Getting there: Drive southeast from Swan Valley on U.S. Highway 26 from Irwin. Turn left on the Palisades Creek Road at the sign for Palisades Creek Campground. Follow this road for 1.5 miles. Just before the campground and creek crossing is a parking area. On the other side of the creek is a horse unloading area. The trailhead is up the creek at the end of the campground. It is also possible to reach Waterfall Canyon from the Little Elk Creek trail. For directions see Hike 68, Little Elk Creek and Mt. Baird.

A great place to view beautiful waterfalls is Waterfall Canyon in the Snake River Mountains near the Idaho-Wyoming border. There are two impressive falls in the upper reaches of the canyon. One runs most of the summer; the second often shrivels to a trickle by late summer. In wet years, both run strong through most of July. The falls resemble those in Yosemite because the large, wide canyon has impressive cliffs on both sides. In the falls, the streams plummet several hundred feet.

In Waterfall Canyon the forest opens into a clearing every 200 to 400 yards. Large block-shaped boulders show that the clearings were created by avalanches. Snow crashes down and wipes the forest clean, then melts, leaving only boulders

151

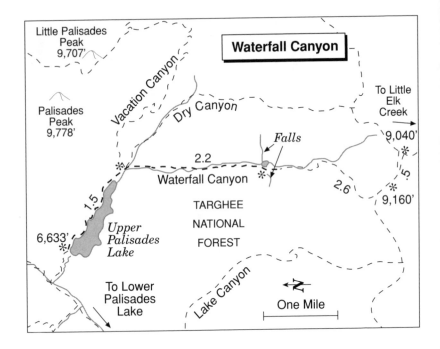

and a few snapped-off trees. Most avalanches occur along the same chutes, but during wet winters, the heavy snow creates new avalanche routes. In July there may still be avalanche snow six feet deep mixed with broken trees.

The biggest drawback to seeing these falls is distance and difficulty. There are three main approaches to Waterfall Canyon. The first and most popular is by the Palisades Creek Trail. This trail is on the east side of the Snake River just north of Palisades Reservoir. From the trailhead to the lower end of the upper lake is 6.2 miles. From there it is 1.4 and 1.5 miles along the lakeshore to junctions with trails up Dry and Vacation canyons. From the second of these junctions it is 2.2 miles farther to the falls, which are about 10 miles from the trailhead.

The second way to reach the waterfalls is from Little Elk Creek. This steep trail is shorter but is less used because it gains 3,600 feet in less than 4 miles and then drops 1,800 feet to the falls in 3 more miles. If you take that route in and out the total climb will be 5,100 feet, about like climbing out of the Grand Canyon. Either route is better as an overnight or three-day hike. Perhaps the easiest would be to backpack to either of the Palisades Lakes the first day, stash your gear and day hike to the falls the second day, and backpack out on the third day. This breaks up the 21 miles into easily managed sections. Or you can set up a car shuttle and go to Palisades Lakes and then up Waterfall Canyon and then come out Little Elk Creek, making a through trip of 17.5 miles with 3,240 feet elevation gain.

On the Little Elk Creek route, the best camping is on the north side of Mount Baird, but after the snow melts, water is hard to find at the top of Little Elk Creek canyon. Be sure to pack extra.

The third way is to take the Sheep Creek Canyon Trail. To reach this trail, drive southeast on Highway 26 from Irwin for 2.8 miles and turn left (north) on the Sheep Creek Road (260). Drive 2.3 miles to the end of this dirt road. From here it is 3 miles to the point where the trail becomes the Lake Canyon Trail and turns north. A half mile past this sharp curve, a trail leads east .8 mile to meet the Waterfall Canyon Trail 1.8 miles above the falls.

70. LITTLE ELK CREEK AND MOUNT BAIRD

Round trip: 9 miles
Elevation gain: 4,105 feet
Highest point: 10,025 feet
Time: 9 1/2 hours or overnight
Difficulty: very strenuous
Maps: USGS topographic: Palisades Dam, Mount Baird; Forest Service: Caribou-Targhee National Forest, Palisades Ranger District
Information: Palisades Ranger District
Getting there: From Idaho Falls, drive 2.5 miles past the Palisades Dam on U.S. Highway 26. Turn left (northeast) at a sign for Little Elk Creek onto a good gravel road (268), which leaves the highway just west of a causeway across the reservoir. Follow this road 1 mile to its end.

Occasionally trips into Idaho's backcountry have a few surprises to remind you of just how wild it is out there. The hike up to Bonneville County's high point,

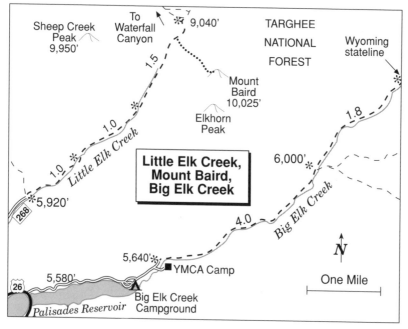

Mount Baird, at 10,025 feet, is one of these hikes. The views, the wildlife, and the route up are all surprising. From the east side, this peaks looks very imposing, but if you follow the ridge on the northwest side it's just a steep walk up. From the summit, the sights are impressive. To the west you can see Palisades Reservoir and the outlines of the Lemhi and Lost River ranges. To the east is a great view of the Tetons with the Grand Teton head and shoulders above its neighbors. Pikas often bleat at you from the rocks. Pikas look like a cross between a large mouse and a rabbit and are often called rock rabbits. They make their homes in the rocky areas along canyons and ridges, where they harvest grasses and plants and cure them in haystacks for winter use. In addition, you may see black bears in the basin below the peak and mountain goats on its slopes.

From the top of Little Elk Creek Canyon 3.5 miles above the trailhead, it is about 1 mile to the summit via the ridge on the northwest side of Mount Baird. The ridge is mostly easy walking — in some places it's even level — until about 200 yards from the summit. Here you walk up steep loose rock.

Directly south of Mount Baird is Elkhorn Peak at 9,940 feet. Probably the easiest way to reach its summit is from the ridge connecting it with Mount Baird.

Just below and to the north is Waterfall Canyon. The Little Elk Creek Trail connects with the trail that leads down this canyon past an impressive falls at 3 miles to Upper Palisades Lake, 5.7 miles below the divide with Little Elk Creek.

The remains of a post with rusted guy wires are strewn about the summit of Mount Baird. This marker may have fallen victim to a nasty lightning strike.

Because the climb is more than 4,000 feet you may find it a strain on your knees unless you do it as an overnight or as part of a multiday trip to or from Waterfall Canyon. There is no water in late summer in the basin below the peak, so if you go up from the Little Elk Creek side you will need to camp farther down along the creek or else carry water.

This mountain would make a good climb for Boy Scouts or families with advanced hikers. Although the trail is open to mountain bikes, it is so steep and rough beyond the first mile it is suitable only for skilled and conditioned bikers.

71. BIG ELK CREEK

Round trip: 10.4 miles to the trail forks
Elevation gain: 640 feet to the trail forks
Highest point: 6,280 feet
Time: 6 to 7 hours
Difficulty: moderate
Maps: USGS topographic: Mount Baird, Palisades Peak; Forest Service: Caribou-Targhee National Forest, Palisades Ranger District
Information: Palisades Ranger District
Getting there: Drive southeast of Swan Valley on U.S. Highway 26 past the Palisades Reservoir Dam. About 3.5 miles past the dam, turn left (east) at the Big Elk Creek sign onto a dirt road (262). Go 2.5 miles to the end of the road.

Here is a mostly easy trail up a scenic canyon with a few connections for longer trips. Big Elk Creek is a good-size creek that runs all year into Palisades Reservoir. Most people on the trail are those camping at the Forest Service campground or staying at the YMCA summer camp at the mouth of the canyon.

Because of these camps, traffic is sometimes heavy on weekends.

Perhaps the canyon's best feature is its wildflowers in early summer. Because of numerous avalanche chutes along the canyon, the area has less timber and more open areas for flowers than most mountain canyons.

For about the first 3 miles of trail, the canyon is wide. Then it narrows and the trail follows the creek closely. The canyon walls are about 600 feet high here. Look for a falls off to the left. At about 2.7 miles a trail turns off to the right (east) up Dry Canyon.

At 5.2 miles the trail forks into three trails. From here the trails become much more strenuous. A half-mile before the fork is the Wyoming border. The left fork trail goes northwest up Cabin Creek to Austin Canyon. This is a fairly tough trail, gaining about 2,000 feet in reaching Austin Canyon. If you want to make a loop, it is easier to take the center trail up the Siddoway Fork north, then take the Austin Canyon Trail west, and return down Cabin Creek. If you're looking for an extended trip, the Austin Canyon Trail also connects with the Little Elk Creek Trail via the Dry Canyon Trail.

The right-hand trail at the fork continues east up Big Elk Creek. In 2.5 more miles the river forks. Trails up both of these forks offer extended trips, all in Wyoming. The North Fork Trail continues on into Jackson Hole. The South Fork Trail connects with the North Fork of Indian Creek Trail, also in Wyoming.

72. OLIVER PEAK (THE MIKE HARRIS TRAIL)

Round trip: 9.6 miles (1 mile cross-country)
Elevation gain: 2,444 feet
Highest point: 9,004 feet
Time: 7 1/2 hours
Difficulty: strenuous at the beginning and end, otherwise moderate
Maps: USGS topographic: Victor; Forest Service: Caribou-Targhee National Forest, Palisades Ranger District
Information: Teton Basin Ranger District
Getting there: To reach the trailhead, drive southeast of Victor on Idaho Highway 33 (or northwest on Wyoming Highway 22 from Jackson) to the turnoff for the Mike Harris Campground, which is 3.5 miles from Victor. Turn right (southwest) onto the dirt campground road. Cross a small bridge over Trail Creek and turn left heading toward the campground. Before reaching the campground park and walk left on a rough dirt road that parallels Trail Creek and the highway. This road is closed to motor vehicles. Follow this road for .5 mile. The trail begins at an intersection of trails where there is a post.

The trail to the top of Oliver Peak near Victor, Idaho, makes for a nice day trip with connections into the topside of the Snake River Range. There's a payoff for all the steep uphill walking: a wonderful view of the surrounding mountain ranges and the beautiful farms of Teton Valley. You can easily make out most of the region's mountain ranges. The Grand Teton dominates the northern skyline, and southwest of Oliver Peak you look far into the Snake River Range, also known as the Palisades.

At the intersection of old jeep trails take the right (west) fork up Mikesell Canyon, avoiding the other trails that continue up Trail Creek parallel to the high-

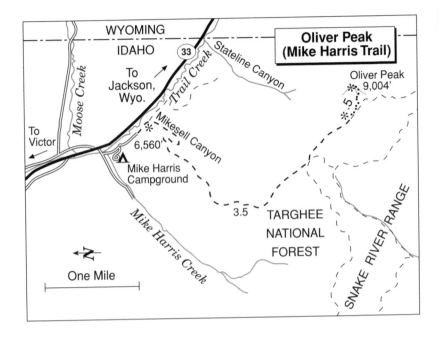

WYOMING

IDAHO

33

Stateline Canyon

Trail Creek

To
Jackson,
Wyo.

Oliver Peak
9,004'

.5

Moose Creek

To
Victor

Mikesell Canyon

6,560'

Mike Harris
Campground

3.5

TARGHEE
NATIONAL
FOREST

SNAKE RIVER RANGE

Mike Harris Creek

N

One Mile

way. The correct trail becomes a footpath after 100 yards.

The canyon at this elevation is thick forest of mostly fir and lodgepole pine with occasional aspen. For the first .3 mile the trail is easy. A small stream flows through this canyon in the spring and early summer, but disappears after the snow above melts.

The trail begins to climb at a huge but gentle switchback. It heads uphill, turns back on itself, then turns back up the canyon again and steepens. From the canyon bottom to the top of the ridge is a 1,600-foot climb. In about the second mile the trail begins to leave the thicker timber behind. This allows you to see more of the canyon but also leaves you exposed to the sun, which can be uncomfortable on a hot summer day.

By 2.5 miles the trail nears the top of the canyon and then follows a nearly level ridge for the next mile. Along this ridge is a view of the Teton Valley to the northwest and the Teton Mountains to the northeast. Southwest are the tops of the canyons in the Palisades Creek drainage.

On the ridge grow brush, grasses and patches of fir as well as midsummer wildflowers. From here it is easy to see Oliver Peak to the southeast. The trail goes straight toward the peak, passing to the right (southwest) of it at 3.5 miles. Past Oliver Peak the trail continues 3.5 miles to a junction with a trail east down Mosquito Creek into Jackson Hole and a trail west down the East Fork of Palisades Creek.

To reach the top of Oliver Peak, leave the trail at 3.5 miles and zigzag up the southeast side of the peak. It is about .5 mile and a 575-foot climb from the ridge to the summit. Game and sheep trails will make this steep section a bit easier. The peak's northern side is covered with thick forest and undergrowth and is also much steeper. In a large grassy area a rock cairn stands on the summit.

156

Caribou Mountains

73. BEAR CREEK

Round trip: 8.6 miles to the North Fork, 9.6 miles to Warm Springs Creek; opportunity for several longer loop trips
Elevation gain: 240 feet to the North Fork; 320 feet to Warm Springs Creek
Highest point: 6,000 feet at Warm Springs Creek
Maps: USGS topographic: Palisades Dam, Red Ridge, Commissary Ridge, Big Elk Mountain, Herman; Forest Service: Caribou-Targhee National Forest, Palisades Ranger District
Information: Palisades Ranger District
Time: 6 hours to Warm Springs Creek
Difficulty: easy to moderate in the first 5 miles; moderate to tough on the side trails
Getting there: Take U.S. Highway 26 to Palisades, Idaho. Cross over the reservoir dam and continue south around the reservoir on Forest Road 058. Look for Bear Creek about 6 miles after crossing the dam. Turn right on a side road north of the creek and follow it past the campground (about .2 mile).

The Bear Creek Trail on the west side of Palisades Reservoir is a multi-use path for hikers, bikers, and horseback riders. A large parking area at the trailhead

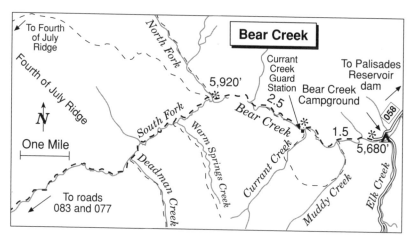

provides facilities for unloading horses. Anglers fish the creek when it opens in July. The area is sandwiched between Grays Lake National Wildlife Refuge on the southwest and Palisades Reservoir to the northeast. There are enough side trails to keep most people busy for many weekends.

The Bear Creek Trail is mostly easy for the first several miles. The trail forks after 4 miles into the North and South forks. After this, there are more stream crossings and some tougher stretches.

Here are a few possibilities for loop trips depending on your mode of transportation. Bikers looking for an all-day trip can take the South Fork Bear Creek trail up to the Skyline Road 077 and go south to the McCoy Creek Road 087 and then circle back on the Jensen Creek-Elk Creek Road 058.

Near the beginning of the Bear Creek Trail, hikers can turn off up Muddy Creek or Currant Creek (which meet on a saddle about 1.5 miles up either trail) and then go over a 7,911-foot peak and down Forest Service Trail 148 to the South Fork of Bear Creek Trail. Along this trail are some good campsites, especially beside a Jacuzzi-size hot pool at the top of Warm Springs Creek.

The side trails off the Bear Creek trail are tougher to follow and steeper hiking. Most climb up and above the deep Bear Creek Canyon. If you're on a bike, stick to the main Bear Creek trails.

Horse riders can go up Bear Creek to the North Fork Trail and over Fourth of July Ridge and Commissary ridges to Skyline Road 077 and south to pick up the South Fork Trail on the return trip. However, the Skyline Road is not graveled, so it is bad when wet.

Remember the area is popular during hunting season, so if you go in the fall, be sure to wear blaze orange.

---

74. CARIBOU MOUNTAIN

Round trip: 3.6 miles
Elevation gain: 1,763 feet
Highest point: 9,803 feet
Time: 5 hours
Difficulty: moderate
Maps: USGS topographic map: Caribou Mountain; Forest Service: Caribou National Forest
Information: Soda Springs Ranger District
Getting there: Take Sunnyside Road in Idaho Falls east into the foothills. Drive all the way to the Bone Road and turn right (south). Drive 8 miles to the village of Bone and continue south. Keep left at the intersection with the Blackfoot Reservoir Road. Take this road, the Long Valley Road, southeast 25 miles to Herman at the northeast corner of Grays Lake. At Herman turn left (east) on the McCoy Creek Road (Forest Road 087) and drive 4.2 miles to the Barnes Creek Road (188). Turn right on this road. From here on, a high-clearance vehicle or mountain bike is recommended. Don't attempt to drive this road when wet. Trailers are not recommended because there road is too narrow to turn around. Drive 4 miles to the Monte Cristo Mine area and park.

If you want to come in from the south, continue south from Herman and turn left (east) on Road 119 (the Bridge Creek-Tincup Road) next to the ranger station.

Checking out the comments in the register box on top of Caribou Mountain.

Two miles along this road turn left on Road 189 to Morgan Meadow. From here, an ATV trail goes northwest.

Caribou Mountain is for hikers and horse riders looking for a fun mountain-climbing experience without paying a high physical price. The mountain sits just east of the Grays Lake National Wildlife Refuge and is the high point of the Caribou Range, which parallels Palisades Reservoir on the west. The peak appears isolated from nearby mountains by basins and valleys, making it seem larger than it is and allowing it to offer super views.

The area is also known for its abundant wildlife, such as deer and moose along the Barnes Creek Road and sandhill cranes on the Grays Lake marshes. Go early in the morning to increase your chances of seeing wildlife.

This area has a storied past. Settlers heading west on the Lander Cutoff of the Oregon Trail could easily spot the big mountain. Some stayed to farm the valleys around Grays Lake and the Portneuf and Blackfoot rivers. In 1871 Carriboo Jack, a.k.a. Jesse Fairchild, discovered gold here. He was called Cariboo because he had

159

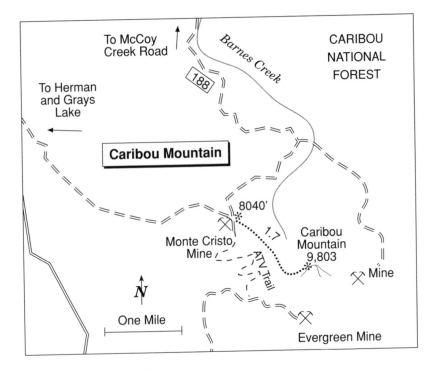

To McCoy Creek Road

To Herman and Grays Lake

Barnes Creek

188

CARIBOU NATIONAL FOREST

Caribou Mountain

8040'

Monte Cristo Mine

1.7

ATV Trail

Caribou Mountain 9,803

Mine

N

One Mile

Evergreen Mine

been at the mines in Cariboo, British Columbia. He mined here for 14 years until he was killed by a bear. His gold discovery led to the thriving gold-mining town of Caribou at the base of the mountain. By 1874 eight hydraulic nozzles were being used to wash gravel down to run through the sluices. Because most of the ore was found around 9,000 feet, the season was so short it was hard for mining to succeed here. A few foundations and acres of rubble are all that remain of Caribou City, even though it had 1,500 residents in the 1880s, and work on the lode continued on and off until 1955.

The Monte Cristo Mine on the northwest side of the mountain tried to make a go of copper mining during World War II. Mining claims remain active, but the area hasn't been seriously worked for decades. During the summer you will likely see a sheepherder's wagon along the Barnes Creek Road.

One way to the top of the mountain is from the Monte Cristo Mine on the north side. Part of the adventure of this route is driving the bumpy Barnes Creek Road to the mine. The road crosses the creek three times. Even though a Forest Service sign urges drivers to stay off the road when it is wet, early spring and late fall travelers have left deep ruts and holes.

There is no trail to the top on this side of Caribou Mountain, but there is an obvious route. From the end of the Barnes Creek Road walk south up a .2-mile side road that is closed to motor vehicles.

Then bushwhack up through the talus to the top of the spur ridge leading east. The spur leads to a north-south ridge that connects the three highest points of the peak. As you approach the summit ridge by way of the spur, you look down to the north on a grassy basin, known as "Grassy Gulch" by the locals and as "House

Basin" by the Forest Service. It is at 9,100 feet, but once held several mining buildings. From above you can spot a few decaying walls. On the spur when you see House Basin on your left, the two lower summits of Caribou Mountain are visible to your right. Continue east along the spur to the top of a shoulder of the mountain (9,642 feet) at 1.5 miles. From here the ridge slopes down about 50 feet and then climbs 150 feet to the summit, 9,803 feet, at 1.8 miles. It is at the north end of the summit ridge.

Some stretches of the ridge are covered by large boulders, making progress slow. As you hike along the ridge you are treated to occasional great views of the Grays Lake Valley. On top of the mountain the views are fantastic. From it you can see most of the surrounding ranges such as the Tetons, and even make out the faint line of the Centennial Mountains on the Idaho-Montana border. The summit is marked with a U.S. Geological Survey benchmark and a metal register box.

Another route up comes from the south. This route climbs from Morgan Meadows to the Evergreen and Monte Cristo mines, but is not shown on the topographic map. The Eagle Creek Road (119) 6 miles south of Herman is no longer open to motor vehicles, but is open to trail bikes and ATVs.

Before or after your hike you may want to consider staying in the old Caribou Basin Guard Station on Road 087 east of Herman. The Forest Service rents it out, but you must make arrangements in advance.

Webster Range

75. HISTORIC LANDER CUTOFF OF THE OREGON TRAIL

Round trip: 7 miles to Road 358, 11 miles to Road 107.
Elevation gain: 985 feet
Highest point: 7,400 feet
Time: 5 1/2 to 7 1/2 hours
Difficulty: easy to moderate but trail is overgrown and requires some route

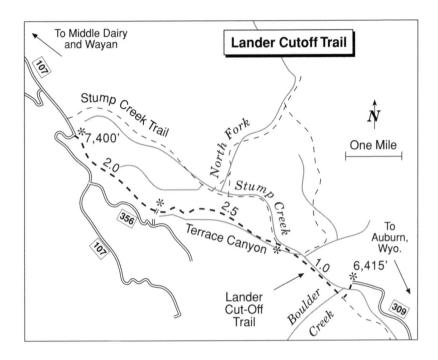

Lander Cutoff Trail

To Middle Dairy and Wayan

107

Stump Creek Trail

*7,400'

2.0

North Fork

Stump Creek

356

107

Terrace Canyon

N

One Mile

To Auburn, Wyo.

2.5

1.0

6,415'

Lander Cut-Off Trail

Boulder Creek

309

finding

Maps: USGS topographic: Diamond Flat, Stump Peak, and Wayan East; Forest Service: Caribou National Forest

Information: Soda Springs Ranger District

Getting there: Drive 23 miles south of Alpine, Wyoming, on U.S. Highway 89 and turn right (southwest) on Highway 238. Drive 4 miles to the town of Auburn, Wyoming, and turn right (west) on Forest Road 110. Drive 3.5 miles and turn right on the second dirt road (109) heading to the Stump Creek Guard Station. Keep right at each intersection and drive 5 miles to the end of the road. If gates are closed, open them and close them after passing through. Most of this access road goes through private land, so stay on the road; that is what the No Trespassing signs mean.

There are times when you come across a great trail and wonder why you are the only one on it. A section of the historic Lander Trail near the Idaho-Wyoming border just north of Afton, Wyoming, is one of those rarely used trails. The Lander Cutoff is an Oregon Trail alternate built with $300,000 provided by Congress in 1858 as a shortcut from Wyoming's Salt River Valley to Grays Lake and the Snake River. Mormon settlers did the work with hand tools for $1 a day. It was north of the main trail and saved a week of the emigrants' time. It also provided much more water and grass than the main trail through the alkaline desert between South Pass and Green River. The Lander Trail was named for Frederick Lander, the man who surveyed its route in 1858.

Now the trail is mostly a single-track footpath. The Forest Service obviously

162

intends the Lander Trail to be a showcase trail. Signs along the route point out interesting features, like wagon wheel ruts, rock work, and old tree carvings. But so few people take advantage of this on-the-ground history that some short sections are completely overgrown by thick grass. The trail isn't near any large towns, but it is worth the drive.

From the informal trailhead you immediately wade across Stump Creek to the left (southwest) side and follow a jeep trail for about 100 yards. In mid- and late summer you can drive across the creek to the end of the jeep trail. In June, Stump Creek is only calf-deep. The creek is named for J.H. Stump, who established a salt works in 1866 near the Salt River on the Wyoming border.

On the far side of the creek, a large sign says "Wagon Wheel Ruts" with an arrow pointing left. After you check out the ruts, continue on the trail northwest up Stump Creek on its left side (southwest), wading across a side creek, Boulder Creek, right away. This creek can't be driven across.

The trail follows the left (southwest) side of Stump Creek for 1.2 miles. In some places stream-bank erosion has erased the trail. In other places game trails leading down to the creek are more prominent than the Lander Trail. About every 100 to 200 yards is a brown plastic Forest Service post. They are especially helpful where grass has overgrown the path. A thick forest of fir and lodgepole pine grows on the southwestern side of the canyon, but on the northeastern side there are only grasses, brush, and a few scattered junipers.

After 1 mile the trail forks. The left fork, which goes up Terrace Canyon, is the Lander Cutoff. A log rail fence marks the entrance to the canyon. The trail going right continues up Stump Creek.

Terrace Canyon is surprisingly narrow for the route of a major wagon road, but the elevation gain is so gentle that walking up it is almost easy. There are huge beaver ponds about a mile up it. Some of the dams are ten feet high. Just above the ponds the trail disappears in a large meadow. Keep to the right of the meadow and the trail will soon reappear. A quarter-mile above the meadow, a sign indicates the trail's rock ledge work was done by the builders of the Lander Road. These ledges are the terraces for which the canyon is named. Within 100 yards a sign points out more wagon wheel ruts. A few hundred yards farther on look for a sign that points out a huge, dead aspen with several carvings. One carving reads: "F.P. 7-6-47."

At the top of the canyon is another log rail fence with a sign telling motorized vehicles to keep out. The trail continues faintly to the northwest. A more prominent jeep trail heads south to Road 358. This road goes northwest to Road 107 after 2 miles. Road 107 passes the top of Stump Creek Canyon as it winds northwest to Middle and Upper Dairy canyons.

Mountain bikers may find these forest roads a good route back to the Stump Creek Trail, which you can descend to your car. However, that trail is in poor shape and would be tough biking, so it is not recommended for mountain bikers. It would be best for them to return the way they came.

Foot travelers can take an alternate route for the return. To do this use your topographic map to find a cross-country route down Noon Creek. First climb to the top of the left (north) ridge of Noon Creek Canyon and follow a game trail for 1.5 miles down to the confluence of Noon Creek and Stump Creek.

The trail down Stump Creek is in poor shape. It is flat and easy, but has been washed away in several places by the meandering creek. Just keep following the water flowing downstream. The Forest Service map shows that the trail should be on the south side most of the time, but it really crosses back and forth several times.

163

As you're going down Stump Creek, once you reach Bechler Creek, which flows into Stump Creek from the east, you are .5 mile from your vehicle. Bechler Creek is easily jumped, and the rest of the trail is in good shape.

As a place to stay before or after your hike, you can rent the old Stump Creek Guard Station on Road 140 just off the Stump Creek Road (109). This must be done by prearrangement with the Soda Springs Ranger District.

Preuss Range

76. SNOWDRIFT MOUNTAIN

Through trip: 7.2 miles from mine road to Trapper Cabin
Elevation gain: 1,877 feet
Highest point: 9,577 feet
Time: 6 hours
Difficulty: strenuous to top of ridge, easy from there on
Maps: USGS topographic: Harrington Peak, Snowdrift Mountain, Meade Peak; Forest Service: Caribou National Forest
Information: Montpelier Ranger District
Getting there: From Soda Springs drive south on U.S. Highway 30 for 19 miles to Georgetown and turn east on the Georgetown Canyon Road. The road is paved for the first 3 miles. Keep right at the intersection and crossing of Georgetown Creek. At this point the road gains the Forest Service number 102. Drive 5.5 miles to just beyond the strip mine dump. Park north of the fenced area.

The main attraction on Snowdrift Mountain is the great views from the top. If you're interested in solitude and in seeing wildlife, this mountain's ridgeline trail is a good bet.

Snowdrift Mountain is a high north-south ridge about 13 miles north of Montpelier that gets its name from the snow that piles up on top and lingers year-round. In winter, the snow often avalanches down chutes on the east and west slopes.

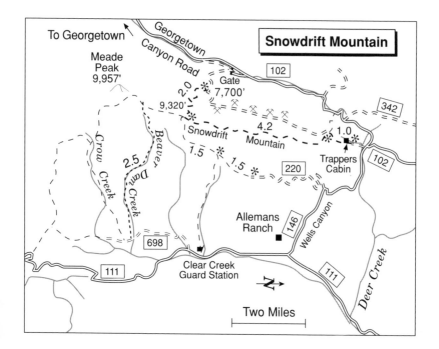

Most of the ridge is well above 9,000 feet.

South of Snowdrift Mountain on the same ridge is Meade Peak. At 9,957 feet it is the highest point in the southeastern corner of Idaho. You can reach the peak from the Snowdrift Mountain trails. It dominates the southern view from the top of the ridge.

Another dominant feature on the mountain is manmade. A large phosphate strip mining operation runs almost the entire length of the ridge on its western side on the 8,000-foot level.

The least obvious, but interesting, feature of the ridge is that it separates the Great Basin and Columbia River watersheds. All water that flows to the east eventually goes into the Snake River by way of Wyoming's Salt River, and all water west of the divide flows into the Great Salt Lake by way of the Bear River.

The range that Snowdrift Mountain and Meade Peak are in is called the Preuss Range. It was named for Charles Preuss, the cartographer on John C. Fremont's 1843 expedition to map the Oregon Trail.

Four main trails lead to the top of the Snowdrift Mountain ridge. The most gradual route starts at the north end and heads south along the top of the ridge. The other three routes come up from the east and west and gain elevation quickly — at least 2,000 feet in 1.5 miles.

To reach the ridge from the old mine, hike up the gated dirt road until the west-side trail is seen, and then go up that trail. The trail switchbacks up and is easy to follow in many places, but disappears in others. Don't worry about losing the trail. Just get to the top of the ridge. Once at the top, the trail is well-used and easy to follow.

From the junction with the west-side trail, the ridge-top trail going south leads

1.5 miles to Meade Basin, dropping 300 feet. To reach Meade Peak, when the trail begins to descend into the basin, turn off the trail and climb along the ridge top west and south to the summit. From Meade Basin the trail descends to the Crow Creek trailhead on the east side of the ridge. A short distance down it, a new trail leads 2 miles to the Right Hand Fork of Georgetown Canyon trail about .7 mile above its trailhead. This trail provides a very short but very steep way to climb Meade Peak.

To reach the summit of Snowdrift Mountain and Trapper Cabin from the junction of the west-side trail on top of the ridge, walk north along the ridgetop trail. Along the way, the trail passes through grasses, brush, and scattered firs and aspens. In the summer, the brushy areas boast plentiful wildflowers. What the ridge top lacks in forest it makes up in views of the surrounding countryside. On clear days you can see Wyoming's Salt River Range to the east and the Bear River Range to the west and southwest.

Immediately below on the east side is the deep and wide Crow Creek valley at 6,700 feet, with a large ranch near the valley floor. On the west side is the deep, narrow Georgetown Canyon.

Once on the top, to make the through trip to Trapper Cabin walk north along the ridgeline trail, which is mostly easy. Some parts of the trail wind around rocky outcrops that offer superior perches for looking at the view. The ridge gradually descends, about 200 feet every mile for 3.8 miles. Then it widens and begins to switchback down the west side. At 8,300 feet, 6.2 miles from the trailhead, the trail forks. The left fork continues down the west side to the mining road and below it to the Georgetown Canyon Road. The right fork, which is not shown on any map, leads north down a canyon with a little stream in it. This creek is a branch of the South Fork of Deer Creek that flows into the Crow Creek valley. The trail follows this canyon for 1 mile to Trapper Cabin. Trapper Cabin sits at 7,600 feet at the mouth of the canyon. It is a medium-size picturesque cabin with a Keep Out notice that says it is used by federal natural science researchers.

Twenty yards from the cabin a jeep road heads north for .2 mile to intersect Road 146, the Wells Canyon Road, which is a good gravel road. The jeep road at the cabin is under water much of the year and can be very muddy. West on Road 146 about 200 yards is an intersection with the Georgetown Canyon Road (105) which is the road you took to reach the mine dump at the beginning of the hike. From the intersection with Road 146, Road 105 climbs south uphill for 1.25 miles, then goes 4.5 miles down to the mine area.

If you'd like to take one of the east-side trails to the top of the Snowdrift Mountain Ridge, drive along Road 146 beyond the Trapper Cabin turnoff for 4 miles. Then turn right on Road 111 and drive 2.5 miles to the Clear Creek Guard Station. (If you need information get it ahead of time, for the station usually is not staffed.) From it a trail leads west up Clear Creek to the top of the Snowdrift Mountain ridge and the trail along it. To reach Meade Peak from this side, drive .3 mile south of the guard station on Road 111 and turn right (west) on a jeep road (698). Go 1.5 miles to the trailheads for the Beaver Dam and Crow Creek trails, which are about .2 mile apart. Both trails lead to Meade Basin and Meade Peak. Going up one of these trails and down the other makes a 9.5-mile loop.

Bear River Range

77. BLOOMINGTON LAKE AND THE HIGH LINE TRAIL

Round trip: 1.6 miles for lake, 3 miles more for viewpoint on High Line Trail
Elevation gain: 120 feet for lake, 540 feet for viewpoint
Elevation loss (return climb): 40 feet for lake, 120 feet for viewpoint
Highest point: 8,000 feet at viewpoint
Time: 1 to 2 hours for lake, 3 hours for viewpoint
Difficulty: easy
Maps: USGS topographic: Paris Peak; Forest Service: Caribou National Forest
Information: Montpelier Ranger District
Getting there: From U.S. Highway 89 on the west side of Bear Lake, turn west at Bloomington on the Bloomington Canyon Road (409), which is washboard gravel for 4.3 miles. Beyond that, the road is primitive with rocks, ruts, and steep sections. A high-clearance vehicle is recommended, but four-wheel drive isn't needed. Avoid turnoffs to Paris Peak at 7.8 miles and the Middle Fork of Bloomington Canyon at 8.1 miles. At 10.5 miles, in a big grassy basin called Telegraph Flat, the road splits. Take the left branch to the trailhead at 11.5 miles.

Striped 600-foot limestone cliffs fall into the south side of Bloomington Lake. Above the emerald water, the trunks of subalpine firs, Englemann spruces, and limber pines grow from cracks in the cliffs. To the right of the big cliffs, snowbanks cling to the mountain wall until late summer. The near side of the lake is choked with willows, grasses, and wildflowers, which in August include purple horsemint and lupine, lavender aster, yellow arnica, red paintbrush, and pink wild geranium.

A high point on the nearby High Line Trail samples the view from this trail with only modest effort. The High Line Trail runs north and south for 55 miles along the crest of the Bear River Range from Soda Point near Soda Springs at the north end to the Beaver Creek Campground 2 miles from the Utah border. From this high point you can see a corner of Bear Lake's brilliant turquoise water. The lake was first named Black Bear Lake by fur trapper Donald McKenzie in 1818.

The Bear River Range is unique because the Bear River runs on both sides of it. The source of the river is in Utah. It flows north into Wyoming and Idaho, where it picks up water flowing out of Bear Lake and continues north. Then it makes a great curve west and south near Soda Springs. From there it flows south

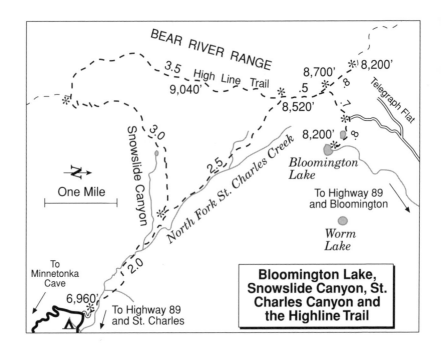

into the Great Salt Lake. The valley along the lower part of the river in Utah and Idaho near Preston and Franklin west of Bear Lake is the Cache Valley. The valley got its name when a man working for the Rocky Mountain Fur Company was buried alive while excavating a cache of furs in a cave. The Cache Valley was first settled in 1859 by Mormon settlers sent by Brigham Young.

From the high point on the High Line Trail near Bloomington Lake, miles of ridges covered with pale green grass, sagebrush, and wildflowers extend north and south. In August the wildflowers include magenta fireweed, purple horsemint, yellow cinquefoil, lavender Englemann aster and blue delphinium. In the distance to the east shimmers the tip of Bear Lake.

To reach Bloomington Lake from the trailhead, take the signed trail, which is shown on the topographic map as a road. It is a rock-strewn path that goes east up a ridge. From the top of the 100-foot ridge, a round pond appears below. The topographic map shows the trail going to the right around the south side of the pond. However, a better and shorter trail leads from the end of the old road to the left around the east side of the pond. On that side at .5 mile a side trail joins from the South Fork of Bloomington Creek. That trail provides access to the lake when the higher part of the road is muddy or snow-covered. Beyond this junction, the main trail passes a smaller pond and joins the trail shown on the map. Then it leads up the right (west) side of the outlet to the lake at .8 mile.

To reach the High Line Trail viewpoint from the Bloomington Lake trailhead, turn right (southwest) up a jeep trail that enters the woods and becomes a pack trail at .4 mile. The trail climbs steeply, curving south to the High Line Trail at .7 mile. From here it is .6 mile south to the junction with the trail down St. Charles Canyon, which is covered in Hike 78.

168

To reach the viewpoint, go north instead. The High Line Trail goes along the side of an open ridge. At .8 mile beyond the junction the trail jogs west. Here 1.5 miles from Bloomington Lake the trail is on a high point with an excellent view. A 6-mile loop hike can be taken from here by continuing north along the High Line Trail to a jeep trail at 2.7 miles and then descending it to the Bloomington Lake Road in Telegraph Flat and hiking back up the road to the trailhead.

78. ST. CHARLES CANYON, THE HIGH LINE TRAIL, AND SNOWSLIDE CANYON

Round trip to Bloomington Lake: 13 miles
Loop trip up North Fork of St. Charles and back down Snowslide Canyon: 11 miles
Elevation gain: 1,780 feet for Bloomington Lake, 2,080 feet for loop trip
Elevation loss (return climb) on route to Bloomington Lake: 500 feet
Highest point: 8,700 feet on Bloomington Lake trip; 9,040 feet on loop trip
Time: 8 hours for Bloomington Lake, 7 hours for High Line Trail loop
Difficulty: strenuous
Maps: USGS topographic: Paris Peak, Egan Basin; Forest Service: Caribou National Forest
Information: Montpelier Ranger District
Getting there: Drive south toward St. Charles on U.S. Highway 89 and turn right (west) at the sign for Minnetonka Cave, .5 mile north of St. Charles. Drive 7 miles west on the paved road (412) and turn right on the first dirt road past the Big Creek Group Area sign about 50 yards down the road. There is no sign for the North Fork Canyon; only for the Middle Fork Canyon beyond it. Drive .2 mile to a large turnaround and parking area with a pit toilet.

Every year thousands of visitors flock to the campgrounds and boat docks of giant Bear Lake, which straddles the Idaho-Utah border south of Montpelier. This area boasts beautiful state parks, good fishing, great water sports, giant caves, interesting historical sites, and a surprisingly large mountain range, the Bear River Range, just to the west.

If you make Bear Lake a summer destination, set aside some days to explore trails in this range, such as the trail up the North Fork of St. Charles Canyon and the trail up Snowslide Canyon. You can made a loop by going up one of these trails, then along an up-and-down section of the High Line Trail, and down the other trail. The High Line Trail runs 55 miles along the crest of the range, up and down forested and wildflower-covered hills. A side trip will take you to Bloomington Lake, a popular subalpine lake halfway surrounded by steep slopes and cliffs. St. Charles Canyon is named for the nearby town that commemorates Charles Rich, who was sent by Brigham Young to colonize the Bear Lake Valley.

The trail up the North Fork of St. Charles Canyon is off the same road that leads to the Minnetonka Cave. There are four Forest Service campgrounds up this canyon. One is a group site. The trail is an interesting route to the popular Bloomington Lake. A couple of large boulders mark the trailhead on the northwest end of the parking area. The creek is on your right at the trailhead. Most of the first two miles is wide enough for two people to walk side by side.

169

One of the giant trees in Snowslide Canyon in the Bear River Mountains

The trail follows the creek west for .2 mile and crosses it on a sturdy footbridge to the right (north) side. Then the trail climbs 100 feet and crosses a small side creek. Most of the canyon is heavily forested with firs and occasional aspens. Willows and cottonwoods choke the banks of the creek.

After 1.2 miles the trail crosses the creek back to the south side on another nice footbridge. Fords for horses are nearby at each of these footbridges. Within .2 mile the trail crosses the side creek coming from Snowslide Canyon. Here the bridge is just logs laid across to islands. On the other side of this creek the trail is much narrower.

The trail forks at 2 miles. One trail goes up Snowslide Canyon from here and one goes up the North Fork of St. Charles Creek. To begin this loop, take the trail to the right. It goes on the left side of St. Charles Creek for 1.2 miles and then crosses the creek. After this crossing the route continues on the right side of the creek for the next mile. At the top of the canyon it turns west and begins to climb. Near the top of the ridge, the trail meets the High Line Trail in a four-way intersection at 4.5 miles. To the west 2 miles is the Willow Flat campground. To the south, the High Line Trail goes 4 miles over an unnamed pass to Road 415 in Egan Basin.

To reach Bloomington Lake, turn north at the four-way intersection and go .5 mile to where a side trail turns right (east) toward the lake. Take this trail, which heads downhill off the ridge, becomes a jeep trail, and reaches the trailhead for the lake in .7 mile. From there it's .8 mile more to the lake. For a description of the lake and hiking to it from the trailhead, see Hike 77, Bloomington Lake and the High Line Trail.

To complete your loop, after seeing the lake retrace your steps to the four-way intersection at the top of the trail up St. Charles Canyon. Then hike south up and down along the High Line Trail for 3.5 miles to a junction with Snowslide Canyon Trail. Take this trail, which descends steeply for a mile, then more gently in thick forest for 2 miles to the junction of the Snowslide and St. Charles Canyon trails, where you started the loop. Some of the trees are more than three feet in diameter.

In the second mile there is a cave off the trail that is difficult to locate, especially if there is still much snow. Look for the cave to the right (south) of the trail a few hundred yards up the side of the canyon.

Bannock Range

79. CITY CREEK

Round trip: 6 miles to camping area; 10 miles to top of Kinport Peak
Elevation gain: 3,242 feet
Highest point: 7,222 feet
Time: 9 hours for top of peak
Difficulty: strenuous for top of peak
Maps: USGS topographic: Pocatello South; Forest Service: Caribou National Forest
Information: Department of Recreation, City of Pocatello
Getting there: In Pocatello, find Benton Street. This road crosses Highway 30/91 in the center of town. Drive southwest on Benton Street and cross the overpass over the railroad tracks. Two blocks past the bridge over the river turn left on Johnson Avenue and drive one block to Grant Avenue where there is a small parking lot at the trailhead accessible from May 15 to November 15. In other months, park at nearby Centennial Park on Grant Avenue. Parking is not allowed in the LDS Church parking lot on Grant Avenue. Additional parking can be found along the paved part of the City Creek Road which is reached by turning onto Lincoln Street from Johnson Street.

The City Creek Trail is a fun half-day or day trip right out of the town of Pocatello into the nearby foothills. This trail attracts hikers and mountain bikers throughout the spring, summer, and fall.

Because this trail leaves from a city street it can get a lot of use, especially on weekends. To avoid crowds, go early in the morning, preferably before 8 a.m. At that time you are more likely to see deer, elk, grouse, and even moose. On fall weekends, go during an Idaho State University football game and there will be a

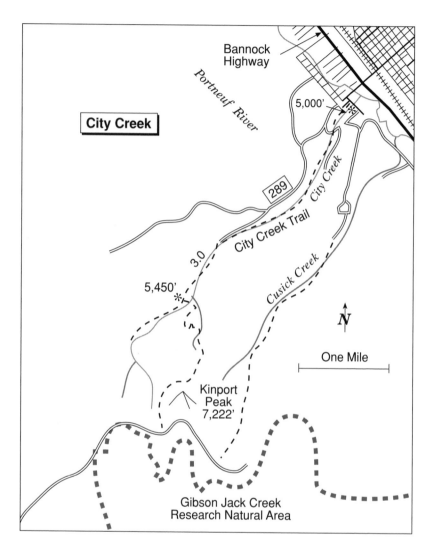

City Creek

Bannock Highway

Portneuf River

5,000'

289

City Creek Trail

City Creek

3.0

5,450'

Cusick Creek

N

One Mile

Kinport Peak 7,222'

Gibson Jack Creek Research Natural Area

mere two or three people.

City Creek flows northeast and enters town on the southeast side before join-ing the Portneuf River. The creek is small and shallow, but runs year-round except maybe in drought years. It can easily be jumped in most places.

From the trailhead on Grant Avenue, the trail starts out paralleling the south (left) side of the creek and heads up the draw. You will pass a much larger sign announcing the City Creek Trail. About 200 yards from the start, the wide trail forks. Keep right and cross the footbridge over the creek.

Unlike many mountain streams, City Creek doesn't traverse a deep wooded canyon. Instead it flows though a shallow draw. Along the draw is a thick ribbon of maples, aspens, and willows. Outside of the draw it is practically barren, with only grasses and brush growing on the hillsides. For the most part, the trail winds along next to the creek inside this ribbon of lush growth. In the fall, you'll walk on a carpet of fallen leaves.

The trail is mostly a gentle up and down, but it has a steady uphill gain. Mountain bikers will probably have to push their bikes from time to time.

After the first mile, the trail comes out onto a dirt road. Follow the dirt road about 100 yards. Take the footbridge on your left and re-enter the ribbon of forest on the single-track trail.

Here there are more aspens with occasional firs mixed in. This section feels like a tunnel through the thick canopy. The trail winds along with some nice downhill stretches to help hikers catch their breath and keep bikers on their toes.

After another mile the trail opens into an obvious camping and picnic area between the trail and the nearby dirt road. This is a good turnaround point.

We suggest that bikers not ride back down the trail. Instead, take the dirt road back to town. The potential for head-on collisions on the trail is great. The next blind corner may hide a hiker or another biker. If you can't resist riding back down the trail, be very cautious and go slowly.

From the camping/picnic area you can extend your trip by riding or walking up the dirt road to another side trail. This trail follows the creek to where it forks. At the fork, the left trail heads south uphill toward Kinport Peak (7,222 feet). This trail eventually hooks into a dirt road that accesses radio transmission facilities near the summit of Kinport Peak.

The trail to the right, which follows the main flow of City Creek, continues to parallel the stream for another half-mile before disappearing into a game trail. Both of these extensions receive much less use, especially by bikers. Expect the going to be rougher and steeper. There is also a jeep trail in Cusick Creek just southeast of City Creek that provides a loop trip from near the summit of Kinport Peak.

80. SCOUT MOUNTAIN NATURE TRAIL AND THE EAST MINK TRAIL

Round trip: 4 to 7 miles (11 miles to top of mountain)
Elevation gain: 800 feet to pond, 1,200 feet to Scout Mountaintop Road, 2,400 feet to top of mountain
Highest point: 8,600 feet at top of mountain
Time: 4 1/2 hours to pond, 9 hours to top of mountain
Difficulty: easy to strenuous
Maps: USGS topographic: Scout Mountain; Forest Service: Caribou National Forest
Information: Westside Ranger District
Getting there: Go south on Interstate 15 from the junction of Interstate 86 with Interstate 15 at Pocatello for 10 miles to Exit 63, signed Portneuf and Mink Creek Recreation areas. Turn right (south) on the Fort Hall Mine Road; then follow the signs to the recreation area. At .6 mile turn right onto the Bannock Highway (North Old Highway 91). At 1.8 miles turn left onto the paved Mink Creek Road (281). At 6.5 miles turn left on the Forest Service road (001). Continue up

173

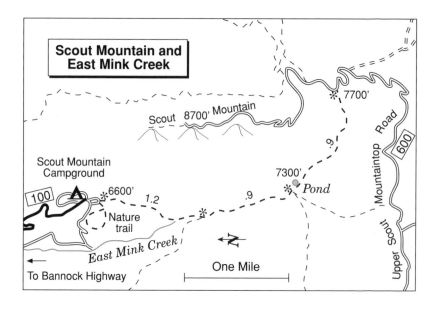

Scout Mountain and East Mink Creek

the East Fork of Mink Creek on this paved road to the Scout Mountain Campground at 11.8 miles. Instead of turning into the campground, keep right on Road 002. In 100 yards, turn left up to the day-use picnic area and park in the trailhead parking lot.

From this parking area a half-mile nature trail winds west up onto a low ridge, giving a quick overview of Scout Mountain. Brochures for the trail are available at the Caribou National Forest office in Pocatello. The trail features aspen, pine grass, Douglas fir, shrubs such as chokecherry and serviceberry, the limestone, quartzite, dolomite and shale of the bedrock, and a squirrel food storage site, or midden. You also get a view of the crumbled cliffs of Scout Mountain.

The wildflowers grow tall and thick along both the nature trail and the East Mink Trail, and they are one of the rewards of hiking these trails. In June they include yellow arrowleaf and balsamroot and mule's ears, pale blue wild forget-me-not, red scarlet gilia, pink wild rose, and white flowering shrubs like serviceberry. By August there are purple lupine, pink wild geranium, purple horsemint, yellow groundsel, and lavender aster.

The East Mink Trail offers a closer view of Scout Mountain. The mountain is a long flattish ridge with jumbled cliffs near the top, and shrubs, aspen, and talus below them. This trail leads from the trailhead to the Scout Mountain Top Road south of the peak. A pond along the trail is pretty in June when it is full and has little algae.

To reach the trailhead for this trail follow the access directions above. Beside the first access road is the Portneuf River, which was named for one of Peter Skene Ogden's Hudson Bay Company trappers who was killed there in 1826.

From the parking area for Scout Mountain, walk a few yards beyond the nature trail trailhead to the end of the loop road. The trail starts in a forest of Douglas fir, aspen, willow, elderberry, and bracken fern. It climbs gently, then contours along

174

the side of the ridge. At .9 mile it drops into a little canyon and crosses two small streams. There is no evidence of the trail shown on the map coming up this canyon from the scout camp, but at 1.2 miles the Valve House Draw Trail comes in from the right (west).

At 1.5 miles is an open ridgetop with a view east of Scout Mountain. From here the trail contours along in aspens and firs to a junction at 2 miles. Here a trail that has come up Box Canyon from the west crosses the main trail and continues a short distance above the grassy banks of a pond. From this junction, a trail leading southwest cuts directly south to the Scout Mountain Top Road. The main trail passes the pond and curves east in the brush with a beautiful view of the top of the mountain. At 3 miles it joins the Scout Mountain Top Road. From there it is 2.5 miles farther to the top of Scout Mountain on this road.

81. WEST FORK OF MINK CREEK TRAIL

Round trip: 13.2 miles at Wild Horse Divide
Elevation gain: 1,326 feet
Highest point: 6,526 feet
Time: 9 hours
Difficulty: moderate to strenuous
Maps: USGS topographic: Clifton Creek, Pocatello South; ForestService: Caribou National Forest
Information: Westside Ranger District

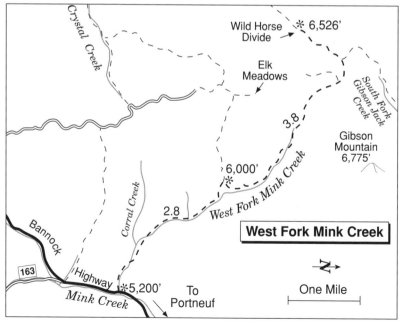

Relaxing on Gibson Mountain in the Mink Creek Recreation Area

Getting there: From Pocatello drive south on Interstate 15 from the junction of Interstate 15 with Interstate 86 for 10 miles and turn off at Exit 63, signed Portneuf and Mink Creek Recreation Area. Turn right (south) on the Fort Hall Mine Road and follow the signs to the recreation area. At .6 mile turn right onto the Bannock Highway (North Old Highway 91) and go north. At 1.8 miles turn left (west) onto the paved Mink Creek Road (281). Go 6.5 miles to the West Mink Creek trailhead about 50 yards south of the Valve House Draw trailhead. There is no sign except for the trail number, 059.

The West Fork of Mink Creek Trail follows the creek up a canyon forested with Douglas fir and aspen. Footbridges take care of the three stream crossings. A side trail turns west to Elk Meadows at 2.8 miles. The springs at the head of the creek at 4 miles are used for municipal water. That is the reason dogs are not allowed on the trail. At 5.5 miles, the trail joins a trail into the South Fork of Gibson Jack Creek. Then it curves southwest and climbs to the Wild Horse Divide at 6.6 miles. Part of the trail runs through the West Fork Mink Creek Research Natural Area. For this reason there is no motorized travel or camping in the area. However this trail, like the others in the area, is open to mountain bikes from mid-May through November.

Research Natural Areas are areas specially designated to preserve, in conditions as undisturbed as possible, representative biotic communities and their natural processes. These areas provide reference areas for study, for measuring ecological changes, and for determining the effects of management. This particular one was established to preserve the springs.

The Mink Creek Recreation area features year-round attractions including camping, biking, hiking, horseback riding, cross-country skiing, snowmobiling and other outdoor activities. There are two self-guided nature trails, one at Cherry Springs and the other near the Scout Mountain campground. In winter there are six snowmobile and ski trailheads. These winter trails are well-marked to keep the skiers and snowmobilers apart. To park at one of these trailheads in winter you need a Park 'n Ski sticker for your vehicle. Most sporting goods stores in Idaho sell the stickers.

176

82. OXFORD PEAK

Round trip: 12.6 miles from Davis Basin; 11 miles from Rockslide Canyon; 10 miles from Cherry Creek Campground
Elevation gain: 2,182 feet from Davis Basin; 3,442 feet from Rockslide Canyon; 3,482 feet from Cherry Creek Campground
Elevation loss (return climb): on Davis Basin route: 400 feet
Highest point: 9,282 feet

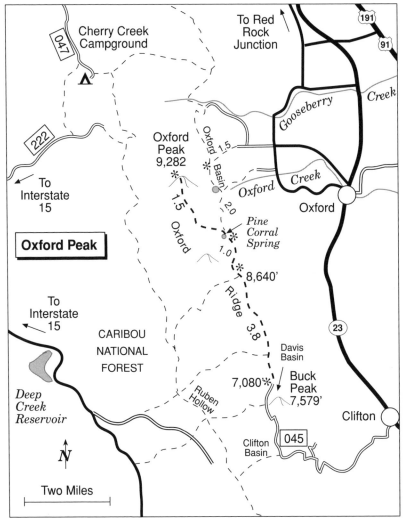

Time: 9 1/2 hours from Davis Basin; 10 hours from Rockslide Canyon
Difficulty: strenuous
Maps: USGS topographic: Oxford, Clifton; Forest Service: Caribou National
   Forest
Information: Westside Ranger District
Getting there: From Pocatello, drive south on Interstate 15 and take a left
(east) onto U.S. Highway 91 at the town of Virginia. Follow the signs southeast to
Downey. Drive 12 miles south from Downey to Red Rock Junction at Red Rock
Pass and keep straight ahead at the junction, following the signs to Oxford. From
the junction, drive 14 miles south past Oxford to the town of Clifton. Turn right
(west) on 100 South Street (follow the sign to the cemetery) and drive 7 miles on
the winding, steep road (Forest Road 045) to the Davis Basin trailhead. There are
three other ways to reach Oxford Peak and they are discussed below at the end of
the description.

Oxford Peak is the summit of a long mountain ridge near the Idaho-Utah border that sits off by itself surrounded by valleys. It appears as though it was made
by two giant hands scooping the landscape together into a long, steep peak with
deep valleys on both sides. West of the 9,282-foot peak is Malad Valley; on the
east is Cache Valley with Oxford and Clifton. Although Oxford Peak is not as high
as most Idaho or Utah mountains, the deep valleys on either side of it make the
views and the dropoffs dramatic.

Red Rock Pass, where the road to Oxford turns off, is the place where prehistoric Lake Bonneville burst through to cause the Bonneville Flood on the Snake
River about 30,000 years ago.

The hike, bike or horseback ride to the top of Oxford Peak makes a great day
trip. It's a good beginner trip for aspiring mountain climbers and Boy Scout
groups. There isn't anything technical about the trip, but it can be a serious workout.

The route with the least climb goes from Davis Basin north along the crest of
the range to the summit. At Davis Basin the trail begins at the end of Road 045.
The vegetation in this area is a mixture of scrubby aspens, firs, and brush. Willows
surround the springs that feed tiny Davis Creek near the trailhead. The area shows
signs of overgrazing, so expect to see cattle.

The trail starts out in some gullies and climbs toward the Oxford Peak ridge
line. After nearly a mile the trail leaves the scrubby trees and climbs steeply to the
top of the bald, grassy ridge.

Once on the ridge you are rewarded with stunning views of the surrounding
valleys. The east side is impressive because the drop is much more abrupt. While
on the ridge, look for Devil Creek Reservoir, Deep Creek Reservoir, and Elkhorn
Peak to the west; and Twin Lakes Reservoir and the north end of the Bear River
Range to the east. You can see for more than 50 miles even on a hazy day.

The ridge is a continuous series of ups and downs. The trail follows the very
top of the ridge most of the way. There are a few shortcut trails around high points
that can save you some of the pain of gaining elevation only to lose it again. Much
of the trail has taken on the width of an ATV trail, but you will probably see more
horseback riders than ATVs.

For the first 3 miles Oxford Peak can't be seen because it is blocked by intermediate bumps along the ridge. It first comes into view as you approach Pine Corral Spring, which is below on your right. The spring can be recognized from afar
because it has been piped and feeds a large cattle trough that is usually surround-

178

ed by cows. The spring runs year-round and is clear and cold, but must be filtered or boiled to be safe for drinking.

Beyond the spring, the ridge climbs abruptly. Within a mile it has climbed to an intermediate peak that is only about 100 feet shorter than Oxford Peak. Here the trail becomes fainter. Beyond this peak the ridge drops steeply for .2 mile before resuming its final upward march to the top. Some of these ups and downs drain you psychologically as much as physically. Just when you've huffed and puffed up a short peak on the ridge, you find yourself heading back down and losing most of the height you just gained. Most of the ups and downs have to be endured because rocky, steep terrain off the sides of the trail makes shortcuts too difficult.

The nearer you get to the summit, the narrower the ridge becomes. When you are finally close enough to see the rock cairn that marks Oxford Peak, the ridge is only 10 to 20 yards wide. This allows you to see the views on both sides by simply turning your head.

Next to the cairn marking the high point is a jar stuffed with notes and business cards from climbers.

There are other approaches to the top. One more adventurous route takes off near the Cherry Creek Campground on the west side of the range north of the peak. It follows a trail east and south along the Middle Fork of Cherry Creek, passing the Left Fork at .5 mile and Mine Creek at 1.2 miles. Where Cherry Creek forks again at about 3 miles, turn northeast off the trail up onto a prominent ridge. Go east along this ridge, which climbs steeply to a point just north of the summit of Oxford Peak. This route requires a great deal of bushwhacking and path finding, but is only a 10-mile round trip. It isn't as visually interesting, but is an adventure. A topographic map is essential.

There are two more ways to reach Oxford Ridge. One is from the Third Creek Campground, which is reached from Malad via Forest Road 038. The other is from Aspen Hollow at the north end of the range, which is reached by the Cedar Knoll Road from Downey and Forest Road 050. Both are farther from the summit and have a greater elevation gain than the other routes.

83. WRIGHT CREEK NATIONAL RECREATION TRAIL

Round trip: 11 miles to top of Wakley Peak, 7.5 miles to top of Elkhorn Peak

Elevation gain: 2,721 feet to top of Wakley Peak; 2,495 feet for Elkhorn Peak

Highest point: 8,801 feet on summit of Wakley Peak; 9,095 feet on summit of Elkhorn Peak

Time: 10 hours for Wakley Peak, 7 hours for Elkhorn Peak

Difficulty: strenuous

Maps: USGS topographic: Wakley Peak, Elkhorn Peak; Forest Service: Caribou National Forest

Information: Westside Ranger District

Getting there: Eight miles north of Malad City on Interstate 15 take the Devil Creek Reservoir Exit 22. Drive north past the reservoir. Go 3 miles north of the reservoir on the paved road and turn left at the sign for Summit Campground.

179

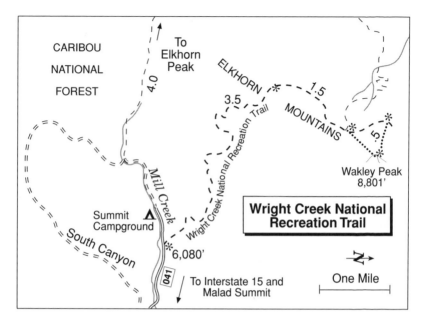

Cross the bridge over Interstate 15 and drive west on a dirt road for 1.5 miles (Forest Road 041). At that point, the road turns north and goes .5 mile before turning due west again. After another mile you will come to a fork in the road. The right takes you to the trailhead for the Wright Creek Trail. The left takes you 200 yards to the Summit Campground, a Forest Service campground that fills quickly on weekends.

The Wright Creek National Recreation Trail winds through a "mini" mountain range just north of Malad City. This range, the Elkhorn Mountains, is only 16 miles long and about six miles wide at its widest. Although not high by Western standards, the tallest peaks are all around a respectable 9,000 feet. They spawn dozens of creeks that run down into the surrounding dry valleys and grasslands. Because the range is small, it appears like an island surrounded by flat land. This means the view from the top is exceptionally good. You get impressive views of the Malad River valley to the west and the Marsh Valley to the east. The large reservoir on the west side is Daniels Reservoir. The two reservoirs on the east and southeast sides are Devil Creek and Deep Creek reservoirs.

The Wright Creek trailhead is on the right (north) side of the access road about .2 mile before you get to Summit Campground. There is a large parking area. The trail is open to hikers, horses, motorcycles, and ATVs. It is too steep to be good for mountain biking. Most of the trail has the wide-track ATV trail look, but relatively few people use it on the average early summer weekend.

The path quickly climbs into forest. The first 2 miles are steep, climbing from 6,100 to 7,500 feet. It is best to start out in early morning before the heat of the day makes the steep sections more difficult.

Most of the trail passes through scrubby aspens and firs until reaching the first saddle 2 miles up. From then on the trail begins to mellow out and even go downhill some. The trees are bigger and the forest thicker. For impressive views of the

180

valley below, turn around and look back occasionally.

At 3 miles the trail begins to swing north toward Wakley Peak and then climbs steeply again. Soon it crosses the crest of the range and continues along the other side of it just below the crest for the next 2 nearly level miles. Hiking become mostly easy as the trail becomes fairly level. Along this stretch the trail is in a thick spruce-fir forest — welcome shade on hot summer days. There are two springs along this section that have been piped into small troughs for cattle. Although it is spring water, you should filter or boil it.

At less than 5 miles take a faint side trail that heads up to the prominent ridge to your right. This route is not open to motorized travel. This trail fades away once you reach the ridge, but the route to the top of 8,801-foot Wakley Peak is obvious: Just follow the ridge for .5 mile to the top. The going is steep in places, but it is essentially a walkup.

At the top, a cairn marks the highest point. Inside the cairn is a jar stuffed with notes from previous visitors.

Below Wakley Peak on the west side, the main trail takes a right turn and descends a mile down a steep canyon to just above the base of the range. Here the trail heads south and connects with other trails at the base. You can reach Wakley Peak from this, the Wright's Creek side, via roads 044 and 043 and a connecting trail, which is not on the topographic map. By this route, Wakley Peak is about 2.5 miles and a 2,200-foot climb, but the access road is rough once you leave Wright Creek.

If you want to climb Elkhorn Peak, which is the highest point in the range, the most straightforward approach is by way of the trail up Mill Canyon, which starts 1 mile past Summit Campground on a poor dirt road.

From that trailhead, cross a bridge, take the trail to the right (northwest) and follow this steep path 1.5 miles to the crest of the range. Once on the ridge, follow the crest south 1.5 miles to the top of Elkhorn Peak. There is no trail along the ridge to the summit. This mountain is 9,095 feet and offers the best view of the entire area.

Portneuf Range

84. BOUNDARY TRAIL

Loop trip: 35 miles for the whole trail; 6.2 miles one way from Pebble Creek

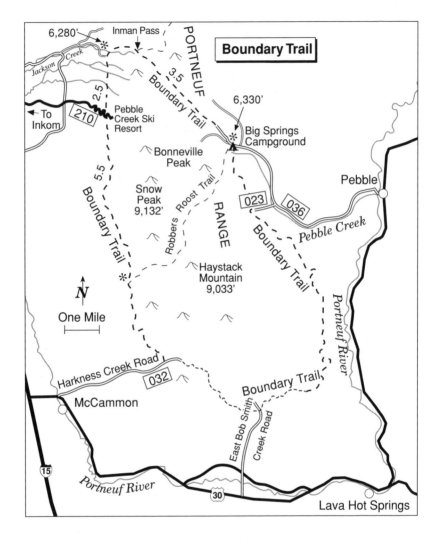

Ski Area to Big Springs Campground; 5.5 miles one way from the ski area to the Robbers Roost Trail

Elevation gain: 1,200 feet for section from Pebble Creek to Big Springs; 500 feet for section from ski area to Robbers Roost

Highest point: 7,600 feet at Inkom Pass

Time: 5 hours for going from Pebble Creek to Big Springs; 4 hours for going from Pebble Creek to Robbers Roost

Difficulty: Moderate to strenuous

Maps: Bonneville Peak, Bearcamp Gulch, McCammon, Haystack Mountain, Caribou National Forest

Information: Westside Ranger District

Getting there: From Pocatello, drive 12 miles south on Interstate 15 and take the Inkom exit to the Pebble Creek Ski Resort. This road passes under the interstate. Turn left, following the signs up to the ski resort on Green Canyon Road. Drive 3.5 miles to the first big parking area where there is a sign for the Boundary Trail. In spring, summer, and fall there is plenty of parking, but in winter downhill skiers crowd the parking lot, especially on weekends. To reach the trail from the east side, drive 21 miles south of Pocatello on Interstate 15 and take the exit to McCammon onto Highway 30. Drive 12 miles from McCammon to Lava Hot Springs. One mile past town turn left (north) and go 10 miles to the railroad siding of Pebble. Here turn left (west), enter the national forest at 1 mile and go 7 more miles on Forest Road 036 to Big Springs Campground, where there are signs for the trail. There are several other access points for the trail, and they are mentioned below.

The Boundary Trail in the Portneuf Range east of Pocatello offers attractions for most interests and abilities. It is open to hikers, bikers, horseback riders, motorcyclists, ATVers and skiers. The views of the Portneuf River valley are pretty: peaceful farms and quiet curves of river. The Portneuf River makes a U-shaped bend at the south end of the range. Thus the river runs on both sides of the range, and you will have the curious experience of looking out into the valley of the same river from both the west and the east sections of the trail.

The slopes beside the west-side trail are mostly sagebrush and grasses highlighted with a few junipers. Beside the streams in the little canyons grow aspen and fir. From near Inkom Pass at the north end you get views of the Bannock Range to the west. The east-side trail offers welcome shade but fewer views because it is mostly in the forest. From it you look out to the Chesterfield Range on the east. The southern part of the trail has almost no trees except along the creeks, so that section is best for cool days. In spring, wildflowers color the landscape all along the trail. Fishing in Pebble Creek near the Big Springs Campground is good.

From the ski resort parking lot, the trail travels north under a ski lift. After 200 yards, it winds down the steep gully of Green Canyon. (This section is not recommended for skiers when it is icy.) After the trail climbs back out of the canyon, it continues due north. Two miles from the parking lot the trail crosses Road 314 and then Jackson Creek.

From here the trail climbs up the north side of Jackson Creek canyon and heads east to Inkom Pass. During the one mile from where the trail crosses Jackson Creek to the pass it climbs 800 feet. This is the steepest section of the hike.

The higher you get, the nicer the views become, especially of the Bannock Range to the west. As the trail climbs Jackson Creek Canyon you see thick forests of fir and aspen down in the canyon and on the north-facing slopes. You are likely to see tracks of moose and deer in this section.

About two-thirds of the way up the canyon, the trail begins to switchback to the top of Inkom Pass. About .2 mile below the top there is a short side trail to an overlook of a section of the Portneuf River valley. At the top the trail levels. Near the pass in winter a yurt is operated by the ISU Recreation Department. The program operates three yurts in the Portneuf Range for a fee. The yurts sleep 6 to 8.

From Inkom Pass, the trail drops as it begins to swing southeast along the other side of the range. After less than .5 mile it enters thick forest, with breaks now and then that let you look out at the valley below. The trail continues southeast for 3.5 miles before reaching Big Springs Campground. There is a pleasant nature trail around Big Springs.

183

Backpackers looking for a loop trail back to the ski area can take the Robbers Roost Trail up and over the mountains. This 7-mile route starts at the Big Springs Campground and connects with the Boundary Trail on the west side of the range 5.5 miles south of the ski area. It is about a 1,900-foot climb to the top of the range from Big Springs Campground on the Robbers Roost Trail.

The southern section makes up the longest stretch of trail. It is about 2 miles from the Big Springs Campground to the intersection with the Robbers Roost Trail. This is a good trip for experienced mountain bikers. The route can be broken up into more manageable pieces with a little planning. Some possible routes such as East Bob Smith Creek and Reed Creek have no public access. Be sure to inquire first.

Access points from north to south on the west side of the range are Lower Rock Creek (Road 319), Upper Rock Creek (543), Robbers Roost, and Harkness Creek (032). On the east side from north to south there are Clear Creek (023), South Fork Pebble Creek (022), and Beach Hollow (034).

Albion Mountains

85. INDEPENDENCE LAKES

Round trip: 6 miles to end of trail at second lake; Add 1 mile round trip and 130 feet gain for higher lakes.
Elevation gain: 1,110 feet
Highest point: 9,168 feet
Time: 6 hours; add 1 hour for higher lakes.
Difficulty: moderate; expert for upper lakes
Maps: USGS Topographic: Cache Peak; Forest Service: Sawtooth National Forest
Information: Burley Ranger District
Getting there: On Idaho Highway 27, 17 miles south of Burley turn left (east) at Oakley. Drive past a turnoff to the City of Rocks at 1 mile. Continue to a junction at 6 miles where the pavement ends. Here, turn left on a dirt road (548), which leads to the Basin-Elba Pass at 11.4 miles. From the pass, turn right (southeast) onto a primitive road (562). After 1.7 miles in a little basin called The Pot Holes, turn left again on Road 728 and drive to the trailhead at 16.2 miles.

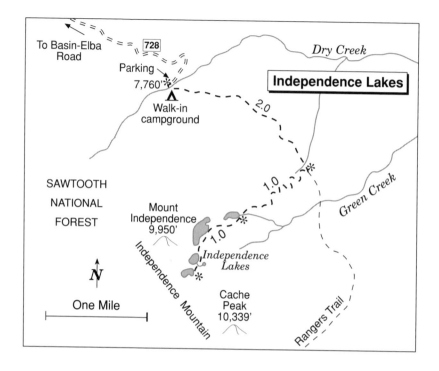

The forest around Independence Lakes is unique because it is only aspen at lower elevations and only subalpine fir higher up. At similar elevations elsewhere, there would also be Englemann spruce, and lodgepole and whitebark pine. In addition, some of the flowers, such as the brilliant magenta Parry primrose, are typical of Utah and Colorado. Except for Bloomington Lake near Paris, these lakes are the only high-elevation lakes in southeastern Idaho. They nestle under a long level ridge of granite ledges. In the center of the ridge, a square rock hat marks the summit of Independence Mountain, 9,050 feet.

At the trailhead there are walk-in campsites. The trail begins by going south between the campsites, which are beside Dry Creek, to join an old road at a T-intersection. Turn left (east) on this track, which soon dwindles to a trail. Follow it east and then south, through forest and across open hillsides. In the first 2 miles the trail climbs only 200 feet. From this first section, Mount Harrison can be seen to the north and the sagebrush-covered Jim Sage Mountains to the east.

At 2 miles a side trail to the lakes turns off the main, or Rangers, trail. The Rangers Trail makes a circle around both peaks and the lakes. It is mostly level and out in the open and gives you the feeling of being in a helicopter overlooking the valley along the way. Improvements are planned on this trail and on the lakes trail, so the Rangers Trail will be easier to find and the lakes trail less steep than described here.

To see the lakes, turn right (west) on the lakes trail. This trail has been rerouted into the band of trees north of where it is shown on the topographic map. It switchbacks over a dry creek, then in the last .2 mile rejoins the old trail shown on the map and goes straight up through thick fir forest. At 3 miles is the first lake,

185

which is surrounded by a wide band of marsh grass.

To reach the upper lakes, cross the outlet of the first lake on rocks and take the signed trail up a wooded ridge above the south side of the lake. On the open ridge top, the path becomes less distinct. At 3.5 miles the lower end of the second lake appears through the trees to the right (west). There are campsites here. Surrounded by big blocks of granite, the blue-green lake stands beneath the summit of Independence Mountain.

To reach the third lake, return to the dwindling path and follow it among granite boulders to the east side of the small round lake at 3.7 miles, which lies among turf and wildflowers. To reach the fourth lake, go south cross-country up a tiny inlet. The small lake in the subalpine firs and boulders is at 4 miles. Above it, snowbanks climb to a saddle between Independence Mountain and Cache Peak, 10,339 feet.

86. SKYLINE TRAIL ON MOUNT HARRISON

Through trip: 9 miles to Basin-Elba Road
Elevation gain: 720 feet
Elevation loss: 1,920 feet
Highest point: 8,300 feet
Time: 7 hours
Difficulty: moderate to strenuous
Maps: USGS topographic: Connor Ridge, Mount Harrison; Forest Service: Sawtooth National Forest
Information: Burley Ranger District
Getting there: From Idaho Highway 77, 5.3 miles south of Albion turn right (west) on the Pomerelle Ski Area Road (Forest Road 549), which is paved as far as the ski area. Continue beyond the ski area turnoff at 8.2 miles. Drive to the

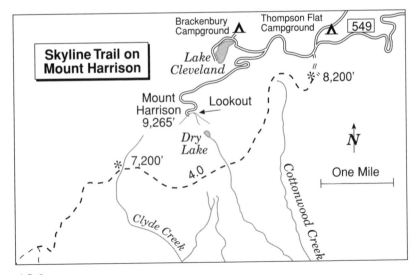

turnoff for the Twin Lakes trailhead. Turn left (south) here and go .3 mile on a dirt road to the trailhead.

This trail begins at rock outcrops resembling stacks of pancakes and goes along under the orange cliffs of Mount Harrison. In mid-July the mountainside is purple with lupine and little-leaf penstemon. At times the trail passes through groves of stunted aspen and mats of snowbrush. It overlooks the valley near Almo and Cache Peak and the dark wooded hills around it. This trail is relatively new and is still being worked on. Four and-a-half miles were improved in 1997, and more miles in 1998. Mount Harrison is named for President Benjamin Harrison, who won the election of 1888 over Grover Cleveland, for whom nearby Lake Cleveland is named.

To reach the trailhead, follow the access direction above. Before or after the hike, be sure to drive to the lookout on Mount Harrison for a 360-degree view. Below the peak, Lake Cleveland with its ropy orange cliffs is also fun to visit.

The first half of the trail is not shown on the topographic or forest maps. It descends west from the trailhead at first, to circle the head of Cottonwood Creek at .5 mile. Then it heads southwest, contouring down along the side of Mount Harrison through the lupine and penstemon.

At 1 mile the way goes above thick groves of stunted aspen. At 2 miles it crosses a tiny stream, and at 2.5 miles comes to an open rocky area. The trail continues across brushy slopes and curves into the canyon of Clyde Creek and crosses it at 4 miles. Then the trail climbs a few feet into a 7,600-foot saddle at 4.5 miles.

From here on, the route connects old jeep trails on a wooded ridge, keeping above New Canyon at 5.5 miles and Flat Canyon at 7 miles. At 9 miles the trail descends to the Basin-Elba Road at the summit of that road. From that summit, it travels primarily on an existing low-standard dirt road, eventually ending at the northwest edge of the City of Rocks in the Indian Grove area. From the Basin-Elba summit it is 12 miles to the City of Rocks.

87. CITY OF ROCKS: BOXTOP TRAIL, STRIPE ROCK, LOST ARROW, AND FLAMING ROCK

Loop trip: 3.3 miles
Elevation gain: 620 feet
Elevation loss (return climb): 720 feet
Highest point: 6,320 feet
Time: 3 1/2 hours
Difficulty: easy
Maps: USGS topographic: Almo; City of Rocks trail map
Information: City of Rocks National Reserve
Getting there: From Interstate 84, 9 miles east of Burley, turn south at the exit for the Pomerelle Ski Area. Follow Highway 77 to an intersection (at the Connor Creek Store) at 22.8 miles. Turn right (west) onto the Elba-Almo Road and continue to the City of Rocks headquarters at 38.7 miles. From there follow signs for the City of Rocks, turning right at 39.2 miles, and keeping right at the road to the Twin Sisters at 43.3 miles. At 43.8 miles turn right (north) into campsites 13-26.

Then turn right again and go east to the trailhead.

This loop leads past dramatic rocks such as the Boxtop, Dolphin, Stripe Rock, and the Lost Arrow. It samples the typical trees and plants, such as sagebrush, prickly pear, piñon pine, juniper, aspen and red osier dogwood. Stripe Rock is an enormous rounded triangle set by itself at the edge of the green pastures of the Circle Creek Valley. The return trail passes beside the lopsided Lost Arrow, and the red-streaked cliffs of Flaming Rock. As you approached the City of Rocks you followed the approximate route of the California Trail. The first European to see the City of Rocks was fur trapper Peter Skene Ogden in 1826. Emigrants began to come through on their way to California in 1843. The pass known as Pinnacle Pass, a mile east of the main road at the Twin Sisters, was crossed by 52,000 wagons in 1852. On the pass there are grooves in the granite left by the block and tackle used to let down the wagons, but the pass is not accessible to visitors because of private land. Near a formation known as the Twin Sisters, the route of the Kelton-Boise stage line crosses the California Trail. This stage line from Salt Lake City to Boise and Walla Walla was established by Ben Holladay in 1863.

From the Boxtop Trailhead, the trail out to Stripe Rock curves north and descends through sagebrush, prickly pear, piñon, and juniper. In mid-June the cactus blooms with yellow or magenta blossoms. The path curves left (north) past outcrops into the canyon of the South Fork of Circle Creek. At .5 mile it crosses the tiny South Fork, and at .6 mile the South Fork of Circle Creek Trail leads off to the left (west). The trail climbs a little ridge beside the Boxtop and the Dolphin (which is on private land) and on top of the ridge goes through a gate at .8 mile.

The route then winds downhill, passing a side trail to the Center Fork of Circle Creek at .9 mile. The trail to Stripe Rock keeps straight ahead. At 1.1 miles it crosses the Center Fork of Circle Creek and goes down right out into the sagebrush toward Stripe Rock. On the right (east) now is a table-shaped tower called The Cyclops. To the left the Lost Arrow raises its crooked face.

Just past the Cyclops at 1.2 miles an old road comes in from the east. This is now a trail coming in from the Circle Creek Overlook. Where the road crosses the trail, it jogs 50 feet south. Notice the jog, because it will take you to the Lost Arrow and the return trail. If you go out toward Stripe Rock to about the 1.4-mile point, there is an excellent view of the rock ahead. Cliffs on the left and curved granite on the right make it resemble an ocean breaker. The trail continues .3 mile around the east side of the rock to the North Fork of Circle Creek Road at 1.7 miles. This is an old road that has been converted to a horse and bicycle trail.

To complete the loop go back to the jog in the intersection with the old road at the Cyclops at 1.6 miles. Turn right (west) and go along the faint old road. Within a few yards it becomes definite. The track soon reaches the base of the Lost Arrow and circles it on the south, dwindling to a trail. The trail passes a side path to the Lost Arrow and then an unmarked intersection. (The trail leading south across the creek here is the other end of the one that left the Boxtop Trail at .9 mile.) Keep straight ahead here. At 2 miles, at a sign for the Lost Arrow, the trail curves left down rock steps and crosses to the south side of the Center Fork.

From the creek, the trail switchbacks south up through junipers and aspens and past outcrops to the top of a hill at 2.3 miles. Here it goes through a gate and descends into a valley of aspens.

At an unmarked Y, where a path goes off to the right to the Bumblie Wall, keep straight ahead. Ahead on the left (east) is the high wall of the Transformer. At the next intersection turn right, and then right again. In a few feet, at 2.7 miles, a trail turns left (south) to the South Fork of Circle Creek. Take that trail, which crosses

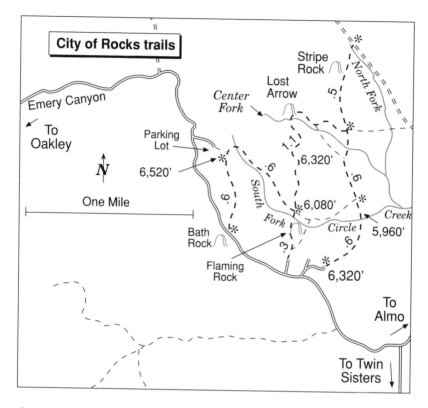

City of Rocks trails

the creek at 2.7 miles and becomes the Flaming Rock Trail.

Now the wall of Flaming Rock is ahead on the left (east), and the trail zigzags up beside it. The route turns right away from the rock and goes through a slot in the granite. Beyond this narrow canyon is a valley of sagebrush. In it at 2.9 miles a side trail turns left down to the creek. Keep straight ahead up a short steep slope to the parking area, and the campground for sites 30-39 at 3 miles. By road from here it is .3 mile back to the Boxtop trailhead. Like other hikes in the City of Rocks, in summer this hike is more enjoyable when taken in the early morning or evening because of the intense heat of midday.

88. CITY OF ROCKS: CREEKSIDE TOWERS AND THE SOUTH FORK OF CIRCLE CREEK

Through trip: 1.5 miles
Elevation gain: 280 feet
Elevation loss (return climb): 480 feet
Highest point: 6,560 feet
Time: 2 1/2 hours
Difficulty: easy

189

Hiking in the City of Rocks National Reserve

Maps: USGS topographic: Almo; City of Rocks trail map
Information: City of Rocks National Reserve
Getting there: Follow directions in Hike No. 87, Boxtop Trail, to campsites 30-39. Continue on the main road .8 mile to Bath Rock.

Under the Creekside Towers, a trail leads along a tiny creek in a grassy swale. Below towers with the fanciful names of The Anteater and Morning Glory Spire this trail joins one that leads down the South Fork of Circle Creek. The creek trail passes walls called The Drilling Fields, the Bumblie Wall, and the Transformer. At the Transformer hikers can climb the Flaming Wall Trail, which was described in the preceding hike, to complete a through trip.

Beginning at Bath Rock, the Creekside Towers Trail leads north. It comes to a five-way intersection in 100 yards. Here bear left, avoiding two paths to the right. The trail descends past a small arch. At .1 mile the route crosses the creek to the right. It then goes along in the grassy swale under the towers, climbing beside the stream. Beyond it, from a low knoll of crumbled granite, you can see the pitted prong of The Anteater ahead. Where the wall of the Creekside Towers ends, two paths go off to the right. Keep straight ahead here. At junctions with a trail and two paths to The Parking Lot on the left, keep straight ahead. The route cuts between the south end of The Parking Lot Rocks and the Anteater. Then it heads downhill along the back side of Parking Lot Rock. Where the trail meets another trail from the Parking Lot to the South Fork of Circle Creek at .5 mile, turn right (southeast) down the creek.

The trail crosses the creek to the left (east) side right away, then continues down the creek through aspens and beside towers. Within five minutes a path leads north to the Drilling Fields wall. Here the main trail turns right down granite steps and crosses back over to the west side of the creek.

On the far side of this crossing, the trail climbs a three-foot ledge, then turns 90 degrees left down the creek. The route continues southeast down the canyon, first through an open area with a view of the Circle Creek Valley and then through

190

aspen meadows. It crosses back to the east side at .8 mile, then passes an unsigned junction with the Stairways Trail to Bath Rock. From a steep hillside covered with mullein stalks you can see the granite wave of Flaming Rock ahead. A couple of paths lead left to the Bumblie Wall. By taking a side trip on the second path you can see a natural arch.

Along the main trail, the long wall of The Transformer sits at right angles to the creek. Just before it, an unsigned trail turns right (south) and crosses the South Fork of Circle Creek. This is the Flaming Rock Trail, covered in Hike 87, Boxtop Trail. Remember that summer hikes in the City of Rocks are more pleasant if taken in morning or evening.

Goose Creek Mountains

89. THIRD FORK OF ROCK CREEK

Through trip: 7 miles with car shuttle
Elevation gain or loss: 1,520 feet
Highest point: 6,727 feet at upper trailhead
Time: 7 hours
Difficulty: moderate
Maps: USGS topographic: Ramshorn Ridge, Trapper Peak; Forest Service: Sawtooth National Forest
Information: Twin Falls Ranger District
Getting there: Turn off Interstate 84 east of Twin Falls at the Hansen exit 182. Go south across the Snake River and turn left (east) at a sign for Hansen at 1.2 miles. At Hansen, at 3.3 miles, go straight ahead across the railroad tracks on the Rock Creek Road (County Road G3). At 24.1 miles turn left onto a gravel road signed "Third Fork Rock Creek" and park at the end of the road, at 24.7 miles.

This canyon is a beautiful place for spring and fall hiking, where lavish wildflowers or red- and yellow-leaved shrubs contrast with dark brown cliffs. The tops of the canyon walls are covered with aspen and the sides with scattered juniper. A curly thread of riparian shrubs and trees follows the creek. As you drive out the Rock Creek Road you cross a side road, which 1 mile to the east passes the Stricker homesite. In 1865 a stage station stood there, and before that travelers on the Oregon Trail stopped there. The emigrants named the creek Rock Creek.

The trail begins among the low grassy hills and benches above the creek. At 200 yards is a junction with a trail into Wahlstrom Hollow. At .5 mile outcrops across the canyon resemble a parade of elephants. At 1.2 miles the trail comes close to the creek in wild roses, clematis, and elderberries. Above is a rounded orange outcrop shaped like a skull.

At 1.7 miles the trail rounds a corner to the left and splits. Here take the middle one of three paths. It leads across the Second Fork of Rock Creek on a bridge to a sagebrush flat. Then the trail climbs a bluff and goes along it above streamside trees. At 2.4 miles it returns to the creek and bridges it to the right (west) side at 2.5 miles. Beyond the bridge, brown outcrops and towers loom ahead. The little meadow beyond the bridge makes a good destination for a day hike.

At 3 miles the trail passes under brown rock towers. At 4 miles a trail turns off to the right up the canyon of A H Creek, and at 5 miles a trail turns off up the Little Fork. At 5.5 miles is a tiny pond on the creek, and here the trail goes into a forest. The trail crosses back and forth over the creek at 6.7 miles, and at 7 miles it reaches Forest Road 500.

90. HARRINGTON FORK

Round trip: 5 to 14 miles (through trip 7 miles)

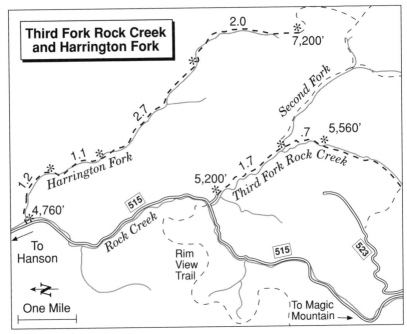

Elevation gain: 2,440 feet
Highest point: 7,200 feet
Time: 4 to 10 hours
Difficulty: easy to strenuous
Maps: USGS topographic: Grand View, Rams Horn Ridge, Trapper Peak; Forest Service: Sawtooth National Forest
Information: Twin Falls Ranger District
Getting there: From Interstate 84 east of Twin Falls take the Hansen exit 182. Go west, crossing the Snake River at .5 mile. At 1.2 miles turn left (south) at a sign for Hansen. At Hansen, at 3.3 miles, go straight ahead across the tracks and past a Sawtooth National Forest sign on Rock Creek Road (County Road G3). At 20.3 miles, at a sign for the Harrington Fork picnic area, turn left into the parking area.

The Harrington Fork of Rock Creek Canyon is smaller than that of the Third Fork, but narrower and more dramatic. It has a bottleneck of close cliffs at the beginning. Farther along, bands of jointed black and brown lava stairstep up the canyon walls. An old fire has left a ghost forest of dead junipers and removed most of the sagebrush. The vegetation consists of grasses, wildflowers, rabbitbrush, elderberry, wild rose, and aspen. Now and then the trail passes under lava outcrops resembling ships or castles.

The first 2 or 3 miles make a pleasant day hike, especially in the spring. Those more ambitious or on mountain bikes may wish to try the whole trail. The unsigned trail begins at the northeast end of the parking lot where it crosses to the north side of the creek on a bridge. By late summer there is water in the creek here but not farther up.

At 200 yards the trail enters the bottleneck amid a thicket of tall plants. Past this, it comes out onto an open grassy slope. At .5 mile are the first dead junipers.

At 1 mile the trail crosses the Dry Fork in a wide side canyon. Ahead the main canyon narrows and steepens. At 1.2 miles the trail fords the four-foot creek to the (right) west side. Below ghost junipers at 1.5 miles it fords back to the east. Now there are aspen and chokecherry, and on the opposite side a tower and a high band of cliffs. At 1.8 miles the trail passes under a 25-foot tower.

At 2.3 miles the route crosses back to the west side of the stream. At 3 miles it passes a large side canyon. A second side canyon is at 4 miles. At 5 and 5.3 miles the trail crosses back and forth over the creek, then enters forest. The spring that is the source of the creek is at 6.6 miles, and at 7 miles the trail crosses a primitive road that connects with Road 527.

Boulder Mountains

91. HUNTER CREEK SUMMIT

Round trip: 6.6 miles
Elevation gain: 1,280 feet
Highest point: 9,400 feet
Time: 6 1/2 hours
Difficulty: moderate
Maps: USGS topographic: Meridian Peak; Forest Service: Challis National Forest
Information: Lost River Ranger District
Getting there: From Idaho Highway 75 at Ketchum, turn east on Sun Valley Road. Go past Sun Valley and drive over Trail Creek Summit at 12 miles on Forest Road 408. (It is numbered 208 past the summit, where it is on the Challis National Forest.) After the end of the pavement at 8.4 miles the road is very bumpy and there are no guard rails. Continue to the North Fork of the Lost River Road (128) at 19 miles. Here turn left (north) and drive to a turnoff for Hunter Creek Summit at 31.4 miles. Turn right (north) and go 1.3 miles on a primitive road (477) to an undeveloped trailhead, which is .4 mile beyond the sign for the trail. In .2 mile, where the road divides, take the left branch. The road crosses a boggy meadow .7 mile beyond this split and then improves. If the meadow is dry enough so vehicles won't damage it, you can drive to the end of the road, at 32.7 miles.

The trail to Hunter Creek Summit gives access to a vast area of backcountry that is unused except by cattle and a few hunters. At the trailhead, you can look up the North Fork canyon to snow-streaked orange and gray peaks at the head of it. The trail climbs through wildflower meadows to a tiny meadow overlooking East Pass Creek. A better view of the canyon can be found on orange outcrops 200 yards north of the pass.

On the way to the trailhead, you drive over scenic Trail Creek Summit. The first European to cross this pass was the fur trapper Alexander Ross in 1825. He crossed it from the valley of the Big Lost River to the Big Wood River, which he called the River Malade. He gave it that name because most of his party got sick from eating some beavers they trapped there.

From the grassy flat at the end of the road, the trail climbs a steep sagebrush hill. Then it contours along through sagebrush and lodgepoles, and fords the creek to the west (left) side at .5 mile. An upstream foot log provides a way across in early summer.

The trail continues up the creek through lodgepoles and grassy swales, crossing a side stream within 150 yards. At 1 mile the route returns to the right (east)

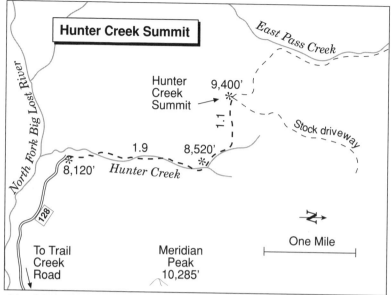

side of the main creek. There are several fords of the creek not shown on the topographic map, and this is one of them. Within a few yards the trail crosses two small side creeks, and then at 1.3 miles returns to the west bank of the main creek. Now dark lava ledges face the creek on the right. At 1.6 miles the way crosses to the right bank once more, and then another side stream.

At 1.9 miles the creek splits. Before the split, the trail crosses to the left side of the creek and turns left (west) up its left branch. It immediately crosses to the right side of that branch. Logs or rocks help with both crossings. At 2.1 miles the track goes over to the left side of the left branch in the last crossing shown on the map. There is now another creek off to the left. The trail switchbacks up well above the main branch in thick forest. The opposite side of the canyon is open sagebrush and outcrops.

At 2.3 miles the trail crosses to the right side of the creek, now only a couple of feet wide. It skirts the right side of a sloping meadow at 2.7 miles and arrives at the meadow on top of the pass at 3 miles.

For the best view be sure to go off to the right (northeast) for a couple of hundred yards on the stock driveway that leads along the ridge. The stock driveway is not on the map and is not the trail into East Pass Creek. That trail is very faint and drops northwest into the canyon from the small meadow on the pass.

92. NORTH FORK LAKE

Round trip: 4 miles
Elevation gain: 994 feet
Highest point: 9,354 feet
Time: 6 1/2 hours
Difficulty: expert

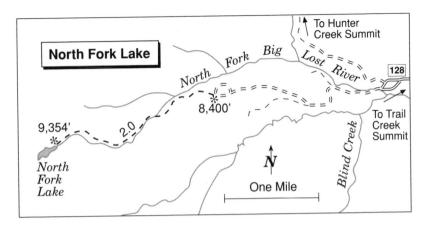

Maps: USGS topographic: Meridian Peak, Ryan Peak; Forest Service: Challis National Forest

Information: Lost River Ranger District

Getting there: From Idaho Highway 75 in Ketchum, turn east on Sun Valley Road. Go past Sun Valley and drive over Trail Creek Summit at 12 miles on Road 408 (208 past the summit). After the end of the pavement at 8.4 miles the road is very bumpy and there are no guardrails. At 20.6 miles turn left (west) on the dirt North Fork of the Big Lost River Road (128) and drive along it to Blind Creek at 30.8 miles. Turn left and cross to the south side of the North Fork on a bridge. Continue on a primitive road and take the right branch at 32 miles. At a split in the road at 32.9 miles, which forms a small loop, go left and park in aspens at 33.3 miles.

The aquamarine water of narrow North Fork Lake separates a gray mountain

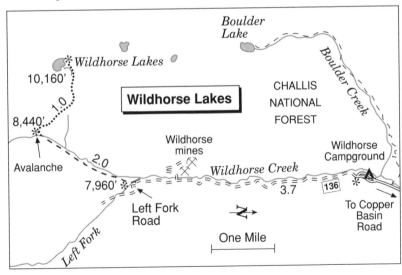

wall from an orange one. At the head of the lake, orange rock meets gray in a row of orange cylinders divided by strips of gray. Gray talus on the south side of the lake rises to a sheer gray wall, and orange talus on the north slopes goes up to a mottled orange mountain. Above the loop road where you park, red, orange, gray and cream stripes scribble the high peaks of the Boulder Mountains. Traces of an old trail exist, mostly on the left side of the creek. Volunteers plan to mark the route soon, so by the time you go to North Fork Lake the route may be a little different.

Begin the hike by walking southwest up the ridge for 200 yards. You can continue along the ridge to the lake, but downed timber and steep talus make it difficult. Instead, turn right off the ridge and gradually descend to the North Fork at .5 mile, where a side branch joins from the west. Once at the creek, climb left (southeast) a few yards onto a wrinkle to stay out of the creek's ravine. At a meadow at 1 mile ford the creek to the right (northwest). From here the route climbs ledges on a steep slope and then goes above a little gorge. Be especially careful here.

Above this, the slope lessens and the gorge widens opposite a slope of tiny firs and downed timber. At 1.3 miles go down to the creek and walk along the grass beside it. Keep well away from the creek at 1.5 miles as you climb a steep grassy hillside. After the ground flattens at 1.7 miles walk through grass to the lower end of the lake at 2 miles.

Pioneer Mountains

93. WILDHORSE LAKES

Round trip: 13.4 miles (2 miles cross-country); 6.0 miles in four-wheel drive
Elevation gain: 2,200 to 2,800 feet
Highest point: 10,160 feet
Time: 7 hours to 2 days
Difficulty: expert
Maps: USGS topographic: Standhope Peak, Phi Kappa Mountain; Forest Service: Challis National Forest
Information: Lost River Ranger District
Getting there: From Idaho Highway 75 at Ketchum, turn east on Sun Valley Road. Go past Sun Valley and drive over Trail Creek Summit at 12 miles on Road

Wildhorse Lake in the Pioneer Mountains

408 (208 past the summit). After the end of the pavement at 8.4 miles the road is very bumpy and there are no guardrails. Turn right (east) on the Copper Basin Road (135) at 21.8 miles. At 24 miles turn right (south) on the Wildhorse Canyon Road (136) and drive to the campground at 29.7 miles. Beyond the campground the road requires four-wheel drive.

After a rugged trip up the Wildhorse Canyon Road toward a Matterhorn-like peak, a trail leads to a meadow with a wonderful view of the dark thumb of Old Hyndman Peak and the rounded triangle and striped orange, cream and gray rock of Hyndman Peak. On the left side of the meadow an avalanche of logs and tiny trees pours into the grasses and wildflowers, which in season includes bistort-flowers that resemble popcorn.

From the end of the trail at the avalanche, a short climb up the side of the canyon brings you to a second meadow. It is enclosed by ledges, talus, and a chain of waterfalls. The first waterfall is wide and fluffy, the second curls in a curving ribbon, and the third draws a faint white line.

A climb over the ledges beside these waterfalls reaches the largest of the Wildhorse lakes. Above the upper end of this lake below a scalloped ridge, white lines on dark gray ledges resemble writing on a blackboard. Across the canyon of Wildhorse Creek from the lake's outlet you can see a pleated wall of gray and orange peaks.

To begin the hike from the campground, continue up the road in four-wheel drive or on foot, ignoring side roads. The trail mileage is figured from the campground. At 2.8 miles the road passes two cabins opposite the old Wildhorse Mine. Keep on to a split in the road at a sign for the Left Fork of Wildhorse Creek, at 3.7 miles. Park here if you haven't already parked.

At this point a blazed trail begins that is not shown on any maps. It starts out by fording the 25-foot-wide Left Fork of Wildhorse Creek to the right (west) side on slimy underwater slabs.

From the ford, the trail climbs along Wildhorse Creek, in a forest of Douglas fir, lodgepole pine and grouse whortleberry. At 200 yards is a fluffy 30-foot waterfall. At 4.7 miles from an open area with willows and a beaver pond you can see the dark tower of Old Hyndman Peak ahead. At 5.2 miles two side streams on the other side of the creek cascade into it 30 feet apart. A few yards later the creek splits in a Y. The trail climbs the left (east) side of the left branch, which is the main creek, to the avalanche of logs and the lower meadow at 5.7 miles.

Cross the creek here to the right (west) side on a logjam 25 yards downstream. Once across, note that any plastic streamers mark mining claims, not a trail. Turn northwest along the edge of the talus and climb .5 mile to the round meadow with

198

the waterfalls, which is shown as a marsh on the topographic map.

To reach the lake, climb the benches and rock ramps on the right side of the waterfalls angling away from them. This requires a little scrambling. On a shelf at 9,600 feet you can see a big waterfall on the creek between the lakes plunging down ledges to your left.

Angle to the right up a ramp towards a cliff face. About 100 feet below the cliff turn straight uphill and then go left up ledges and snowbanks. Soon you come out on another shelf with a creek running in little pools. This is the outlet of the lake, which is just ahead at 6.7 miles. Avoid camping at the lake, for the only sites are grassy and therefore fragile.

94. IRON BOG AND FISHPOLE LAKES FROM ANTELOPE VALLEY

Round trip: 5 miles
Elevation gain: 1,520 feet
Elevation loss (return climb): 80 feet
Highest point: 9,280 feet
Time: 5 to 6 hours
Difficulty: Moderate
Maps: USGS topographic: Smiley Mountain; Forest Service: Challis National Forest
Information: Lost River Ranger District
Getting there: On U.S. Highway 93, 11 miles north of Arco, turn left (west) on the Antelope Valley Road. The pavement ends at 4 miles and the improved road (135) becomes dirt at the turnoff for Antelope Guard Station and Copper Basin at 18 miles. Continue to Iron Bog Campground at 25 miles, and then go .1 more mile to a Y. Here take the left of the two primitive roads, Forest Road 220 signed for Iron Bog Lake. Continue to the unsigned trailhead at 28.2 miles. You may need four-wheel drive for the last .6 mile.

The black mountain rising from a gray rock layer above milky green Iron Bog Lake resembles an iron. Below it, a rocky peninsula extends into the lake. A half-mile farther on, grass and sagebrush hills hold the blue oval of Fishpole Lake. On the shore stand black and orange outcrops. Behind the lake, the cliffs of a triangular mountain drop into a cirque of snow.

The trail begins as an old road angling to the right from a meadow on the Iron Bog Creek Road. It climbs uphill, then turns left up a ridge with a view of snow-capped mountains at the head of the canyon. At .5 mile the trail crosses three tiny streams that may be dry, then comes out onto an open sagebrush ridge and goes along the side of it. It turns right (north) up a gully at 1.2 miles to a meadow. At 1.5 miles the trail climbs a hill and descends to a Y at 1.8 miles. Here the right (north) branch goes a few yards to Iron Bog Lake. The best campsites at this lake are on the opposite side near the peninsula. The trail was recently reconstructed to to avoid marshy areas and two bridges were added. (See Trails of Western Idaho by Margaret Fuller for a description of this trail.) From the lake, a trail climbs over a pass into Muldoon Canyon and down it to the Muldoon Canyon Road in Copper Basin.

Fishpole Lake in the Pioneer Mountains.

To reach Fishpole Lake, return to the Y and take the left (south) branch, which is indistinct. It descends 100 vertical feet to a ford of the outlet of Iron Bog Lake. From the ford, the path switchbacks up through woods. At 2 miles is a little pond below cliffs that drop from the iron-like peak on the north. The route now goes over a sagebrush hill to a second, marshier pond below a huge meadow. It crosses this meadow on the right of the lake's outlet and climbs through trees to the lake at 2.5 miles. There are several campsites on the south and east sides of the lake. A .2-mile side trip to the northwest climbs 100 feet to Bobber Lake.

As the names of these lakes imply, trout are in abundance.

95. BROCKIE LAKE

Round trip: 10.8 miles; 6 miles with four-wheel drive
Elevation gain: 2,000 feet
Highest point: 10,000 feet
Time: 6 hours
Difficulty: Strenuous
Maps: USGS topographic: Smiley Mountain; Forest Service: Challis National Forest
Information: Lost River Ranger District
Getting there: Following directions to Iron Bog and Fishpole Lakes, drive to Iron Bog Campground. From the campground continue to a Y in the road at .1 mile and take the Right Fork of Iron Bog Creek Road. Avoid a side road to the creek at .4 mile. At .6 mile the main road fords the creek to the northeast. The ford requires four-wheel drive only in early summer, so the trail mileage starts at the trailhead. The road is a good but rocky dirt road beyond the ford. It is gated 3 miles from the campground.

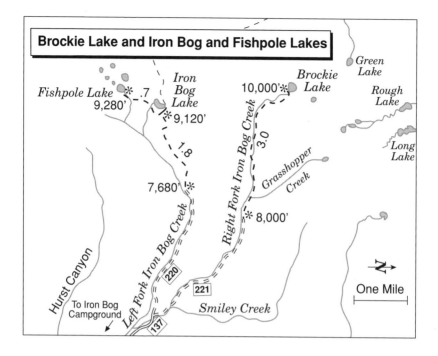

Brockie Lake and Iron Bog and Fishpole Lakes

Green Lake

Iron Bog Lake

Brockie Lake

Rough Lake

Fishpole Lake 9,280'   .7   *9,120'*

10,000'

Right Fork Iron Bog Creek

3.0

Grasshopper Creek

Long Lake

1.8

7,680'

8,000'

Left Fork Iron Bog Creek

Hurst Canyon

220

221

One Mile

N

To Iron Bog Campground

137

Smiley Creek

Below the outlet of round, blue Brockie Lake, dark gray splintery cliffs form a mountain wall. This wall continues along on the left side of the lake to a dark gray tower. Around the lake, whitebark pine, subalpine fir, and bits of meadow edged with pink kalmia and mountain heather soften the talus and ledges.

From the gate, the trail begins as an old road along the creek in a marshy meadow and Douglas fir forest. At .5 mile, the track fords Grasshopper Creek on stones. At .7 mile is an open sagebrush area extending up the mountain. After more forest and another open area, a trail leaves the old road at 1.3 miles. Take this trail down to the creek and across it to the left (south) side.

The path climbs a partly wooded hillside and at 1.4 miles crosses three sections of an intermittent side stream on rocks. After a steep climb through forest, in an open area the trail crosses the creek back to the north side on rocks. Now it goes along the center of a sagebrush ridge, climbs sagebrush hills, and curves back to the left along another sagebrush ridge. From its crest, the route descends into a small meadow and leaps a tiny stream.

On a scree slope at 2.5 miles a marsh with a tea-colored pond appears below. As the path skirts a red outcrop, cascades and waterfalls on the creek appear ahead. After the trail climbs along steep slopes, a tiny meadow leads to the lake at 3 miles. There are only one or two small campsites, so larger parties should turn off at 2.5 miles and camp near the marsh. It has a more beautiful setting anyway.

White Knob Mountains

96. WILDCAT TRAIL TO THE WILDHORSE LOOKOUT

Round trip: 8.4 miles
Elevation gain: 2,546 feet
Highest point: 9,546 feet
Time: 7 1/2 hours
Difficulty: strenuous
Maps: USGS topographic: Harry Canyon; Forest Service: Challis National
Forest
Information: Lost River Ranger District
Getting there: From Idaho Highway 75 at Ketchum, turn east on Sun Valley

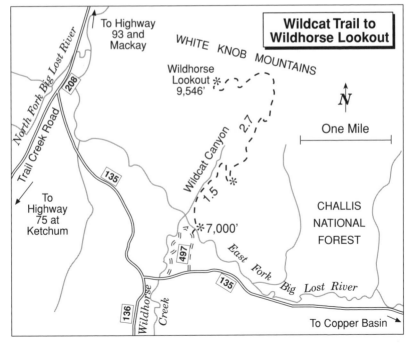

Road. Go past Sun Valley and drive over Trail Creek Summit Road 408 (208 past the summit) at 12 miles. After the end of the pavement at 8.4 miles the road is very bumpy and there are no guardrails. At 21.8 miles turn right (south) on the dirt Copper Basin Road (135). Just past where a road up Wildhorse Canyon turns off at 24 miles, the Copper Basin Road turns east and crosses Wildhorse Creek. Just beyond the creek a primitive road labeled 497 turns left (north) at 24.3 miles, and makes a loop over to the East Fork of the Big Lost River and back. Avoid this end of the loop because it is rough and rocky. Instead, wait and turn left on the other end of the loop, also signed 497, at 24.5 miles. Drive to the signed trailhead at 25 miles.

From this lookout you can look south up Wildhorse Creek at the cirques and high peaks, such as thumb-shaped Old Hyndman and frog-shaped Devils Bedstead. Below them, Wildhorse Creek draws great blue curves through a wide band of willows. You can also look west at the Boulder and White Cloud Mountains, with Castle Peak peering over the gray and red-orange peaks like a breaking wave. North across the Lost River Valley is the high, pale gray cap of Mount Borah, Idaho's highest peak. To the east rolls the rest of the short chain of orange peaks with white outcrops that are called the White Knob Mountains.

To reach the trailhead follow the access directions above, allowing plenty of time for the drive because the roads can be full of potholes. From the trailhead the trail drops to a bridge over the East Fork of the Big Lost River. It then climbs through sagebrush up the right (east) side of Wildcat Creek. Because most of the trail is in the open and the climb is long and steep, it can be hot on a warm day. Therefore, it is a good idea to start early. Carry plenty of water, since the only reliable water source is a spring high up on the peak.

At about 1 mile, after 400 feet of climb, the trail passes through a grove of Douglas firs. Just beyond the grove, the trail switchbacks to the right in the open and then goes back into the trees. By the time it switchbacks left again at 1.5 miles there are no more trees. To the west across the canyon here, sagebrush marks the talus of the mountain with vertical gray-green stripes. At the head of the canyon are brown rock towers.

By 2 miles the trail has climbed 1,200 feet. Here the grade lessens for a half-mile. At 2.4 miles the trail makes two more switchbacks and at 2.7 miles goes through trees above the rock towers to the head of the canyon. At 3.1 miles the route turns west to a fenced spring at 3.4 miles.

The trail goes through Douglas firs and limber pines below a rust-colored cliff. Then it switchbacks up a rocky slope and goes left into trees. At 3.8 miles the lookout and a brown talus slope appear above. The trail switchbacks up the talus to the lookout at 4.2 miles.

The Wildhorse Lookout is the standard white 14-foot-square building with a green roof and a catwalk all the way around it. It was built in 1935 by the Civilian Conservation Corps, so it is a historic building. The Lost River Ranger District asks you to help preserve it.

97. CORRAL CREEK

Round trip: 12.4 miles
Elevation gain: 2,000 feet
Highest point: 10,000 feet

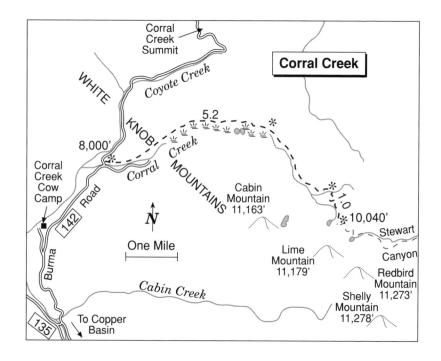

Time: 9 hours
Difficulty: Strenuous
Maps: USGS topographic: Copper Basin Knob, Lehman Butte, Shelly Mountain; Forest Service: Challis National Forest
Information: Lost River Ranger District
Getting there: From Idaho Highway 75 in Ketchum, turn east on Sun Valley Road. Go past Sun Valley and drive over Trail Creek Summit on Road 408 (208 on the Challis National Forest side) at 12 miles. After the end of the pavement, at 8.4 miles, the road is very bumpy and there are no guardrails. Turn right (south) on the Copper Basin Road (135) at 21.8 miles. Keep straight ahead at the Wildhorse Junction at 24 miles and at the junction at 35.2 miles for the Copper Basin Loop Road. At 39.1 miles turn left (east) on the Burma Road (142). Four-wheel drive is sometimes needed beyond here, but when the road is dry a two-wheel-drive, high-clearance vehicle can reach the Corral Creek trailhead. Go 4 miles on this rough road to Corral Creek and across the creek to the trailhead at 43 miles.

This trail takes you through sagebrush hills and alpine meadows to a divide with an excellent view of the little-traveled White Knob Mountains. You also see the Salmon River Mountains and the Lost River Range. Just before the divide a small lake indents a grassy basin beneath a triangular peak ribbed with avalanche chutes. On the far side of the divide, roof-shaped Lime Peak rises above a tea-colored pond and a lush meadow.

On top of the divide you look down into Stewart Canyon, one of the two forks of Alder Creek Canyon. The Alder Creek drainage was the site of the copper and lead-silver mines that gave birth to the town of Mackay. Most of the mines were up the other fork, Mammoth Canyon to the north, or north of it. Copper was discovered on Alder Creek in 1879 and in Copper Basin in 1888. John W. Mackay of San Francisco, one of the developers of the Comstock lode in Nevada, invested in what had come to be called the White Knob Mines. He brought in a branch of the Oregon Short Line and encouraged Wayne Darlington to build a 600-ton smelter. A new town, Mackay, grew up to serve the mines and the railroad.

The trail crosses a sagebrush flat for 1 mile, then climbs along a sagebrush slope above the creek and its willows. At 1.7 miles the trail is opposite a tongue of willows. It goes along a series of sagebrush flats patched with Douglas fir and lodgepole pine. At 2.8 miles, below a talus slope on the opposite wall, beaver ponds interrupt the creek.

The trail climbs through whitebark pines, sagebrush, and granite boulders. At 3.7 miles, on a big sagebrush flat, three wide-triangle peaks appear ahead. At 4.5 miles you can see a high green ridge up the canyon and an orange ridge across it. Now the trail is on grassy slopes. At 5 miles you can look southwest up a side canyon at the hill that hides an unnamed lake.

Now the creek and trail swing left. Across the canyon are the swirled browns and grays of Cabin Peak. Just past a side stream the trail crosses to the right (west) side of the creek at 5.2 miles.

The trail switchbacks up a wooded ridge and a grassy hillside. It would have many wildflowers if there were fewer cows. Ahead are the switchbacks of the divide and two grassy ridges: the one on the right holds in the lake, and the one ahead is the divide. From a sharp switchback at 6 miles, just below the pass, you can descend to the small lake. Its shores are grass and mud. From the divide at 6.2 miles you look over at the tea-colored lake under the banded cliffs of Lime Mountain.

Snake River Plain

98. CRATERS OF THE MOON: NORTH CRATER TRAIL

Through trip: 1.8 miles

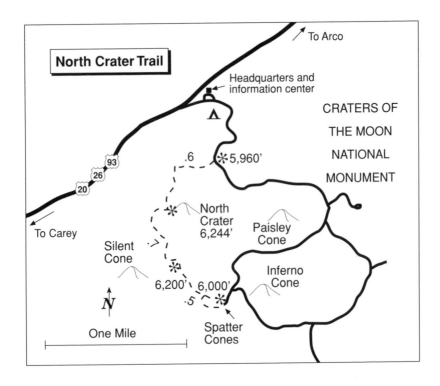

Elevation gain: 340 feet from the Big Crater end of the trail to the North Crater trailhead

Highest point: 6,200 feet

Time: 2 hours

Difficulty: easy, with a few slippery slopes

Maps: Craters of the Moon National Monument (a composite of six USGS quadrangles sold at the visitor center)

Information: Craters of the Moon National Monument

Getting there: Drive to Craters of the Moon National Monument on U.S. Highway 20-26, which is 24 miles east of Carey and 18 miles west of Arco. From the Visitors Center take the paved park road past the north end of the North Crater Trail at .8 mile and park in the lot .1 mile south of it. The climb is 150 feet less if you begin at Big Craters instead of here. At 1.9 miles the road splits in a one-way loop. The trail, called the Big Craters Trail at this end, begins at the parking area for the Spatter Cones, 2.9 miles from the Visitor Center. To walk the trail only one way, a car shuttle is needed.

Hiking or skiing the moon-like landscape of Craters of the Moon National Monument can be an experience unlike any you're likely to have anywhere else in North America. The monument is operated by the National Park Service and features guided walks and talks, easy nature walks, and longer hikes. In winter there are groomed cross-country ski trails. When the snow melts, the black and reddish lava gravel blooms with delicate annuals and perennials.

Exploring lava tubes just off the Echo Crater trail at Craters of the Moon National Monument

The North Crater Trail starts at the small black Spatter Cones and climbs along the rim of the Big Craters complex with a view down into its red depths. Farther along, on the side of North Crater, the trail crosses a flow of smooth pahoehoe lava that resembles a lava lake. This hike samples the vegetation of the monument: limber pine, rubber rabbitbrush, tansy bush, antelope bitterbrush, and dwarf buckwheat. Because the leaves and stems of the dwarf buckwheat are white, the plants resemble pancakes on a cast-iron griddle.

Captain Benjamin Bonneville first explored the edges of the Craters in 1833-34 while looking for fur. U.S. Highway 20-26, which passes Craters of the Moon, follows the approximate route of the Goodale Cutoff of the Oregon Trail. This route left the Snake River at Fort Hall and traveled north to the Lost River then west across the Snake River to Baker City, Oregon. Travelers on this route who described the craters in their diaries gave them their name.

In 1901 I.C. Russell of the U.S. Geological Survey led the first scientific expedition to the Craters. Boise taxidermist Bob Limbert explored the Craters in the 1920s and began writing articles about the area. In 1921, Harold Stearns conducted a more detailed exploration and recommended the creation of a national monument. After Congressman Addison Smith visited the area in 1923 he convinced the Secretary of the Interior to recommend the Craters as a national monument. President Calvin Coolidge established the monument in 1924.

Take time at the trailhead to look at the spatter cones. The one called the Snow Cone holds snow inside it all year long. Then follow the Big Craters Trail west along the base of Big Craters and then up onto its rim at .2 mile. The Big Craters complex is elongated because its lava erupted from a fissure. It is composed of multiple vents.

Walk northwest past a third crater, where at .5 mile the trail turns left and drops

207

120 feet. Then it curves north over small knolls and descends into a depression filled with lava blocks.

Now the trail traverses the side of North Crater. At 1 mile it descends onto an arm of the lava flow and passes the mouth of a small lava tube cave. Here the trail tread disappears, but cairns mark the way. Stay close to the cairns to avoid damaging the lava.

On the other side of the flow, the trail climbs onto the side of North Crater and over a ridge into a small crater at 1.3 miles. After climbing out of the crater, the trail passes a detour to a viewpoint of the North Crater Flow. Then it skirts the north side of North Crater to the North Crater parking lot at 1.8 miles.

99. CRATERS OF THE MOON: BIG CINDER AND ECHO CRATER

Loop trip: 8 miles
Elevation gain: 400 feet
Highest point: 5,847 feet
Time: 5 to 7 hours
Difficulty: Expert, no obvious water sources
Maps: Craters of the Moon National Monument (composite of six USGS quadrangles sold at the visitors center)
Information: Craters of the Moon National Monument
Getting there: Drive to Craters of the Moon National Monument on U.S. Highway 20-26, 24 miles east of Carey and 18 miles west of Arco. From the Visitor Center, take the paved park road. Drive around the loop drive turning off onto

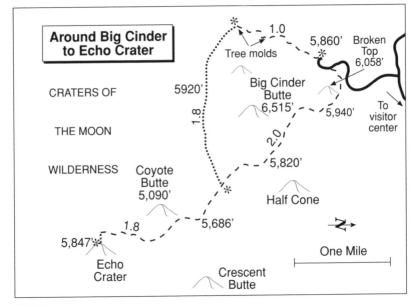

the Tree Molds spur road and go to the end of the road. Park at the Tree Molds trailhead. The main trail used to get into the Craters wilderness begins at Broken Top, .2 mile before the end of the road. You will return that way.

This hike into the wilderness area of Craters of the Moon National Monument gives you an idea of how rugged and beautiful these lava fields are. It isn't the usual route into the wilderness, but it allows you to see more of the plants, trees, and volcanic features. The return follows the usual route. The Tree Molds at the trailhead are imprints of trees charred when lava covered them. The hike includes a cross-country climb around the back of 700-foot-high Big Cinder, the largest cinder cone in the monument. On the cone grow limber pines. In June they are underlain by blue larkspur and pink dwarf monkeyflowers. Farther south, from the burnt orange summit of Echo Crater a row of cones similar to Echo Crater leads southeast along the 5-mile-wide, 60-mile-long Great Rift. The rift is the fault zone that provided a pathway for magma (molten rock) to reach the surface. Most of the Great Rift was added to the monument in 2000.

If you are planning an overnight hike, be sure to carry an adequate supply of water. To stay overnight in the wilderness area, you must first register at monument headquarters.

Compasses don't work well here because of the high magnetite content of many of the rocks. GPS units (Global Positioning Systems) are recommended instead. The park topographic map has the UTM grid on it to make GPS use easy.

In midsummer it is more pleasant to hike in the early morning or evening. It is a good idea to wear a hat and carry at least three to four quarts of water per person per day.

To reach the trailhead, follow the access directions above. At first the Tree Molds Trail is paved, but the pavement soon ends. The trail angles uphill through sagebrush with Big Cinder and its limber pines to the left. At .2 mile the route goes along the rim of a small crater, then continues south through sagebrush and across cinders.

At 1 mile are some of the tree molds. Beyond the molds the trail ends. When it does, turn left and climb southeast cross-country onto the side of Big Cinder. On the cone grow limber pines and a variety of wildflowers, including an unusual larkspur. Continue across the south slopes of the cone and over a small southeast spur. On the other side of it at 2 miles climb down steep cinders into a little valley beside a row of small black cones that are actually vents. Avoiding the sharp blocks of lava called a'a, walk east uphill among the cones. You will soon reach an old road over the cinders that is the main trail leading south into the wilderness area of the monument. After going to Echo Crater, you will return on this trail. Turn right on the trail and follow it south past the cinder cone of Coyote Butte to Echo Crater at 4.5 miles.

To reach the top of Echo Crater, turn off the trail and climb its north rim. Then walk south along the rim to the highest point. From here you can see limber pines growing in the bottom of the crater. Side trips are possible to the more rugged lava flows such as the Sawtooth Flow. A short distance east of the crater, pieces of lava that cooled into weird shapes called volcanic bombs lie on the lava.

To return from Echo Crater, go back to the main trail and follow it north along the cinder road. At 6 miles the track crosses Trench Mortar Flat where you probably intersected it as you came over from Big Cinder. Here dwarf buckwheat resembles lace doilies. The plants are white because they have white hairs that protect them from the heat by reflecting the sunlight. Their roots may spread out around the plant for as much as three feet.

At 7 miles the trail climbs 50 feet between Big Cinder and Half Cone. Now look for volcanic bombs along the trail, but remember it is illegal to collect anything in the monument except photographs. Volcanic bombs are pieces of lava that solidified in midair, so they are often elongated into spindles or ribbons. At 7.5 miles it goes around the north side of Broken Top to the paved road at 7.8 miles. From here it is .2 mile back to the Tree Molds trailhead at the end of the road.

100. HELLS HALF ACRE

Round trip: 9.4 miles to the vent
Elevation gain: roughly 500 feet
Highest point: 5,350 feet
Time: 8 hours
Difficulty: moderate, but requires watching your steps carefully
Maps: USGS topographic: Kettle Butte SW, Morgans Pasture NW; BLM map: Circular Butte
Information: Bureau of Land Management at Idaho Falls
Getting there: From the Broadway Bridge over the Snake River in Idaho Falls go west on U.S. Highway 20 for 23 miles. Look for a sign that says "Lava Trails." Turn left (south) and drive up a gravel road .2 mile to the signed trailhead.

The Hells Half Acre lava flow west of Idaho Falls is a fascinating hiking area, particularly if most of your hikes have been in the mountains. This hike is a good introduction to lava flow exploration. The area ranks right up there with Craters of the Moon National Monument. Hells Half Acre's lava extends from Interstate 15, south of Idaho Falls, west for about 30 miles. The flow lies between U.S. Highway 20 on the north and U.S. Highway 26 on the south. The area is a wilderness study area.

If you traveled east to reach the trailhead, you passed through land belonging to the Idaho National Engineering and Environmental Laboratory. The 900-square

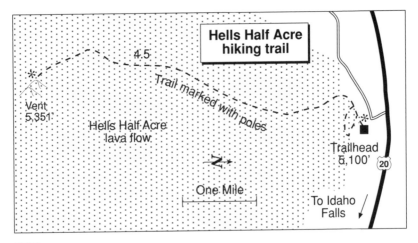

mile laboratory was established in 1949 by the Atomic Energy Commission. Today it is as much temporary storage for nuclear waste as it is an experiment station. Just off the highway stands the first nuclear power plant in the world, the Experimental Breeder Reactor 1, a national historic site open for tours.

Snow patches along the Hells Half Acre trail

Stepping into the lava fields of Hells Half Acre is like stepping onto the surface of another world. The terrain is so rough, contorted and full of cracks that it seems surreal.

A main feature of the flow is the vent, the flow's high point. It is the place where the lava spilled out thousands of years ago. The main vent is about 700 feet long and 100 to 200 feet wide. It rises 500 feet above the rest of the flow and is 50 feet deep, with 13 pits that go deeper. The most recent lava flow from the vent is estimated to be about 2,100 years old, about the same age as the newest flows at Craters of the Moon.

From the trailhead a 1-mile loop trail marked with poles painted blue on top allows you to sample the lava field in a short time. The trail surface is completely undeveloped and you will have to step over cracks in the lava and on rough lava rocks. The trail is for hiking only. So is the longer trail out to the vent. Neither trail is shown on the BLM or topographic maps.

The trail to the vent is marked by red-topped poles about every 50 yards. It starts halfway around the loop trail at an arrow. You can see the vent from the beginning of the trail. It is the low-lying dark hill about 4 miles to the south. Because of the rough lava surface you should expect to be able to follow the trail at only 1 mile an hour. Plan on the hike to and from the vent to take most of the day.

From the beginning you have to walk over cracks in the lava, up and down lava ramps, and over boulders as well as flat lava. At .5 mile there is a deep lava crack containing ferns, and at 1 mile another crack must be negotiated. There are distance markers every mile. From 1 mile on, the route is rougher. At 3 miles there is an area of thick junipers and some rough walking. Then at 4 miles the lava becomes the rough jumbled blocks that are called a'a. After about .2 mile on the a'a you come to the lip of the vent. A ridge to the left leads to the high point of the rim of the vent. Northeast of this point a few hundred feet are some arches, but be very careful if you try to go to them, for this is very rough walking.

If you go in early spring, be aware that snow covering cracks and holes makes "booby traps," so avoid walking on the snow. In any season bring plenty of water and wear good boots.

Spring is probably the best time to hike the lava flow because desert flowers are in bloom then, and they are finished blooming by early summer. Some of the flowers you may see are white evening primrose, pink wild onion, red paintbrush, blue penstemon, pink wild geranium, and yellow cinquefoil. The only trees on the flow are gnarled and twisted junipers in areas where enough soil has gathered to support them. You may see pigeons, rabbits, and the occasional snake.

101. WAPI LAVA FLOW

Round trip: 3 miles to the large holes reached from edge of lava near Rattlesnake Butte, 2 miles for Pillar Butte from Wapi Park, 4 miles for Wood Road Kipuka
Elevation gain: 80 feet for large holes, 180 feet for Pillar Butte, 180 feet for Wood Road Kipuka
Highest point: 5,261 feet on summit of Pillar Butte
Time: 3 hours for largest hole, 2 hours for Pillar Butte, 4 hours for Wood Road Kipuka
Difficulty: easy to moderate – watch for treacherous footing
Maps: USGS topographic maps: Rattlesnake Butte, Pillar Butte, Bear Trap Cave, Schodde Well, Lake Walcott East, Gifford Spring; BLM map: Great Rift and Snake River Plain
Information: Bureau of Land Management
Getting there: There is more than one way to reach the Wapi Lava Flow. One

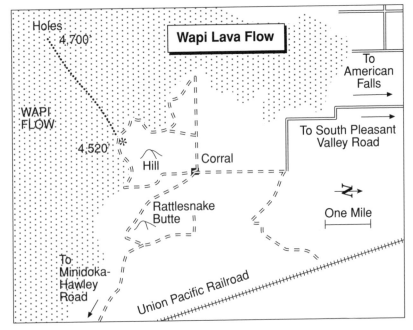

of the authors who hiked the flow drove to the southeast corner of it on county roads and roads through private land. Other ways lead through BLM land and are less likely to cause problems for private landowners.

The author drove to the flow from the east from American Falls. To follow this route, drive 2.5 miles north of American Falls on Idaho Highway 39 across the American Falls Dam. Turn left (west) on South Pleasant Valley Road and drive almost 8 miles to the end of the road and turn left (south) on the gravel road; this is Wapi Road. In .75 mile the road turns right (west); go another 2 miles (passing Schatz Road) and turn left (south); go .25 mile and turn right (west) on a road numbered 2900 South; go 1 mile and turn left (south) on 4100 West (also called Wapi Road) and go 1 mile.

At this point the roads start getting rougher. Turn right (west) and go 2 miles until you come to an old corral. At the corral you can go straight 1.5 miles then north a half-mile to the edge of the lava, or take a slightly better road by going north first for .7 mile and then turning west. The dirt road follows the edge of the flow. A high-clearance vehicle is advised for the last 2 miles of either road. You can also reach this point through mostly BLM land by driving east on the Minidoka-Hawley Road to Wapi Station and going north past Rattlesnake Butte to the corral. However, this route has more miles of primitive road.

To reach the Wapi Flow through BLM land from the west, from Interstate 84 at Rupert go northeast on Highway 24 to Minidoka. Then turn east on the Minidoka-Hawley road and drive about 2.5 miles. Here you can turn north on the Arco-Minidoka Road and go to Bear Trap Cave and then turn east to Kings Bowl, Crystal Ice Cave, and Wapi Park at the north end of the flow. Or you can continue along the Minidoka-Hawley road and find other access routes to the southern edge of the flow to see Baker Cave, Sand Kipuka, and Wood Road Kipuka. There are lots of side roads, so be careful to follow the maps. It may help to have the topographic maps as well as the BLM map, especially if you want to find the Wood Road Kipuka.

Idaho's huge lava flows in the east-central part of the state offer years of exploration and discovery. They are also open more of the year than mountain areas, even in early winter and early spring. During dry years they may be open most of the winter. Probably the best time to go is late spring, when the wildflowers are in bloom.

The Wapi Lava Flow is just north of American Falls. As with many lava flow hikes, any trails are only imaginary. One feature to hunt for is large and deep holes. There are some big holes about 1.5 miles northwest of the edge of the lava from the place the author started out. The biggest is about 80 feet deep. Be extremely careful not to fall into any of the holes. The Wapi Flow is a good place to hike if you like just wandering around and looking at the formations without any destination in mind.

The many deep cracks are fascinating. Some are only a few feet wide but more than 30 feet deep. Some provide a damp microclimate that supports lush ferns and wildflowers. Once on top of the lava you can see for many miles in all directions. The lava has accumulated enough sand and soil to support junipers, grasses, shrubs, and hardy plants.

If you go in the warm months, wear a sun hat, avoid the middle of the day, and be sure to take along plenty of water. Avoid going when the area is snow-covered, and if you go in early spring don't walk on the remaining snowbanks. They could cover a hole or crack and be a "booby trap." Avoid going when the access roads

213

are wet because they will be very soft and slippery and you could get stuck. Any time of year you will need boots. Remember that on lava flows a compass won't work well or at all because of the high metal content of the rock. If your hike is complicated enough to require a way to determine where you are, use a GPS unit. When hiking here always orient yourself by using the buttes, like Big Southern Butte, as landmarks.

The Wapi Lava Flow has many interesting features besides holes in the lava. It is one of three lava flows formed by volcanic activity along the 62-mile-long Great Rift. Just north of the flow is the deep vent called Kings Bowl. Within it is the lava tube cave called Crystal Ice Cave which, when discovered in 1952, had an ice floor and ice stalagmites and stalactites. South of Kings Bowl is an indentation in the flow called Wapi Park, where aspens grow. It is reached by a 2.5-mile-long jeep trail.

A mile southeast of Wapi Park is the summit of Wapi Flow, Pillar Butte. This butte consists of 11 eruptive centers. About 2 miles southwest of Pillar Butte is Old Juniper kipuka. A kipuka is an island of soil and desert vegetation that escaped the lava. This is a 100-foot-high older cone that wasn't covered by the Wapi Flow. On this Kipuka stands the biggest Rocky Mountain juniper in Idaho. It is 11 feet in circumference. Hiking over the lava is so tough it takes three hours to reach this point from Wapi Park.

At the south end of the Wapi Flow the most interesting feature is probably the Wood Road Kipuka. Here an old road leads from near Baker Cave into an area of junipers. People used to drive in here 50 and 60 years ago to get wood. It is a 2-mile hike into the kipuka. Don't try to drive the old road because it isn't safe. See the BLM Great Rift map for more ideas for trips.

102. MASSACRE ROCKS

Round trip: 2.2 miles for the River Trail; 5.6 miles for the Oregon Trail Ruts Trail; .5 mile for the Meadow Trail; .25 mile for the Nature Trail
Elevation gain: about 100 feet for each of the longer trails
Elevation loss: 100 feet for each of the longer trails
Highest point: 4,300 feet
Time: 2 hours for the River Trail; 3 hours for the Oregon Trail Ruts Trail
Difficulty: easy, but the footing is steep and treacherous in a few places
Maps: USGS topographic: Neeley; Massacre Rocks State Park trail map
Information: Massacre Rocks State Park
Getting there: Ten miles west of American Falls turn north off Interstate 86 at Exit 28 to Massacre Rocks State Park and follow signs to the visitor center.

Massacre Rocks State Park takes its name from an Indian attack on two wagon trains traveling along the Oregon Trail in August 1862 just south of present-day American Falls. During the initial attack five pioneers were killed. After a retaliatory strike by the emigrants, four more emigrant men died. Another girl died later from wounds.

Although "massacre" might seem a bit harsh for the events, it was how the term was used during the early history of this nation. Earlier, in 1832, Nathaniel Wyeth built Fort Hall near the park, close to today's American Falls Reservoir. He built it to protect supplies he had been unable to sell at the fur-trapping rendezvous

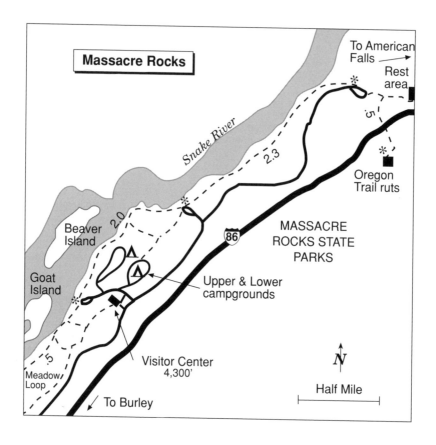

Massacre Rocks

To American Falls →

Rest area

Snake River

2.3

.5

Oregon Trail ruts

Beaver Island

2.0

86

MASSACRE ROCKS STATE PARKS

Goat Island

Upper & Lower campgrounds

Visitor Center 4,300'

.5

Meadow Loop

N

Half Mile

To Burley

that year. Later the fort became a rest stop for travelers on the Oregon Trail.

Today the name Massacre Rocks serves to attract people to an area filled with fascinating rock formations. Hiking a combination of the trails in the park will give you an idea of its beautiful and rugged terrain. The trails wind along past junipers, boulders, and outcrops of black lava down to the river. Along the river are islands, reeds, and marsh grass. Across it, basalt cliffs outline the top of the canyon. Joe Winter's old log cabin stands below them on a grassy flat. A longer trail gives access to Oregon Trail ruts on the south side of the interstate.

This is a great early-season hiking and biking destination because the trails are usually clear of snow by April. In summer, benches in shady spots make the trails at Massacre Rocks more pleasant.

First you will probably want to obtain a booklet on the nature trail and hike it. This quarter-mile trail is just west of the visitor center. This trail features the products of a volcanic vent, basalt boulders rounded by the Bonneville flood, and native plants, such prickly pear cactus.

From the visitor center, the trail along the river may be reached by driving to the lower parking lot or by taking the left branch of the nature trail and descending through a slippery defile to the parking lot. The Meadow and River trails begin at the northwest corner of this lot as one trail and diverge in a few yards.

From here the Meadow Trail leads west along the river, under and over small outcrops and beside wild roses. There is a good view of some islands with meadows and junipers on them. After .3 mile the trail curves south and loops back along the hillside, climbing through rocks to meet the nature trail and returning to the parking lot at .5 mile.

From the lower parking lot the River Trail goes east along the edge of the river between the reeds and cattails of the riverbank and the sagebrush hillside. Then it climbs 60 feet up onto a high outcrop with a fine view of the river at .3 mile. Here a sign gives the history of Joe Winter's cabin on the far side of the river.

Some of the birds that may be seen along the river are pelicans, grebes, ducks, herons, and other waterfowl. If you are lucky, in spring you may see the grebes doing a "mating dance" out in the river.

Most of the River Trail follows along the top of the canyon. In several places, cliffs drop straight down 50 to 100 feet to the water. Here be sure to keep an eye on small children who want to get a closer look. At 1.1 miles the trail descends to the fishing access parking area.

From here you may return to the visitor center the same way, but it is shorter (only .7 mile) to return by way of the shortcut trail and its interesting lava formations to the campground and then walk along the road from there.

From the fishing access parking area, you may instead continue on the Oregon Trail Ruts Trail. Signs help keep trekkers on the right path. This trail swings back along the river for a nice overlook before going southeast to connect with yet another parking lot, 2 miles from the fishing access. From this parking lot the trail is paved and open to wheelchairs. The paved trail forks at 2.3 miles. The east fork of the trail goes .5 mile to the Massacre Rocks Rest Area. The south fork goes through a tunnel under Interstate 86.

On the south side of the eastbound lane of Interstate 86 is a display on the Oregon Trail at 2.8 miles. The display includes journal extracts from pioneers to give a feeling of what it was like to be on the trail more than 100 years ago. Next to the display are old wagon wheel ruts in the dirt. The ruts go for about 50 yards before fading out.

Another area worth the extra bike or drive is the Register Rock picnic area. Register Rock is a large rock with the names and dates of many Oregon Trail pioneers inscribed on it.

Historic charcoal kilns near Bell Mountain Canyon trail (Hike 37) in the Lemhi Range

NOTES ON OTHER SELECTED TRAILS

(Distances given are one-way)

LOST RIVER RANGE
Information: Lost River Ranger District

Big Creek: From U.S. 93, Pass Creek Road 121, and Big Creek Road 121. From end of road to tiny lake in canyon; continues faintly on up Big Creek to Wet Creek-Long Lost Trail. Access road goes through private land and is padlocked. Not maintained. Talus covers trail in places. 1.2 miles to lake, 2.7 miles to Wet Creek-Long Lost Trail. 240 feet gain to lake, 1,000 feet to Wet Creek-Long Lost Trail. Maps: Warren Mountain, Massacre Mountain

Mud Lake: From U.S. 93 near Leslie and Pass Creek Road (122). From Pass Creek Road 8 miles from U.S. 93 to lake. Good view of Lost River Range but lake is surrounded by mud and its water is gray. 1.8 miles, 834 feet gain. Map: Methodist Creek.

Hidden Mouth Cave: From U.S. 93 near Leslie and Pass Creek Road (122). From short spur road (427) to cave. .6 mile, 600 feet gain. Map: Methodist Creek.

LEMHI RANGE / WEST
Information: Challis Ranger District

Morse Creek: Access from road between Ellis and Howe and Morse Creek Road 094. From Morse Creek Campground to crest of Lemhis. It is so wooded there is little view, even from the summit, but you can glimpse Mogg Mountain off to the south. 4 miles, 1,730 feet. Trail continues down other side as the Carol Creek Trail 2.5 miles to the Hayden Creek Trail 3.8 miles from its trailhead. Maps:

Abandoned miner's cabin along the Eightmile Creek trail in the Lemhi Range.

May Mountain, Mogg Mountain.

South Fork Big Creek: Access from road between Ellis and Howe and the Big Creek Road (097). From Big Creek Road to the Snowbank Trail. Can be used to make loop trip with Cabin Creek, Big Timber Creek, Park Fork, and North Fork Big Creek trails. 10 miles, 2,500 feet gain. Maps: Big Creek Peak, Iron Creek Point.

Big Gulch Trail and Iron Creek Point: Access from signed trailhead one mile before end of Big Gulch Road 099. Trail 079 leads to top of ridge where it joins Trail 193 that goes to summit of Iron Creek Point. On the two trails, it is 3.5 miles from the trailhead to the summit of Iron Creek Point with a 2,936-foot elevation gain. Maps: Moffett Springs, Iron Creek Point.

LEMHI RANGE / EAST
Information: Leadore Ranger District

Basin Lake: Access from Highway 28 and Basin Creek Road to jeep trail to Basin Lake is confusing because of private land. Road numbers will help. To reach the jeep road that leads to Basin Lake from Highway 28 take the Hayden Creek Road 008. Then take the Basin Creek Road 199, and the Basin Creek Jeep Trail 210. 2 miles from beginning of jeep trail to lake, 1,090 feet gain. Maps: Lemhi SW, Lem Peak.

Deer Creek Lake: Access from Highway 28 and Road 212. From Salmon Forest boundary to lake. Hike is along 3 miles of four-wheel-drive road (only 1.4 miles of which is driveable even with four-wheel drive because of bogs) plus 1.4 miles of trail. 4.4 miles, 1,920 feet gain. Maps: Purcell Spring, Gilmore.

SALMON RIVER MOUNTAINS / NORTH
Information: North Fork Ranger District

Twin Creek Ridge Trail: Access from Highway 93 between Gibbonsville and Lost Trail Pass. From Twin Creek Campground to Divide Trail. Gives access to

A herd of sheep temporarily clogs an access road in the Centennial Mountains

Scenic Idaho-Montana Divide Trail with views of the North Fork of the Salmon River Canyon. 5 miles, 2,400 feet. Maps: Gibbonsville, Allan Lake, Overwhich Falls.

BEAVERHEAD MOUNTAINS / NORTH
Information: North Fork Ranger District
Blacktail Creek: Access from Highway 93 between Salmon and North Fork and the Fourth of July Creek Road 071 and the Blacktail Creek Road, also 071. From end of short spur road to Continental Divide and along it. Can make a through trip along Continental Divide to the Carmen Creek Trail. Provides new access to planned Continental Divide Trail in non-motorized section. Four-wheel-drive, high-clearance vehicles recommended to reach trailhead. 5.5 miles to Continental Divide, 1,200 feet climb. Map: Shewag Lake.

BEAVERHEAD MOUNTAINS / NORTH CENTRAL
Information: Bureau of Land Management, Salmon
Geertson Creek Lake: Access from Highway 28 south of Salmon and Geertson Creek Road. From end of pavement to the cabin that can be rented from the Bureau of Land Management. Jeep trail that crosses two pieces of private land that require renting the cabin to enter. Fords creek 3 times. 7 miles, .2 mile farther to lake. 1600 feet gain. Map: Bohannon Spring.

CENTENNIAL MOUNTAINS
Information: Dubois Ranger District
Willow Creek-Crooked Creek: Access from Highway 28 north of Lone Pine and Willow Creek Road 189. From end of Willow Creek Road to end of Crooked Creek Road 178. Provides access to trails in Italian and Scott Canyons with less difficult access roads than the roads in those canyons. Gives scenic views of Beaverheads and Lemhis. 13.4 miles, 2,960 feet gain, 3,200 feet loss. Maps: Cot-

tonwood Creek, Italian Canyon, Scott Peak.

Stoddard Creek Loop: Access from Interstate 15 between Spencer and Monida Pass. From Stoddard Campground over divide into Huntley Canyon and then back down the Van Noy Canyon Trail to spur road from campground. 9.1 miles. 1,600 feet gain, 1,000 feet loss. Maps: Spencer North, Paul Reservoir

Big Table Mountain (Continental Divide Trail 004): Access from the Yale-Kilgore Road and the Pete Creek Road 012. From Pete Creek Divide east along the Continental Divide across Big Table Mountain, past Rock Spring and Burnt Canyon, across Coon Creek and down Bear Trap Creek to Road 023. Eight miles, 2,300 feet gain, 940 feet loss. Map: Big Table Mountain.

HENRY'S LAKE MOUNTAINS
Information: Island Park Ranger District

Big Springs Nature Trail: Access from U.S. 20 and Big Springs Road 059 near Mack's Inn. From Big Springs Day Use Area to boat launch. Half a mile paved. 1 mile. Map: Big Springs.

Box Canyon: Access from Highway 20 just south of Island Park and Box Canyon campground, reached by Road 284. From campground .5 mile north to Buffalo River and south 2.5 miles to Henry's Fork access area off Road 134. Beautiful views of the Henry's Fork with some paths to river's edge. No through access to Island Park Reservoir. 3 miles, about 100 feet elevation loss, Map: Island Park Dam.

Sheep Falls: Access from U.S. 20 north of Ashton and Forest Road 163. From end of Road 163 to falls on Henry's Fork. Good trail, easy walk, but not suitable for mountain bikes. In "Hiking and Biking Trails Near Idaho Falls, Vol. II" by Jerry Painter, .6 mile, 240 feet loss. Map: Lookout Butte.

YELLOWSTONE NATIONAL PARK (the small strip in east Idaho)
Information: Yellowstone National Park, backcountry rangers (307) 344-7381

Boundary Trail: Access from Idaho 47 near Ashton, Cave Falls Road 582, and spur road to Bechler River Ranger Station. From Bechler River Ranger Station to the Continental Divide Trail 078 southeast of Big Springs. From here the Continental Divide trail goes east into the park as the Summit Lake Trail, and north along the Idaho border on a series of roads to the Black Canyon Road. The Boundary Trail gives access to Buffalo Lake. 22 miles, 1,400 feet gain. Maps: Bechler Falls, Buffalo Lake.

SNAKE RIVER MOUNTAINS
Information: Palisades Ranger District

Rainey Creek-North Fork Rainey Creek Trail: Access from U.S. Highway 26 at Swan Valley and Rainey Creek Road 257. From trailhead at Road Creek on Rainey Creek Road to North Fork Rainey Creek trailhead, which is at the end of Road 253 off Pine Creek Pass. In "Hiking and Biking Trails Near Idaho Falls, Vol. I" by Jerry Painter. It is 2.3 miles to where the canyon forks. 5.5 miles, 1,070 feet gain. Maps: Fourth of July Peak, Thompson Peak.

CARIBOU MOUNTAINS
Information for Palisades Reservoir area only, Palisades Ranger District

Red Ridge: Access from U.S. 26 at Palisades Reservoir and Road 076. From Road 076 near Palisades Dam and Calamity Campground to Long Gulch Road near Camp Tamanawis northwest of Palisades Dam. The Calamity Trailhead is 200

Trapper Cabin near Snowdrift Mountain in the Preuss Range

yards past Calamity Junction. The Long Gulch trailhead will soon be moved away from the scout camp. Several side trails. Views of the Palisades country. Red Peak is a .2 mile side trip. 13 miles, 2,160 feet gain, 2,950 feet loss if start at Long Gulch end. Maps: Red Ridge, Palisades Dam.

ASPEN RANGE

(a section of the Preuss Range) Information: Montpelier Ranger District

Swan Lakes: Access from U.S. 30 southeast of Soda Springs and Forest Road 127. From end of road to lakes. .5 mile, 160 feet gain to Swan Lake. 1 mile to Lakey Reservoir. Map: Fossil Canyon.

BEAR RIVER RANGE

Information: Montpelier Ranger District

Paris Peak: Access from U.S. Highway 89 at Bloomington and Bloomington Creek Road (409). From junction of Middle and South Forks of Bloomington Creek roads go to within 800 feet of top of Paris Peak. Peak can be reached by going southeast .7 mile from saddle northwest of peak. Trail continues by going down South Fork of Paris Creek to Paris Canyon Road. 3.3 miles to saddle, about 2.8 miles more to Paris Canyon. 1,560 feet gain, 1,800 feet loss. Map: Paris Peak.

Worm Lake: Access from U.S. 89 at Bloomington and Bloomington Creek Road. From South Fork of Bloomington Creek spur road via Midland Trail to Worm Lake. Trail hard to find, lake often dries up by mid- to late summer. 2.7 miles, 1,060 feet gain. Map: Paris Peak.

BANNOCK RANGE

Information: Pocatello Ranger District

Gibson Jack Creek: Access from Bannock Highway (Highway 35) 5 miles southeast of Pocatello. From end of Gibson Jack Creek Road 008 to West Fork Mink Creek Trail. Trails go up both north and south forks, but south fork trail is in better condition and ties in to West Fork Mink Creek Trail. Scenic with stream and

221

beaver dams. No overnight camping. In "Hiking and Biking Trails Near Idaho Falls, Vol. II" by Jerry Painter.) 2 miles to forks, 3 more miles to West Fork Mink Creek, 1,040 feet gain. Map: Pocatello South.

Crestline Trail: Access from Interstate 15, Bannock Highway, Mink Creek (231), and Scout Mountain (001) roads. From Big Fir Picnic Area on Scout Mountain Road to Scout Mountaintop Road. Designed for trail bikes. 8 miles, 2,200 feet. Map: Scout Mountain.

ALBION MOUNTAINS / CITY OF ROCKS NATIONAL RESERVE
Information: City of Rocks

North Fork Circle Creek Trail: Access from main road in the reserve and road to Circle Creek Overlook. From Circle Creek Overlook to Emery Canyon opposite the Bread Loaves. Level for 2 miles at lower end. Passes Stripe Rock, Shangri La, and the Indian Grove Trail. Park ranger says, "This trail gets rave reviews and is arguably the best long hike in southern Idaho." Five miles, 1,920 feet gain. Map: Almo.

GOOSE CREEK MOUNTAINS
Information: Twin Falls Ranger District

Eagle Hiking Trail: Access from Rock Creek Road (515) south of Twin Falls. From Diamondfield Jack Campground to side of ridge south of the Magic Mountain ski resort. Built by Eagle Scouts. A .3-mile nature trail loop that connects with this trail features the wildlife of the area from bats to cougars. 2.6 miles, 400 feet gain. Map: Pike Mountain.

Rim View Trail: Access from Rock Creek Road (515) south of Twin Falls. From confluence of Third Fork and Fourth Fork of Rock Creek below Third Fork trailhead to Rim View trailhead. Non-motorized. Excellent views of Rock Creek Canyon. 9.5 miles, 1,900 feet gain. Maps: Grand View Peak, Pike Mountain.

Ross Falls: Access from Rock Creek Road (515) south of Twin Falls. From Rock Creek Road about 2 miles past the Third Fork trailhead to falls. Nature trail featuring the geology of the Cassia Mountains and the fault along Rock Creek. .2 mile, 120 feet gain. Map: Pike Mountain.

BOULDER MOUNTAINS / EAST
Yankee Fork Ranger District

Herd Creek: Access from Idaho 75, East Fork Salmon River Road, and Herd Lake Road that goes along Lake Creek to Herd Lake. Do not try to descend into the canyon of Herd Creek from the Herd Creek sign. There is no trail at this point and the slope is very steep. Trailhead is well beyond the sign for the creek. There are no signs at the trailhead, just a parking area. Trail begins by climbing over a knob and dropping south into the canyon of Herd Creek. Trail extends to Lake Basin, which contains two tiny lakes. Beautiful in early summer. 8 miles, 2,400 feet gain. Map: Herd Lake.

Herd Peak: Access from Idaho 75 at Ketchum, Trail Creek Road, and North Fork Lost River Road (178). From North Fork road up Toolbox Creek to top of peak. 3.5 miles, 2,460 feet gain. Map: Herd Peak.

PIONEER MOUNTAINS / EAST
Information: Lost River Ranger District

Kane Lake: Access from Highway 75 at Ketchum, Trail Creek Road (408/208), and Kane Creek Road. From end of Kane Creek Road (134) to 1.3 miles below Kane Lake. In "Trails of Western Idaho" by Margaret Fuller. 2.7

miles, 4 miles to lake. 1,640 feet gain. Map: Phi Kappa Mountain.

Boulder Lake: Access from Highway 75 at Ketchum, Trail Creek Road (408/208), Copper Basin Road (135), and Wildhorse Creek Road (136). From Wildhorse Campground to lake. Ford of Wildhorse Creek at beginning. In "Trails of Western Idaho" by Margaret Fuller. 4 miles. 2,200 feet gain. Maps: Standhope Peak, Phi Kappa Mountain.

Moose Lake: Access from Highway 75 at Ketchum, Trail Creek Road (408/208), Copper Basin Road (135), Wildhorse Creek Road (136), and short spur road up Fall Creek and Fall Creek trail. From Fall Creek trail at 3-mile point to lake. In "Trails of Western Idaho" by Margaret Fuller. 2 miles long; 5 miles from trailhead to lake, 2,255 feet gain. Map: Standhope Peak.

Surprise Valley and Lakes: Access from Highway 75 at Ketchum, Trail Creek Road (408/208), Copper Basin Road (135), Wildhorse Creek Road (136), short spur road up Fall Creek, and Fall Creek trail. From Fall Creek trail at the 3.5-mile point to upper lake. In "Trails of Western Idaho" by Margaret Fuller. 3 miles long, 6.5 miles from trailhead to upper lake, 2,340 feet gain. Map: Standhope Peak.

Bellas Lakes: Access from Highway 75 at Ketchum, Trail Creek Road (408/208), Copper Basin Road (135), and Copper Basin loop road (138). From short spur road up Bellas Canyon to first lake. In "Trails of Western Idaho" by Margaret Fuller. 3 miles, 1,660 feet gain. Map: Big Black Dome.

Betty Lake: Access from Highway 75 at Ketchum, Trail Creek Road (408/208), Copper Basin Road (135), Copper Basin loop road (138), and spur road up Broad Canyon (506). From end of road in Broad Canyon to lake. Rerouted in 1995. In "Trails of Western Idaho" by Margaret Fuller. 5 miles, 2,560 feet gain. Maps: Standhope Peak, Big Black Dome.

Round, Long, Rough, Big, and Golden Lakes loop: Access from Highway 75 at Ketchum, Trail Creek Road (408/208), Copper Basin Road (135), and Copper Basin loop road (138). From Copper Basin loop road to trail junction, from which a loop accesses each of the lakes. Has recently seen heavy trail and bridge repairs. In "Trails of Western Idaho" by Margaret Fuller. 12.7 miles, 1,660 feet. Maps: Copper Basin Knob, Smiley Mountain.

Green Lake: Access from Highway 75 at Ketchum, Trail Creek Road (408/208), Copper Basin Road (135), Copper Basin loop road (138), and Muldoon Canyon Road (510). From Muldoon Canyon Road to lake. All but .2 mile is a jeep trail (511). In "Trails of Western Idaho" by Margaret Fuller. 2.7 miles, 1,600 feet gain. Map: Star Hope Mine, Smiley Mountain.

SNAKE RIVER PLAIN

Big Southern Butte: Information: Bureau of Land Management, Idaho Falls. Access from U.S. Highway 20-26 near where they split between Arco and Idaho Falls, Tabor Road, Cox Well-Atomic City Road, and Big Butte-Springfield Road. From Frenchman's Cabin to summit of butte. Jeep trail. In "Hiking and Biking Trails near Idaho Falls, Vol. II," by Jerry Painter. 2.8 miles, 2,000 feet gain. Map: Big Southern Butte.

Milner "Oregon Trail" trail: Information: Bureau of Land Management, Burley. Access from I-84 at the Ridgeway Exit (Hazelton), and U.S. 30. From U.S. 30 follow the signs for the Milner Historic Recreation Area. The recreation area is on the south side of Milner Reservoir, which is on the Snake River. You can walk sections of the Oregon Trail for 4 miles. Elevation gain: 20 to 40 feet. Map: Burley SW.

Useful Addresses and Phone Numbers

Challis National Forest
- Challis Ranger District, HC 63 Box 1669, Challis ID 83227, (208) 879-4321
- Lost River Ranger District, P.O. Box 507, Mackay, ID 83451, (208) 588-2224
- Yankee Fork Ranger District, H/C 67 Box 650, Clayton, Idaho 83226, (208) 838-2201

Salmon National Forest
- Leadore Ranger District, P.O. Box 180, Leadore, ID 83464, (208) 768-2371
- North Fork Ranger District, P.O. Box 160, Highway 93, North Fork, ID 83466, (208) 865-2700
- Salmon/Cobalt Ranger District, RR 2 Box 600, McPherson Street, Salmon, ID 83467, (208) 756-3724

Targhee National Forest
- Ashton Ranger District, Box 228, 30 South Yellowstone Highway, Ashton ID 83420, (208) 652-7442
- Dubois Ranger District, P.O. Box 46, Dubois ID 83423 (208) 374-5422
- Island Park Ranger District, P.O. Box 220, Island Park ID 83429, (208) 558-7301
- Palisades Ranger District, 3659 East Ririe Highway, Idaho Falls, ID 83401 (208) 523-1412
- Teton Basin Ranger District, P.O. Box 777, Driggs ID 83422, (208) 354-2312

Caribou National Forest
- Malad Ranger District, 75 South 140 East, P.O. Box 142, Malad ID 83262 (208) 766-4743
- Montpelier Ranger District, 431 Clay, Montpelier, Idaho 83254, (208) 847-0375.
- Pocatello Ranger District, Federal Building, Suite 187, 250 South 4th Avenue, Pocatello ID 83201, (208) 236-7500
- Soda Springs Ranger District, 421 West 2nd South, Soda Springs, Idaho 83276, (208) 547-4356

Sawtooth National Forest
- Burley Ranger District, Rt. 3 3650 Overland Avenue, Burley, ID 83318, (208) 678-0430
- Twin Falls Ranger District, 2647 Kimberly Road East, Twin Falls, ID 83301-7976, (208) 737-3200

State Parks
- Harriman State Park, HC-66 Box 500, Island Park ID 83429, (208) 558-7368 (har@idpr.state.id.us)
- Massacre Rocks State Park, 3592 N. Park Lane, American Falls, ID 83211, (208) 548-2672

Bureau of Land Management
- Burley District, Route 3, Box 1, Burley, ID 83318, (208) 678-5514
- Idaho Falls office,1405 Hollipark Drive, Idaho Falls, ID 83401, (208) 524-7500

■ Salmon District, Salmon, ID 83467, (208) 756-5400

Other agencies
■ Department of Recreation, City of Pocatello, P.O. Box 4169, Pocatello ID 83205-4169, (208) 234-6232

■ City of Rocks National Reserve, Box 169, Almo, ID 83312, (208) 824-5519

■ Craters of the Moon National Monument, P.O. Box 29, Arco, ID 83213, (208) 527-3257

TIPS FOR LEAVE-NO-TRACE CAMPING

As you plan a trip into the mountains of eastern Idaho, you will want to plan to leave no trace of your ever having been there. Some ways that will help you do this are:
■ Keep your group small.
■ Pack food in plastic bags so there are no cans, bottles, or aluminum foil to carry out.
■ Use a backpacking stove for cooking.
■ Build no new fire rings; use existing fire areas; never build a fire against a large rock or in a meadow.
■ Avoid cutting switchbacks.
■ Let muddy trails and access roads dry out before traveling them.
■ Avoid pitching tents on grass or plants.
■ Move your camp at least every three days.
■ Do not cut standing trees or boughs, whether dead or alive.
■ Wash dishes, clothes, or yourself in a wash pan away from lakes and streams.
■ Bury human waste 6 to 8 inches deep, and burn or carry out toilet paper.
■ Pack out all garbage and trash.
■ Leave artifacts and historical items in place for others to see.

Suggested Equipment Checklist

*Items starred are essential for all trips

CLOTHING:
- ❏ broken-in hiking boots*
- ❏ wool or synthetic boot socks*
- ❏ long-sleeved shirt
- ❏ warm insulated jacket
- ❏ rain jacket or poncho*
- ❏ long pants (not jeans)
- ❏ hiking shorts
- ❏ wool hat and gloves
- ❏ sun hat*
- ❏ mosquito headnet
- ❏ complete change of clothes
- ❏ pullover or jacket
- ❏ sweater*

GENERAL:
- ❏ comfortable backpack: older children should have a child's backpack with padded shoulder straps and padded waistband. Younger children will do best with fanny packs.
- ❏ topographic map*
- ❏ compass*
- ❏ plastic bags*
- ❏ toilet paper
- ❏ unbreakable mirror
- ❏ thread and needles
- ❏ toothbrush
- ❏ twist ties
- ❏ spare clevis rings for packs
- ❏ flashlight*
- ❏ extra batteries and bulbs
- ❏ plastic trowel
- ❏ 50 feet 1/8" nylon cord
- ❏ whistle
- ❏ one quart plastic canteen full of water*
- ❏ dental floss to repair packs and tent
- ❏ a few inches of duct tape
- ❏ patches and glue

COOKING:
- ❏ aluminum cooking pots
- ❏ cup and spoon per person
- ❏ folding plastic washbasin
- ❏ biodegradable soap
- ❏ pot scrubber
- ❏ firestarter
- ❏ extra snack food*
- ❏ protected matches*
- ❏ utensils
- ❏ backpacking stove
- ❏ extra fuel
- ❏ work gloves or pot grippers
- ❏ pocket knife*
- ❏ food
- ❏ water filter

SLEEPING
- ❏ tent (breathable fabric with waterproof fly)
- ❏ down or synthetic fill sleeping bag with stuff sack
- ❏ closed-cell foam mattress or air/foam mattress

FIRST AID*
- ❏ prescription pain pills, and aspirin or Tylenol, antihistamine, antacid, moleskin, Band-Aids, gauze, adhesive tape, antibiotic ointment, cortisone ointment, electrolyte balance restoring powder to treat shock, foil emergency blanket, elastic bandage, wire or air splint, nail scissors, tweezers, moist towelettes in individually wrapped packages, mosquito repellent, sunblock, aloe vera cream, lip salve, prescription medicines such as those for asthma or bee stings, other items recommended by your doctor.

OTHER OPTIONAL ITEMS

- ❏ camera
- ❏ camera batteries
- ❏ notebook and pen
- ❏ field guides
- ❏ razor
- ❏ toothpaste
- ❏ fishing gear
- ❏ head lamp
- ❏ small toys for children
- ❏ film
- ❏ paperback book
- ❏ sketchbook and pencil
- ❏ deodorant
- ❏ comb
- ❏ binoculars
- ❏ walking stick
- ❏ tennis shoes, sandals or water socks
- ❏ altimeter

ABOUT THE AUTHORS

Margaret Fuller is the author of three other Idaho trail guides: "Trails of the Sawtooth and White Cloud Mountains," "Trails of Western Idaho," and "Trails of the Frank Church – River of No Return Wilderness." She has also written three books of natural history: "Mountains: a Natural History and Hiking Guide," "Forest Fires: An Introduction to Fire Behavior, Management, Firefighting, and Prevention," and with Betty Derig, "Wild Berries of the West." She and her husband, retired district judge Wayne Fuller, live in Weiser. They have five children and four grandchildren.

Jerry Painter is the author of other trail guides: "Great Trails for Family Hiking: The Tetons," "Hiking and Biking Trails in the Idaho Falls Area," "Hiking and Biking Near Idaho Falls, Vol. II," and "10 Peaks in 10 Weeks." He writes a weekly outdoor column for the Idaho Falls Post Register (a daily newspaper). He also draws maps for guidebooks published by The Mountaineers Books in Seattle and Wilderness Press Books in Berkeley, Calif. He and his wife, Julie, live in Idaho Falls. They have five children and one grandchild.

Sam Painter, 8, on the summit of Borah Peak with the southern end of the Lost River Range behind him

Guide to Trail Features

TRAILS	Easy	Moderate	Strenuous	Expert ability	Foot travel only	Recommended for biking	Packing in recommended	Campground on access road	High-clearance access	Four-wheel-drive access	Open three seasons	Open summer only	No water	Gets heavy use	Fishing	Historical sites	Nearby hike-up peaks
1. Mount Borah			✔		✔			✔					✔	✔			✔
2. Leatherman Peak			✔		✔			✔	✔	✔			✔	✔			✔
3. Mount Church and Donaldson Peak				✔	✔								✔				✔
4. Diamond Peak			✔		✔								✔				✔
5. Mount Breitenbach			✔		✔								✔				✔
6. Peak 12,078 (Lost River Peak)			✔		✔								✔				✔
7. Mount Idaho			✔		✔								✔				✔
8. Hyndman Peak			✔		✔			✔							✔		✔

228

TRAILS	Easy	Moderate	Strenuous	Expert ability	Foot travel only	Recommended for biking	Packing in recommended	Campground on access road	High-clearance access	Four-wheel-drive access	Open three seasons	Open summer only	No water	Gets heavy use	Fishing	Historical sites	Nearby hike-up peaks
9. Carlson Lake		✔				✔			✔						✔		
10. Bear Creek Lake		✔		✔				✔	✔						✔		
11. Wet Creek, Long Lost Trail to Big Creek				✔				✔									
12. Ramshorn Canyon	✔								✔				✔				
13. Natural Arch				✔	✔				✔				✔				✔
14. Merriam Lake	✔									✔					✔		
15. Pass Lake		✔								✔					✔		
16. East Fork of the Pahsimeroi				✔						✔							
17. Unnamed Lake, 9,682				✔	✔					✔							
18. Dry Creek Trail			✔							✔					✔		
19. Swauger and Copper Lakes			✔							✔					✔		
20. Upper Long Lost Creek	✔						✔			✔							
21. Shadow Lakes	✔						✔			✔							
22. North Fork of Big Creek		✔						✔							✔		
23. Devils Basin and the Park Fork Loop From Yellow Lake				✔	✔		✔										
24. Timber Creek Pass	✔							✔									
25. Mill Creek Lake	✔				✔			✔			✔			✔	✔		✔
26. Bear Valley Lakes and Buck Lakes	✔	✔				✔		✔	✔		✔				✔		
27. Mill Lake	✔					✔					✔				✔		
28. Stroud Lake	✔					✔		✔	✔						✔		
29. Everson Lake	✔					✔		✔	✔						✔		
30. Dairy Lake	✔					✔		✔	✔						✔		
31. Big Eightmile Creek		✔			✔			✔							✔		
32. N. Fork of Little Timber Creek Lake	✔									✔					✔		
33. Middle Fork of Little Timber Creek and Yellow Lake		✔						✔									
34. Big Timber Creek	✔					✔		✔	✔						✔		✔
35. Nez Perce Lake	✔			✔					✔						✔		✔
36. Meadow Lake	✔			✔				✔						✔	✔		✔

TRAILS

TRAILS	Easy	Moderate	Strenuous	Expert ability	Foot travel only	Recommended for biking	Packing in recommended	Campground on access road	High-clearance access	Four-wheel-drive access	Open three seasons	Open summer only	No water	Gets heavy use	Fishing	Historical sites	Nearby hike-up peaks
37. Bell Mountain Canyon	✔					✔							✔			✔	
38. Rocky Canyon			✔						✔								
39. Pass Creek Lake		✔							✔					✔	✔		
40. Challis Creek Lakes			✔					✔		✔					✔		
41. Opal Lake	✔								✔						✔		
42. Hat Creek Lakes		✔						✔	✔						✔		✔
43. Old Thunder Mountain Trail			✔						✔							✔	
44. Pine Creek Ridge Trail and the Clipper Bullion Mill	✔							✔				✔				✔	
45. Divide Trail from the Spring Creek Road		✔						✔									
46. Allan Lake		✔			✔										✔		✔
47. Lewis and Clark Trail at Lemhi Pass				✔	✔			✔		✔						✔	
48. Gilmore and Pittsburg RR Grade				✔				✔								✔	
49. Hawley Creek, the Continental Divide, and Morrison Lake		✔						✔		✔					✔		
50. Divide Creek Lake			✔					✔							✔		
51. Divide Creek Lake to Webber Creek			✔									✔					
52. Webber Lakes			✔					✔							✔		
53. Salamander Lake		✔			✔							✔			✔		
54. Aldous and Hancock Lakes	✔					✔						✔			✔		
55. Blair and Lillian Lakes		✔				✔			✔			✔			✔		
56. Mt. Jefferson and Rock Creek Basin			✔		✔							✔					
57. Targhee Creek and Lakes				✔	✔	✔						✔			✔		✔
58. Tygee Creek Basin		✔				✔								✔	✔		
59. Coffee Pot Rapids	✔				✔			✔			✔			✔	✔		
60. Golden Lake	✔					✔					✔			✔	✔		
61. Warm River Rail Trail	✔					✔		✔						✔	✔		

TRAILS	Easy	Moderate	Strenuous	Expert ability	Foot travel only	Recommended for biking	Packing in recommended	Campground on access road	High-clearance access	Four-wheel-drive access	Open three seasons	Open summer only	No water	Gets heavy use	Fishing	Historical sites	Nearby hike-up peaks
62. Big Hole Crest			✔				✔										
63. Thousand Springs Valley and Castle Lake		✔												✔			✔
64. Hell Hole Trail		✔								✔							
65. South Fork Snake River		✔							✔					✔			
66. The Black Canyon, Little Burns Creek, Burns Creek		✔												✔			
67. Packsaddle Lake	✔					✔								✔	✔		
68. Palisades Lakes		✔				✔		✔						✔	✔		
69. Waterfall Canyon			✔		✔			✔									✔
70. Little Elk Creek and Mount Baird			✔		✔												✔
71. Big Elk Creek	✔					✔		✔							✔		
72. Oliver Peak (the Mike Harris Trail)		✔						✔				✔					✔
73. Bear Creek	✔					✔		✔							✔		
74. Caribou Mountain			✔		✔				✔			✔				✔	✔
75. Historic Lander Cut-off Oregon Trail		✔														✔	
76. Snowdrift Mountain			✔									✔					✔
77. Bloomington Lake, High Line Trail	✔								✔					✔	✔		
78. St. Charles Canyon, the High Line Trail, and Snowslide Canyon			✔						✔								
79. City Creek	✔					✔				✔				✔			✔
80. Scout Mountain Nature Trail and East Mink Trail	✔					✔					✔			✔			✔
81. West Fork of Mink Creek Trail		✔				✔								✔			✔
82. Oxford Peak			✔							✔							✔
83. Wright Creek National Rec. Trail			✔					✔									✔
84. Boundary Trail	✔					✔				✔							✔
85. Independence Lakes	✔							✔	✔					✔	✔		✔
86. Skyline Trail on Mt. Harrison								✔				✔					

TRAILS	Easy	Moderate	Strenuous	Expert ability	Foot travel only	Recommended for biking	Requires packing in	Campground on access road	High-clearance access	Four-wheel-drive access	Open three seasons	Open summer only	No water	Gets heavy use	Fishing	Historical sites	Nearby hike-up peaks
87. City of Rocks: Boxtop Trail, Stripe Rock, the Lost Arrow, Flaming Rock	✔			✔				✔	✔		✔		✔	✔		✔	
88. City of Rocks: Creekside Towers and the South Fork of Circle Creek	✔			✔				✔	✔		✔		✔	✔		✔	
89. Third Fork of Rock Creek		✔				✔		✔			✔		✔				
90. Harrington Fork		✔				✔		✔			✔		✔				
91. Hunter Creek Summit		✔						✔	✔								
92. North Fork Lake				✔				✔		✔					✔		
93. Wildhorse Lakes				✔				✔		✔							
94. Iron Bog and Fishpole Lakes from Antelope Valley		✔						✔	✔						✔		
95. Brockie Lake			✔					✔							✔		
96. Wildcat Trail to Wildhorse Lookout			✔					✔					✔			✔	✔
97. Corral Creek			✔				✔	✔	✔								✔
98. North Crater Trail	✔				✔			✔			✔		✔	✔			✔
99. Big Cinder and Echo Crater				✔	✔			✔			✔		✔	✔			✔
100. Hells Half Acre		✔			✔						✔		✔				
101. Wapi Lava Flow		✔			✔						✔		✔				✔
102. Massacre Rocks	✔							✔			✔		✔			✔	